Fodor's 2000

New York City

Fodor's Travel Publications, Inc. • New York, Toronto, London, Sydney, Auckland
www.fodors.com/nyc

CONTENTS

MAPS

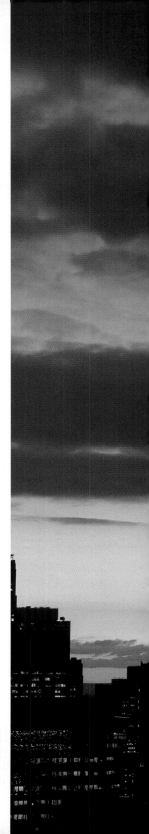

Circled letters in text correspond to letters on the photographs. For more information on the sights pictured, turn
to the indicated page number Ⓐ on each photograph.

DESTINATION
NEW YORK CITY

It's been called the "greatest city in the world" so many times—usually by its own politicians, its own media figures, its own men and women in the street—that the claim may seem empty. But that slogan takes on new life when inverted: New York is civilization's greatest *world within a city*. It feels as though *everything* is here. It's not, of course, but that's a trifling observation. What truly matters is the overpowering impression that New York gives of being both a mirror and a magnet for all of humanity and all that humanity does. Come and see for yourself: New York is the world's beating heart.

SKYSCRAPERS

Years back, the story goes, a sightseer stood on 5th Avenue ogling the ⒶⒷ**Empire State Building** (1931). After a minute or so he pronounced, deadpan, "It gives the impression of height." Yes, it certainly does. It's no longer the world's tallest building—not even New York's—but it *feels* tall, especially to anyone on the 86th-floor observation deck. Year-round its summit is floodlit in honor of holidays and events. The tallest-building title has also been held by the Ⓔ**Chrysler Building** (1930), a midtown study in Art Deco; downtown's lacy Woolworth Building (1913); and the World Trade Center's twin

Ⓒ▷ 40

D⟩152

E⟩52

towers (1972–73), which anchor Manhattan near the concrete canyons of the ⒹFinancial District. Skyscraper fashions change. Park Avenue's Seagram Building (1958) ushered in an era of large plazas and deep setbacks. The tilted top of the ⒸCiticorp Center (1977) introduced whimsy to the city skyline, which now includes the Sony Building (1984), scalloped like a Chippendale highboy.

CLASSIC
ARCHITECTURE

For a city so young, New York is home to an impressive number of architectural classics. When you're talking early 20th-century American architecture, it doesn't get any better than this. In the shadow of the gleaming Chrysler Building on 42nd Street near Lexington Avenue, Ⓐ**Grand Central Terminal** sparkles, fresh from its years-long renovation. Step onto its concourse and let yourself be dazzled by the immensity of the space, the human energy, and the zodiac fresco twinkling

FEDERAL EXPRESS

benignly overhead. Two stone lions guard the Beaux Arts–style New York Public Library immediately to the west, on Fifth Avenue. Marking the foot of the avenue is the Ⓓ**Washington Arch,** stellar for the people-watching to be had in the park below. Everywhere, blocky high-rises contrast with church spires: St. John the Divine, the world's largest Gothic cathedral, uptown; St. Patrick's Cathedral, opposite Rockefeller Center; St. Mark's-in-the-Bouwerie, in the East Village; and an emblem of godliness near Wall Street, Ⓑ**Trinity Church.** Among the small wonders in the vicinity of Trinity are colonnaded Federal Hall, the handsome U.S. Custom House (now housing the Museum of the American Indian), and the exquisite Ⓒ**Brooklyn Bridge,** one of the world's great spans. Views from its walkway are incredible— across the spiky ship masts at South Street Seaport into the thicket of Manhattan skyscrapers. Make the trip late in the day, when the sun is low and pinkish-gold light coats the cityscape like honey.

Ⓑ⟩152

Ⓒ⟩157

Ⓓ⟩122

CITY OF IMMIGRANTS

(A) 391

(B) 417

For many who love New York, this, above all else, is what makes the city special: From the beginning it has opened its doors to those from other lands who would make America their home. For millions in the late 19th and early 20th centuries (D)**Ellis Island** meant landfall. The island's former immigrant-processing center is now a museum, accessible via the same excursion boat that takes you to the Statue of Liberty. Even if your ancestors didn't come through Ellis Island you will be stirred by the exhibits. Many immigrants traveled no farther into the New World than New York. The French, disembarking on the midtown piers, started restaurants right there, on 52nd Street. Italians stopped in (F)**Little Italy,** which is now squeezed by New York's increasingly robust (C)**Chinatown.** Go Chinese for dinner then wrap up your

(C) 138

Ⓓ›148

evening with cannolis and espresso. Or step a few blocks uptown to the East Village, or to Little India on Lexington Avenue in the 20s, for an aromatic feast. Farther north, the Irish pubs in Turtle Bay prove that the greening of New York continues: when the city salutes its Irish heritage at the annual Ⓑ**St. Patrick's Day Parade,** many a recent Irish arrival joins in, and the crowd is full of lilting accents. Nowadays many newcomers hail from outside Europe. They season the melting pot at flea markets on the Ⓐ**Upper West Side** and march in Brooklyn's Ⓔ**West Indian American Day Parade.** About the only group that hasn't emigrated to New York yet is extraterrestrials (although some days you wonder).

Ⓔ›419

Ⓕ›139

Est. 1919

11

Even if some Hollywood renditions of New York cross the line into cliché, there's a lot of truth to the image of the city as elbow-to-elbow and high-voltage, seething with the nervous energy of so many people crowded into so little space. Think about it: Elsewhere in America, pedestrians appear eccentric, if not

(A) 389

NEW YORK ON THE MOVE

(B) 359

subversive; a gathering of two or three constitutes a throng, perhaps warranting a slow pass by a police cruiser. By contrast, New York is a city of foot traffic, and walking—say, along (B)**5th Avenue**—is often the smartest way to get around, despite the crowds on the sidewalks. Except when stuck in bumper-to-bumper traffic in (C)**Times Square** or elsewhere, New Yorkers keep up a relentlessly brisk pace. Could anyone but a Zen master remain mellow at (A)**F.A.O. Schwarz,** particularly during the Christmas shopping season, or meander languidly through Penn Station, Grand Central, or the subways at rush hour? On a turbulent trading day the floor of the (D)**New York Stock Exchange** is the scene of bellowing and flailing that suggest an aerobics class

(C) 58

in hell. Thank goodness for green spaces like Central Park, Riverside Park, and Brooklyn's Prospect Park, where cars are sometimes banned, and a guy and his dog can own the road if they move fast enough.

For some, what New York is really all about is Stuff, from budget to off-the-charts, from armoires to zippers. Everywhere, the ambience is part of the experience, and stores are stage

ⓐ 362

sets—the elaborate Ralph Lauren mansion, the minimalist Calvin Klein boutique, super-hip NikeTown, endlessly eclectic ABC Carpet & Home. Bookstores are legion, including big names and

SHOPPING

ⓑ 359

wonderful secondhand specialists like the Strand, with 8 miles of books, and alfresco bookstalls like ©**Green Arc** in Union Square. The mother ship of all department stores may be Bloomingdale's, an institution at 59th Street and Lexington Avenue, or maybe ⓐ**Macy's** in Herald Square, whose famous sign reminds you how big the store is. Jog around it three times, and you can easily cover more than a mile. (Some people cover more ground because they get lost.) Fifth Avenue is home to scattered electronics micro-stores (where haggling is expected),

© 108

Ⓓ 363

Ⓔ 372

D&G
DOLCE·GABBANA

Lord & Taylor, Ⓓ**Saks Fifth Avenue,** and, in its upper reaches around the Ⓑ**Plaza Hotel,** to Henry Bendel and Bergdorf Goodman. All of these specialize in clothing—very, very nice clothing, of a type that also hangs in stores along Madison Avenue. Between 60th and 72nd streets this avenue is New York's answer to Beverly Hills' Rodeo Drive, and to Monaco in general. In the rarefied Barneys New York and designer emporiums like Prada, Cerruti, and Ⓔ**Dolce & Gabanna,** regulars who shop 'til they drop are apt to be caught by their chauffeurs before they hit the floor. Come to look even if you know you won't buy. Everything is gorgeous, including the people. If your ancestors arrived at Ellis Island they may have shopped on the Lower East Side, specifically on Ⓕ**Orchard Street.** The languages on the street are different now, but the feeling is the same. As you admire the Stuff—some of it waving in the breezes outside, some of it in chic shops, and all of it discounted—think of your walk as part of your Ellis Island tour. And while you're philosophizing, keep your eyes peeled for bargains.

Ⓕ 355

Many people who move to New York bring good kitchen skills and a fondness for cooking. Soon they're eating in restaurants as often as they can afford it. And who can blame them? The variety of cuisines makes the senses reel: You'll find everything

DINING OUT

from great steaks to the freshest of fish, spaetzle to tapas, roti to farofa. For breakfast, go native and start the day with a bagel. Understand, though, that bagel quality varies widely, even in New York: some taste like cardboard, others like heaven. For lunch and dinner, study all the options before you choose. The inventiveness of menus around town is almost novelistic. You might be tempted to play it safe with pasta in an Italian trattoria. But give your adventurous side free rein, and you might end up sampling kimchee at a Korean lunch counter, trying the crispest-ever

Ⓐ 288

Ⓑ 260

© >280

french fries at a Belgian bistro, gobbling a pastrami sandwich on the Lower East Side, perusing the wine list at ®**Tabla,** or feasting on sea bass in a potato crust or tuna carpaccio at Ⓐ **Daniel.** Tucked into Central Park, ©**Tavern on the Green** occupies a tiny, magical principality of its own, a wonderland of tiny white lights. And, in Chelsea, the Ⓓ**Empire Diner** is a wee-hours stalwart, open 24/7. To create a picnic, seek out Fairway or Zabar's on the Upper West Side, a stone's throw from Central Park, or look up Ⓔ**Balducci's** on 6th Avenue at 9th Street.

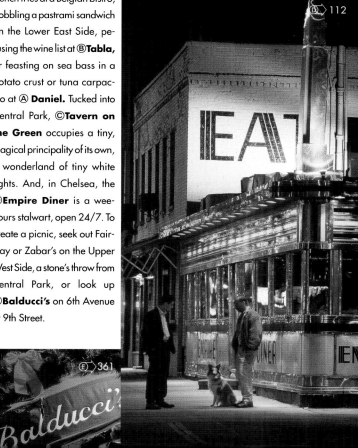
Ⓓ >112

Ⓔ >361

New York's museums span interests from modern armaments—at the Ⓑ***Intrepid Sea-Air-Space Museum,*** aboard a giant aircraft carrier—to

MUSEUMS

Ⓐ 42 Ⓑ 32

photography, film, and 20th-century painting and design at the Ⓐ**Museum of Modern Art.** Repositories of art are the dominant species of museum, but if the city housed no other museum than the colossal ©**Metropolitan Museum of Art,** you would sense nothing amiss. You could spend whole years happily roaming its labyrinthine corridors and still not see it all. Weather permitting, go up to the roof garden at sunset for a drink and a nice angle on Central Park. Some museums also distinguish themselves as works of architecture. Marcel Breuer designed the stark, square Whitney Museum of American Art,

© 64

PAINTINGS

and the Ⓔ**Solomon R. Guggenheim Museum** is Manhattan's only building by Frank Lloyd Wright. At the borough's northern tip the Ⓓ**Cloisters** was cleverly assembled from chunks of European monasteries to look like a monastery itself, a perfect showcase for one of the world's best collections of medieval art. Go on a weekday—preferably a rainy one—and you'll have the tranquil garden walkways a bit more to yourself. Equally unusual is the Ⓕ**Frick Collection,** in Henry Clay Frick's fine limestone 5th Avenue mansion. It seems impossible that so many masterpieces of the stature of Holbein the Younger's portrait of Thomas More could have been amassed by just one man. After the Frick there's the Museum of Television and Radio (a treasure). And the American Museum of Natural History (an adventure). And the Lower East Side Tenement Museum. And many more. As a New Yorker might say, "You want museums? We got museums."

Ⓔ 67

Ⓕ 63

GUGGENH

19

THE GREAT WHITE WAY

Ⓐ 217

There are places in this world where telling someone to "break a leg" might get you some fractures of your own. Not so in New York City's Ⓓ**Theater District,** where theater people wish each other luck in perverse ways. Radiating mainly north and west from Times Square, this is a tight little zone of bright lights and big dreams—the latter belonging to everyone from the well-heeled backers who finance the productions to your bartender, who might have auditioned for the show you just saw. He may have heard the three words actors hate, "We'll call you," but for some the dream comes true. They can quit waiting tables, at least for a while, and tread the boards in style at the Ⓐ**Ford Center for the Performing Arts** or snag a role in a hit such as Ⓑ*Rent* or Ⓔ*Phantom of the Opera.* Some tickets are

Ⓑ 219

Ⓒ 217

Ⓔ 217

impossible to get unless you plan years in advance—one case in point is Ⓒ*The Lion King.* But to see great theater you've only to join the line at the Ⓕ**TKTS** discount ticket booth at 47th Street. Message boards at the head of the line tell you what shows are available that evening; with luck, your first choice won't sell out before you get to the window. Then again, pot luck can be fun. And the price is right. Once you step inside the theater, the magic really begins. Musical, drama, comedy, or revival, a Broadway show will transport you far beyond the city even as you sit at its very heart. And no moment is more purely New York than when the curtain rises. As the lights go down and the audience hushes, you know without a doubt that you're not in Kansas anymore.

Ⓕ 209

OUTDOORS & SPORTS

Ⓐ 122

Ⓑ 351

You may not think of New York as a place of exquisite green spaces. But these are far more plentiful than you might expect—and city dwellers find many ways to enjoy them. The chess tables permanently set up in Ⓐ**Washington Square Park** lure players from all five boroughs; you may be able to get a game. Sign up early enough and, with luck, you can join the more than 30,000 New Yorkers and other runners from all over the world in the Ⓑ**New York City Marathon,** which begins with an epic stampede across the Verrazano-Narrows Bridge. If you're a less competitive runner, don't miss Central Park. Run the 1½-mile reservoir or make the 6-mile circuit on the road, known as the Loop. Or stroll among the park's many landmarks: the

Ⓔ**Sheep Meadow,** which along with the Ⓓ**Lake** is one of the park's loveliest areas; John Lennon's memorial, Strawberry Fields; and the Ⓕ**Wollman Memorial Rink,** where you can take a spin on the ice under the watchful gaze of the Pierre and Plaza hotels. If you just want to watch, head for the basketball court at 3rd Street and 6th

Ⓒ 350

Avenue, which attracts some of the city's best asphalt hoopsters. Or catch the Knicks at Madison Square Garden. Or head out to ©**Yankee Stadium,** where multimillionaires dress up in pinstriped pajamas to entertain you, or to any of the many other big-time sports venues. If you're a fan, the New York area's 10 major-league franchises won't let you down.

Ⓔ 82   Ⓕ 347

THE CITY THAT NEVER SLEEPS

Ⓐ 328

If night is your element, New York is your playground—and not just on Halloween, when the ⒹGreenwich Village Halloween Parade clogs 6th Avenue with some of the campiest, most outrageous street theater on *any* planet. This event will remind you, in case you'd forgotten, of New York artists' amazing creativity, their talent, and their passion for doing what it takes to make each performance the best. As examples, just watch the Rockettes high-kick at ⒷRadio City Music Hall or study the ballerinas fouettéing through performances at City Center, the Joyce Theater, or Lincoln Center's American Ballet Theatre or the ⒸNew York City Ballet; the latter is famed for its phenomenal yuletide *Nutcracker*. Afterward, all over the Theater District and around Lincoln Center, restaurants are aclatter with latenight diners and bars are shoulder-to-shoulder and hip-to-hip.

Ⓑ 43

Ⓒ 214

Ⓓ➤420

Ⓔ➤312

You might discuss the marvels you've just seen over expensive martinis and the suavest live piano music at a swank spot like the Carlyle Hotel's Bemelmans Bar. Or go catch a rising star or two at a comedy club. Hit the dance clubs, a rock dive, a cabaret, or a doormanned lounge. Or take in some R&B or salsa. If New York nights have a sound track, though, it's jazz. Walk the streets after dark and you can almost hear it. Settle into a seat at any Manhattan jazz club and you *will* hear it—the Ⓐ**Village Vanguard** is only one of the greats. Swing by the Royalton or the Ⓔ**Paramount Hotel** in the Theater District, purpose-built to be cool. Bend an elbow here and call it a night, or keep going: Grab a bite, then ride the Staten Island Ferry until dawn. When you start doing the town after dark in New York, you won't want the night to end.

25

GREAT ITINERARIES

New York in 5 Days

Enjoying everything New York City has to offer during a short trip is more than a challenge, it's an impossibility. The city's riches can seem as overwhelming as they are exhilarating: Whether your bent is sightseeing or shopping, museums or music, New York does indeed have it all. In five days you can see only the best of the best.
☉ So that you don't show up and find your destination closed, shuffle itinerary days around as suggested.

Ⓐ▷ 57

DAY 1
Launch your exploration with a visit to the top of the Empire State Building to take in the entire city in one panoramic glance. Stroll up 5th Avenue past the leonine guardians of the Ⓐ New York Public Library Humanities and Social Sciences Library and step inside to take a look at the gleaming Main Reading Room. Forty-Second Street takes you to the newly restored Grand Central Terminal, a hub of frenetic activity and architectural wonder. Move on to the Chrysler Building, an Art Deco beauty, and continue east to the United Nations. Make your way back west to Ⓑ Rockefeller Center for more grandeur, then across 5th Avenue to St. Patrick's Cathedral and into Saks Fifth Avenue. The Museum of Modern Art stands a few

blocks away, and to the south Times Square lights up as night falls. Walk down 7th Avenue to take in all the bright sights on your way to a Broadway show.
☉ Don't do this on Wednesday.

DAY 2
Go in search of history via ferry to Ellis Island and the Statue of Liberty. An early start helps you beat the crowds, though it's impossible to visit both in a single morning. When you return, head northeast for a tour through the Wall Street area; on the way you'll pass colonial-era Fraunces Tavern and Trinity Church. Then follow your nose to no-longer-so-fishy South Street Seaport, a great place to shop, have a bite, and soak up New York's seafaring history along with views of the Brooklyn Bridge. Head back past ornate City Hall, the neo-Gothic Woolworth Building (don't miss the splendid gilded lobby) and 18th-century St. Paul's Chapel on your way to the towering World Trade Center, where you can take in the sunset. For dinner, choose among TriBeCa's many restaurants.
☉ This is fine any day.

DAY 3
Fine art and the finer things in life beckon, starting at the magnificent Metropolitan Museum of Art. You could easily spend a whole day here, but tear yourself away and choose between the Guggenheim and the Whitney. If you choose the Solomon R. Guggenheim Museum, the giant spiral filled with 20th-century art, meander over to pricey and chic Madison Avenue afterward and shop your way down to 59th Street. If, instead, you walk southeast from the Met to the modern Whitney Museum of American Art, Bloomingdale's is just a quick southeast jaunt

away. After exploring the museums, find nearby Grand Army Plaza, its western edge graced by The Plaza hotel, across the way from F.A.O. Schwarz. After dinner, hail a hansom cab for a carriage ride in Central Park.
☉ This won't work on Monday, Tuesday, or Thursday, depending on what you want to see.

DAY 4
First thing this morning, head west to the American Museum of Natural History. Take a gander at the dinosaurs and stop by John Lennon's last home, the Dakota apartment building on Central Park West at 72nd Street. Walk into lush, green Central Park itself to see its Shakespeare Garden, Belvedere Castle, Bethesda Fountain, and Wildlife Center (more familiarly known as the Central Park Zoo). After your dose of fresh air, shop 'til you drop along 5th Avenue and 57th Street. Then treat yourself to dinner followed by a performance at Carnegie Hall or Lincoln Center for the Performing Arts.
☉ Do this any day.

DAY 5
Make your way downtown and wander around Chinatown, where you can enjoy a dim sum breakfast or brunch. From here head north to SoHo and NoLita for galleries and the crème de la crème of both shops and restaurants. Next, take a walk on the Lower East Side, a former immigrant enclave where you'll find the Lower East Side Tenement Museum and bargain shopping on Orchard Street. If you haven't eaten by now, hit a café a few blocks away in the happening East Village, home to yet more shopping. Head west from here to see the historic sights and pretty streets of Greenwich Village; a quick stroll north will take

Solomon R.
Guggenheim
Museum

Metropolitan
Museum of Art

Belvedere
Castle

American
Museum of
Natural History

Shakespeare
Garden

The Dakota

Bethesda
Fountain

Whitney Museum
of American Art

Central
Park

Lincoln
Center

Central Park
Wildlife Center
(Zoo)

Grand Army
Plaza

Bloomingdale's

Plaza Hotel

59th St.

F.A.O. Schwarz

57th St.

Carnegie
Hall

Museum of
Modern Art

53rd St.

Rockefeller
Center

St. Patrick's
Cathedral

Saks Fifth Avenue

49th St.

United Nations

Grand Central
Terminal

42nd St.

Times
Square

Chrysler
Building

Public
Library

Empire State
Building

34th St.

Herald
Square

Madison
Square

22nd St.

23rd St.

Flatiron
Building

Chelsea

Flatiron
District

20th St.

Union
Square

Greenwich
Village

St. Marks Pl.

Washington
Square

East
Village

Houston St.

Prince St.

NoLita

SoHo

Lower East Side
Tenement Museum

Canal St.

Chinatown

TriBeCa

City
Hall

Woolworth
Building

Fulton St.

Brooklyn
Bridge

World Trade
Center

St. Paul's
Chapel

Wall
Street

South Street
Seaport

Trinity
Church

Fraunces
Tavern

Ferry to Ellis Island
and Statue of Liberty

Ellis
Island

To Statue of Liberty

Roosevelt
Island

you to Chelsea and its galleries, and to the fashionable Flatiron District with its inimitable Flatiron Building. After dark, haunt one of the Village's many jazz clubs or slink into a SoHo or East Village hipster lounge.
🕐 *Don't do this on Monday, Friday, or Saturday; some galleries are closed Sunday.*

If You Have More Time

Take a break from Manhattan with a day trip to Brooklyn, where you'll find the Brooklyn Museum of Art right next to the lush Brooklyn Botanic Garden. Adjacent to the gardens is Prospect Park, which forms the southeastern boundary of the vibrant neighborhood of Park Slope. The Slope's main street, 7th Avenue, is lined with distinctive cafés and shops. For entertainment, see what's happening at the Brooklyn Academy of Music or spend the evening in Brooklyn Heights, strolling the Promenade at sunset. Back in Manhattan, another day sees another side of the city uptown. In Morningside Heights you'll find Riverside Park overlooking the Hudson and the Gothic work-in-progress Cathedral of St. John the Divine, as well as the ivory towers of Columbia University. Come back down to earth in Harlem, whose rich history is documented at the Schomberg Center near the famous Abyssinian Baptist Church. Other landmarks include the legendary ©Apollo Theatre, the Langston Hughes House, the Studio Museum of Harlem, and soul-food restaurants such as Sylvia's.

If You Have 3 Days

An abbreviated visit can give you a tempting taste of the Big Apple. Follow the itineraries for days 1 and 3 above, then zip downtown for your third day. Start early, with a visit to Ellis Island or the Statue of Liberty, and take a quick spin around the Wall Street area and South Street Seaport. Next head north-west to bustling, colorful Chinatown on your way to gallery- and shop-filled SoHo. Cruise through trendier and less expensive NoLita, then up to the East Village. When you've had your fill of funky, walk west to the historic sights and winding streets of Greenwich Village. Stay downtown for dinner in a budget Village eatery or a SoHo hot spot, then dance the night away before you bid the city good-bye.

A Kid's-Eye View of New York

New York City can make a kid's eyes pop and his jaw drop. The playgrounds in Riverside and Central parks are world-class, and just walking down the street can be an adventure for tots and teenagers alike. New York bursts with fantastic activities and sights for kids. Best of all, these stops appeal to adults as well.

DAY 1

Start off with a trip to that perennial favorite, the Ameri-can Museum of Natural History, to see the genuinely awesome dinosaurs. After-ward take a rumbling ride down to 34th Street on the subway's B line, in the front car for a cool view of the tracks. You'll find all kinds of action in Herald Square,

home of Macy's. Shop if you like, or walk to the nearby Empire State Building. Take in the view and stop in the lobby to purchase a three-day double-decker bus ticket to get around the rest of this itinerary. Ride down to SoHo, location of the New York City Fire Museum and the Chil-dren's Museum of the Arts. Adventurous eaters love dinner in colorful Chinatown, where the whole family can play tic-tac-toe with the celebrity chicken in the Mott Street arcade, just off the Bowery.

DAY 2

Greet the day at the World Trade Center and take the elevator trip of your life to the "Top of the World." Back on the ground, catch a free ride across New York Harbor on the Staten Island Ferry past such famous sights as the Statue of Liberty and Ellis Island. The round trip will put you in a suitably nautical mood for a visit to South Street Seaport, which offers food and fun of every description. Next take the double-decker bus up to Rockefeller Center; in winter the ice-skating and Christmas tree are special treats. There's more fun to be had at the nearby Museum of Television and Radio and at the high-tech Sony Wonder Technol-ogy Lab in the Sony Building. And no kid's trip to N.Y.C. is complete without a pilgrim-age to F.A.O. Schwarz. An evening at a Broadway musical such as *Cats* or *The Lion King* thrills many young-sters. Or see what's on the child-friendly program at the New Victory Theater.

DAY 3

Cruise around Manhattan island this morning on the Circle Line, and when your tour's completed stop by the *Intrepid* Sea-Air-Space Museum. Next take in some of the wild energy of the cleaned-up Times Square. If weather permits, look for more outdoor magic in Central Park. There, check out the Children's Zoo, take a ride on the famous carousel, catch a performance at the marionette theater in the Swedish Cottage, and watch

the miniature boats on the Conservatory Water. If you still have energy to burn, visit the playground near the zoo or near the carousel. After-ward stop in at the Metropoli-tan Museum of Art to see the Temple of Dendur, the arms and armor, and other fun stuff. As night falls, try one of the special kids' music offerings at Lincoln Center for the Performing Arts or take in a movie on the huge screen at the nearby ⒹSony IMAX Theater.

Art Attack!

For art lovers of every taste, there's no place like New York. You have so much to choose from, whether you favor the classic, the experi-mental, or the outrageous. This itinerary allows you to try a little of everything.

DAY 1

The first stop on every aes-thete's schedule should be the Metropolitan Museum of Art. Although you could easily while away whole weeks here, limit yourself to a morning, then head for the many galleries along Madi-son Avenue between 80th and 70th streets—be sure to stop in at both Gagosian and Knoedler & Co. Don't miss the masterpiece-heavy Frick Collection before strolling east to view the art collec-tions at the Asia Society. In the evening attend a perfor-mance at Lincoln Center for the Performing Arts, City Center, or Carnegie Hall. Then catch a cabaret act at Café Carlyle or the Oak Room.

DAY 2

Spend a thoroughly modern morning at the Solomon R. Guggenheim Museum and the Whitney Museum of American Art. With visions of de Kooning and Klee danc-ing in your head you'll be ready for a visit to the Mu-seum of Modern Art. Spend the rest of the afternoon at the galleries along 57th Street, whose standouts include the Marlborough Gallery and Pace/Wildenstein. Depend-

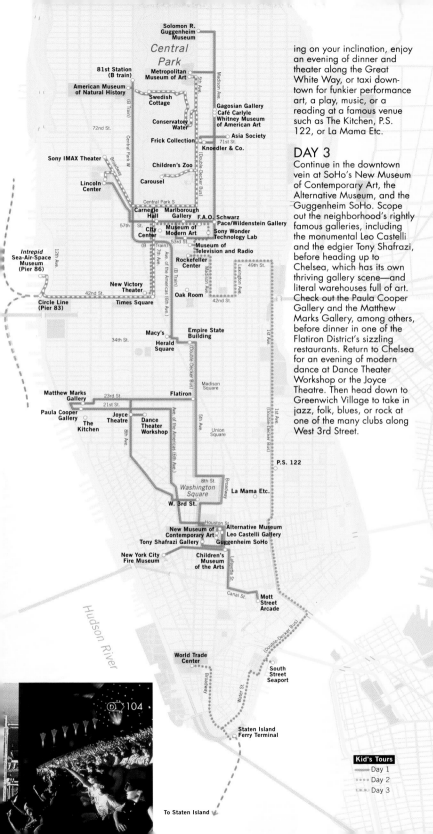

ing on your inclination, enjoy an evening of dinner and theater along the Great White Way, or taxi downtown for funkier performance art, a play, music, or a reading at a famous venue such as The Kitchen, P.S. 122, or La Mama Etc.

DAY 3
Continue in the downtown vein at SoHo's New Museum of Contemporary Art, the Alternative Museum, and the Guggenheim SoHo. Scope out the neighborhood's rightly famous galleries, including the monumental Leo Castelli and the edgier Tony Shafrazi, before heading up to Chelsea, which has its own thriving gallery scene—and literal warehouses full of art. Check out the Paula Cooper Gallery and the Matthew Marks Gallery, among others, before dinner in one of the Flatiron District's sizzling restaurants. Return to Chelsea for an evening of modern dance at Dance Theater Workshop or the Joyce Theatre. Then head down to Greenwich Village to take in jazz, folk, blues, or rock at one of the many clubs along West 3rd Street.

Central Park

Solomon R. Guggenheim Museum

81st Station (B train)
Metropolitan Museum of Art
American Museum of Natural History
Swedish Cottage
Gagosian Gallery
Café Carlyle
Whitney Museum of American Art
Conservatory Water
Asia Society
Frick Collection
Knoedler & Co.
Sony IMAX Theater
Children's Zoo
Lincoln Center
Carousel
Carnegie Hall
Marlborough Gallery
F.A.O. Schwarz
City Center
Pace/Wildenstein Gallery
Museum of Modern Art
Sony Wonder Technology Lab
Museum of Television and Radio
Intrepid Sea-Air-Space Museum (Pier 86)
Rockefeller Center
New Victory Theater
Oak Room
Circle Line (Pier 83)
Times Square
Empire State Building
Macy's
Herald Square
Matthew Marks Gallery
Flatiron
Paula Cooper Gallery
The Kitchen
Joyce Theatre
Dance Theater Workshop
P.S. 122
La Mama Etc.
Washington Square
W. 3rd St.
New Museum of Contemporary Art
Alternative Museum
Leo Castelli Gallery
Tony Shafrazi Gallery
Guggenheim SoHo
New York City Fire Museum
Children's Museum of the Arts
Mott Street Arcade
Hudson River
World Trade Center
South Street Seaport
104
Staten Island Ferry Terminal
To Staten Island

Kid's Tours
Day 1
Day 2
Day 3

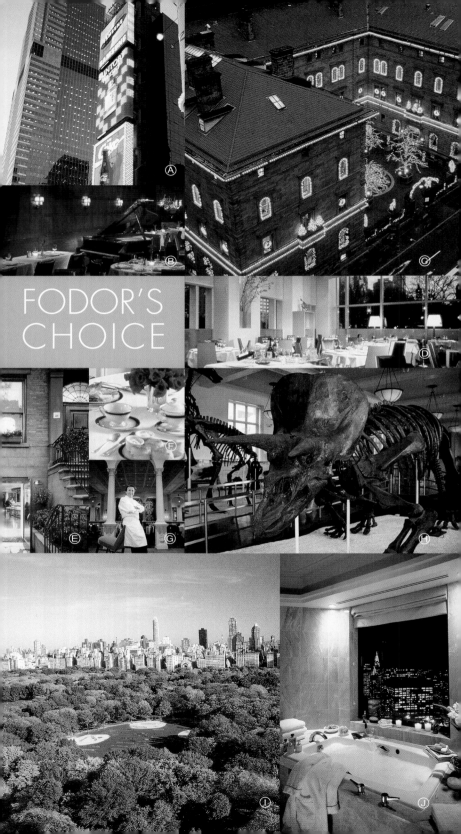

FODOR'S
CHOICE

Even with so many special places in New York City, Fodor's writers and editors have a few that stand out.

MOMENTS

The Cloisters at sunset. Nestled in enchanted gardens far above the urban din, the medieval Cloisters are most gorgeous as the sun sets over the Hudson River and the soaring Palisades. ☞ p 93

New York City Marathon. The city unites in a cheering, breathless mass as thousands of runners dash through the five boroughs to the finish line in Central Park. ☞ p 351

⑧ Romance at the Supper Club. On a Friday or Saturday evening, slip into your white tie or black satin and sip champagne to the strains of a big band. Then take to the dance floor to glide and whirl and hold your sweetheart close. ☞ p 326

④ Times Square at night. As daylight wanes, New York's energy seems to concentrate here and erupt in brilliant display. ☞ p 58

A walk on the Brooklyn Heights Promenade. For stunning views of downtown Manhattan and the Brooklyn Bridge nothing beats a stroll along this elegant esplanade, especially in early morning with sun glinting off Wall Street's glass monoliths. ☞ p 173

PLACES

⑧ American Museum of Natural History. Whether you are among the dinosaur fossils, beneath the 94-ft blue whale, or admiring the dioramas depicting human evolution, you can't help but be awed. ☞ p 86

Brooklyn Botanic Garden. In one of the city's loveliest spots, savor the tranquillity of the Japanese Garden, commune with the Bard in the Shakespeare Garden, or get lost in a profusion of pink at spring's Cherry Blossom Festival. ☞ p 178

① Central Park. Dusted with snow or awash in autumn colors, humming with weekend athletes or silent but for the clip-clop of a carriage horse, this oasis offers citified outdoor pleasures and a skyline spiked with skyscrapers. ☞ p 74

NoLita. Tiny designer boutiques, velvet-upholstered lounges, and bold new restaurants are popping up all over this tenement neighborhood east of SoHo. This is New York as downtowners think it should be, with nary a chain store nor T-shirt shop in sight. ☞ p 355

West Village. Historic town houses and hidden courtyards charm one and all along winding, tree-lined lanes—most notably St. Luke's Place and Commerce, Bedford, and Grove streets. ☞ p 117

FLAVORS

⑥ Daniel. Daniel Boulud's grand dining room presents French classics as well as the chef's own brilliant inventions, such as scallops in black tie (dressed with truffles). $$$$ ☞ p 288

⑩ Jean Georges. Dramatic picture windows give you a view of Central Park from this sleek, modernist dining room as Jean-Georges Vongerichten casts his culinary spell over some of the most astonishing dishes you'll ever taste. $$$$ ☞ p 282

Lespinasse. The service is exquisitely refined and Christian Delouvrier's French cuisine marvelously innovative in this gilded dining room. $$$$ ☞ p 267

Nobu. Reservations are hard to come by at this striking, contemporary Japanese-inspired restaurant, but persevere: flawless sushi and sashimi and Nobu creations like seared black cod with sweet miso are utterly delicious. $$$$ ☞ p 237

Babbo. This is Italian food as it was meant to be, updated, and after your first bite of the ethereal homemade pasta or tender suckling pig you'll know why critics rave. $$$–$$$$ ☞ p 251

Gramercy Tavern. If wild Scottish partridge in consommé and fondue of sea urchin and Maine crabmeat sound good, head for this urbanely rustic restaurant. $$$–$$$$ ☞ p 259

Union Pacific. Exotic ingredients and unusual flavor combinations work beautifully here. Anyone for seared duck liver on pickled green papaya with toasted pistachio oil and tamarind glaze? $$$–$$$$ ☞ p 260

COMFORTS

③ Four Seasons. Towering over 57th Street, this I. M. Pei spire houses palatial, soundproof guest rooms with 10-ft ceilings, English sycamore walk-in closets, and blond-marble baths whose immense tubs fill in 60 seconds. $$$$ ☞ p 304

© New York Palace. Sleep amid glamorous deco or traditional Empire-style furnishings. The health club's views of St. Patrick's cathedral are terrific. $$$$ ☞ p 305

The Carlyle. Everything about this landmark suggests refinement, from the first-rate service to the artfully framed Audubons in the rooms. Bemelmans Bar and Café Carlyle are destinations unto themselves. $$$–$$$$ ☞ p 315

⑥ The Lowell. Many rooms and suites have working fireplaces in this gem on a quiet, tree-lined Upper East Side street. The Pembroke Room serves a stunning tea, and the Post House is renowned for steaks. $$$–$$$$ ☞ p 315

⑤ Inn at Irving Place. The tea salon of this grand pair of 1830s town houses near Gramercy Park evokes a gentler New York, as do the ornamental fireplaces, four-poster beds, and embroidered linens. $$$ ☞ p 317

Mercer Hotel. The hotel of the moment for unconventional travelers, this SoHo minimalist is all dark African woods and high-tech light fixtures. The decadent two-person tubs, surrounded by mirrors, steal the show. $$$ ☞ p 320

1 EXPLORING MANHATTAN

Around the next corner, a visitor to New York will always find something new to discover uptown and down—world-class museums and unusual galleries, breathtaking skyscrapers, multicultural color, historic town houses, vibrant neighborhoods, parks and gardens. From the Battery in the south to Harlem in the north, this chapter uncovers the essential places to see in each part of Manhattan, as well as worthwhile sights off the tourist track. Be sure to stop and rest along the way so you have a chance to observe the fabulous street life that makes this city unique.

Updated by
Barbara
Blechman,
Hannah
Borgeson,
Karen Deaver,
John J.
Donohue,
Rachel King,
Heather Lewis,
and Margaret
Mittelbach

MANHATTAN IS, ABOVE ALL, A WALKER'S CITY.
Along its busy streets there's an endless variety
of sights everywhere you go. Attractions, many
of them world famous, crowd close together on this narrow island, and
because the city can only grow up, not out, the new simply piles on
top of the old. Manhattan's character changes every few blocks, so quaint
town houses stand shoulder to shoulder with sleek glass towers, gleaming gourmet supermarkets sit around the corner from dusty thrift
shops, and chic bistros inhabit the storefronts of soot-smudged warehouses. Many visitors, beguiled into walking a little farther, then a little farther still, have been startled to stumble upon their trip's most
memorable moments.

Our walking tours cover a great deal of ground, yet they only scratch
the surface of the city. If you plod dutifully from point to point, nose
buried in this book, you'll miss half the fun. Look up at the tops of
skyscrapers, and you'll see a riot of mosaics, carvings, and ornaments.
Step into the lobby of an architectural landmark and study its features;
take a look around to see the real people who work, live, or worship
there today. Peep down side streets, even in crowded midtown, and
you may find fountains, greenery, and sudden bursts of flowers. Find
a bench or ledge on which to perch and take time just to watch the
crowd passing by. New York has so many faces that every visitor can
discover a different one.

Orientation

The map of Manhattan has a Jekyll-and-Hyde aspect. The rational Dr.
Jekyll part prevails above 14th Street, where the streets form a regular grid pattern, imposed in 1811. Numbered streets run east and west
(crosstown), while broad avenues, most of them also numbered, run
north (uptown) and south (downtown). The chief exceptions are Broadway and the thoroughfares that hug the shores of the Hudson and East
rivers. Broadway runs the entire length of Manhattan. At its south-
ernmost end it follows the city's north–south grid; at East 10th Street
it turns and runs on a diagonal to West 86th Street, then at a lesser
angle until 107th Street, where it merges with West End Avenue.

Fifth Avenue is the east–west dividing line for street addresses: on either side, addresses begin at 1 where a street intersects 5th Avenue and
climb higher in each direction, in regular increments. For example, 1
East 55th Street is just east of 5th Avenue, 99 East 55th Street is at
Park (the equivalent of 4th) Avenue, 199 East 55th Street is at 3rd Avenue, and so on; likewise, 1 West 55th Street is just west of 5th Avenue, 99 West 55th Street is at 6th Avenue (also known as Avenue of
the Americas), 199 West 55th Street is at 7th Avenue, and so forth.
Above 59th Street, where Central Park interrupts the grid, West Side
addresses start numbering at Central Park West, an extension of 8th
Avenue. Avenue addresses are much less regular, for the numbers begin
wherever each avenue begins and increase at different increments. An
address at 552 3rd Avenue, for example, will not necessarily be anywhere near 552 2nd Avenue. Even many New Yorkers cannot master
the complexities of this system, so they give addresses in terms of intersections: 5th Avenue and 55th Street, for instance, or 55th Street
between 9th and 10th avenues.

Below 14th Street—the area settled before the 1811 grid was decreed—
Manhattan streets reflect the disordered personality of Mr. Hyde. They
may be aligned with the shoreline, or they may twist along the route

Manhattan Neighborhoods

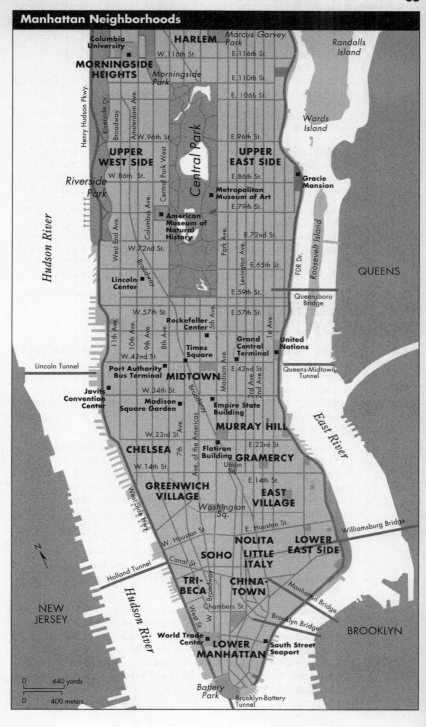

Columbia University

HARLEM

Marcus Garvey Park

Randalls Island

W. 116th St.

E. 116th St.

MORNINGSIDE HEIGHTS

Morningside Park

E. 110th St.

E. 106th St.

Henry Hudson Pkwy.

Riverside Dr.

Broadway

Amsterdam Ave.

W. 96th St.

E. 96th St.

Wards Island

UPPER WEST SIDE

Central Park

UPPER EAST SIDE

Riverside Park

W. 86th St.

Central Park West

E. 86th St.

Gracie Mansion

West End Ave.

Columbus Ave.

Metropolitan Museum of Art

American Museum of Natural History

E. 79th St.

W. 72nd St.

Park Ave.

E. 72nd St.

Roosevelt Island

Broadway

Lexington Ave.

E. 65th St.

FDR Dr.

QUEENS

Lincoln Center

E. 59th St.

W. 57th St.

Queensboro Bridge

Rockefeller Center

E. 57th St.

11th Ave.

10th Ave.

9th Ave.

8th Ave.

5th Ave.

Times Square

Grand Central Terminal

1st Ave.

United Nations

W. 42nd St.

MIDTOWN

E. 42nd St.

Queens-Midtown Tunnel

Lincoln Tunnel

Port Authority Bus Terminal

Madison Ave.

East River

Javits Convention Center

W. 34th St.

Broadway

3rd Ave.

2nd Ave.

Madison Square Garden

Empire State Building

MURRAY HILL

W. 23rd St.

Ave. of the Americas

E. 23rd St.

CHELSEA

7th

Flatiron Building

GRAMERCY

W. 14th St.

Union Sq.

E. 14th St.

GREENWICH VILLAGE

Washington Sq.

EAST VILLAGE

West Side Hwy.

E. Houston St.

Williamsburg Bridge

N

W. Houston St.

NOLITA

LOWER EAST SIDE

Holland Tunnel

Canal St.

SOHO

LITTLE ITALY

TRI-BECA

Broadway

CHINA-TOWN

Manhattan Bridge

NEW JERSEY

Chambers St.

West St.

Brooklyn Bridge

Hudson River

World Trade Center

LOWER MANHATTAN

South Street Seaport

BROOKLYN

0   440 yards

0   400 meters

Battery Park

Brooklyn-Battery Tunnel

Hudson River

of an ancient cow path. Below 14th Street you'll find West 4th Street intersecting West 11th Street, Greenwich Street running roughly parallel to Greenwich Avenue, and Leroy Street turning into St. Luke's Place for one block and then becoming Leroy again. There's an East Broadway and a West Broadway, both of which run north–south and neither of which is an extension of plain old Broadway. Logic won't help you below 14th Street; only a good street map and good directions will.

You may also be confused by the way New Yorkers use *uptown* and *downtown*. These terms refer both to locations and to directions. Uptown means north of wherever you are at the moment; downtown means to the south. But uptown and downtown are also specific parts of the city. Unfortunately, there is no consensus about where these areas are: Downtown may mean anyplace from the tip of lower Manhattan through Chelsea; it depends on the orientation of the speaker.

A similar situation exists with *East Side* and *West Side*. Someone may refer to a location as "on the east side," meaning somewhere east of 5th Avenue. A hotel described as being "on the west side" may be on West 42nd Street. But when New Yorkers speak of the East Side or the West Side, they usually mean the respective areas above 59th Street on either side of Central Park. Be prepared for misunderstandings.

ROCKEFELLER CENTER AND MIDTOWN SKYSCRAPERS

Athens has its Parthenon and Rome its Colosseum. New York's temples, which you see on this mile-long tour along six avenues and five streets, are its concrete-and-glass skyscrapers. Many of them, including the Lever House and the Seagram Building, have been pivotal in the history of modern architecture, and the 19 limestone-and-aluminum buildings of Rockefeller Center constitute one of the world's most famous pieces of real estate.

Conceived by John D. Rockefeller during the Great Depression of the 1930s, the Rockefeller center complex—"the greatest urban complex of the 20th century," according to the *AIA Guide to New York City*—occupies nearly 22 acres of prime real estate between 5th and 7th avenues and 47th and 52nd streets. Its central cluster of buildings consists of smooth shafts of warm-hued limestone, streamlined with glistening aluminum. Plazas, concourses, and shops create a sense of community for the nearly quarter of a million people who use it daily. Restaurants, shoe-repair shops, doctors' offices, barbershops, banks, a post office, bookstores, clothing shops, variety stores—all are accommodated within the center, and all parts of the complex are linked by underground passageways.

Rockefeller Center helped turn midtown into New York City's second "downtown" area. The neighborhood now rivals the Wall Street area in its number of prestigious tenants. The center itself is a capital of the communications industry, containing the headquarters of a TV network (NBC), several major publishing companies (Time-Warner, McGraw-Hill, Simon & Schuster), and the world's largest news-gathering organization, the Associated Press.

Numbers in the text correspond to numbers in the margin and on the Midtown map.

A Good Walk
The heart of midtown Manhattan is **Rockefeller Center** (☎ 212/632–3975 for information), one of the greatest achievements in 20th-

century urban planning. A fun way to navigate among its myriad buildings is to move from east to west, following a trail past three famous figures from Greek mythology. Atlas stands sentry outside the classically inspired **International Building** ①, on 5th Avenue between 50th and 51st streets. Head one block south on 5th Avenue and turn west to walk along the **Channel Gardens** ②, a complex of rock pools and seasonal flower beds. Below these are the **Lower Plaza** ③ and, towering heroically above, the famous gold-leaf statue of Prometheus. The backdrop to this scene is the 70-story **GE Building** ④, originally known as the RCA Building, whose entrance is guarded by another striking statue of Prometheus. Straight across bustling 50th Street is America's largest indoor theater, the titanic **Radio City Music Hall** ⑤.

Two other notable Rockefeller Center buildings are on the west side of 6th Avenue: the **McGraw-Hill Building** ⑥, between 48th and 49th streets, and the **Time & Life Building,** between 50th and 51st streets.

Continue north on 6th Avenue, leaving Rockefeller Center. On the east side of 6th Avenue between 52nd and 53rd streets, the monolithic black **CBS Building** ⑦ (also known as Black Rock) stands out from the crowd. From here it's a short stroll to three museums enshrining contemporary culture. Go east on 52nd Street to the **Museum of Television and Radio** ⑧, devoted to the two key mediums of the modern era; here, you can screen favorite television shows from your childhood using the museum's huge library. Right next door is the landmark **"21" Club** ⑨. A shortcut through the outdoor public space close to the CBS Building or through a shopping arcade farther east, at 666 5th Avenue, takes you to 53rd Street's museums: on the south side, the **American Craft Museum** ⑩, and on the north side, the **Museum of Modern Art (MoMA)** ⑪. A block east of MoMA, across 5th Avenue at 3 East 53rd Street, is **Paley Park,** ⑫ a small vest-pocket park with a waterfall.

The true muse of midtown is not art, however, but business, as you'll see on a brisk walk east on 53rd Street across 5th Avenue, where you'll encounter four office towers named after their corporate owners. First head north on Madison Avenue to 55th Street and the elegant rose-granite tower known as the **Sony Building** ⑬, immediately recognizable from afar by its Chippendale-style pediment. Farther east and a little south on Park Avenue stand two prime examples of the functionalist International Style: **Lever House** ⑭ and the **Seagram Building** ⑮, the only New York building designed by Ludwig Mies van der Rohe. Finally, go one block east to Lexington Avenue where, between 53rd and 54th streets, the luminous silvery shaft of the **Citicorp Center** ⑯ houses thousands more New Yorkers engaged in the daily ritual that built the city—commerce. To end your walk on a less material note, return to Park Avenue and turn south to 51st Street and **St. Bartholomew's Church** ⑰, an intricate Byzantine temple struggling to be heard in the home of the skyscraper.

TIMING

To see only the buildings, block out an hour and a half. Allow more time depending on your interest in the museums en route. At minimum you might spend 45 minutes in the American Craft Museum; the same in the Museum of Television and Radio; and 3½ hours in the Museum of Modern Art—even then you'll only dip briefly into the collections; it would be easy to pass an entire day there, ending with a movie in the museum's theater. Keep in mind that some parts of Rockefeller Center are open only during the week.

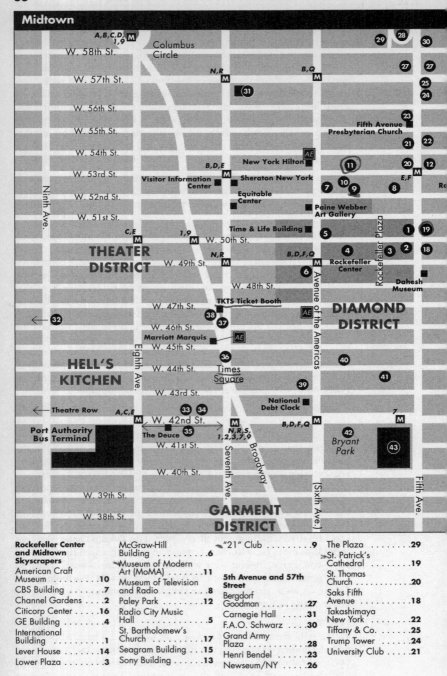

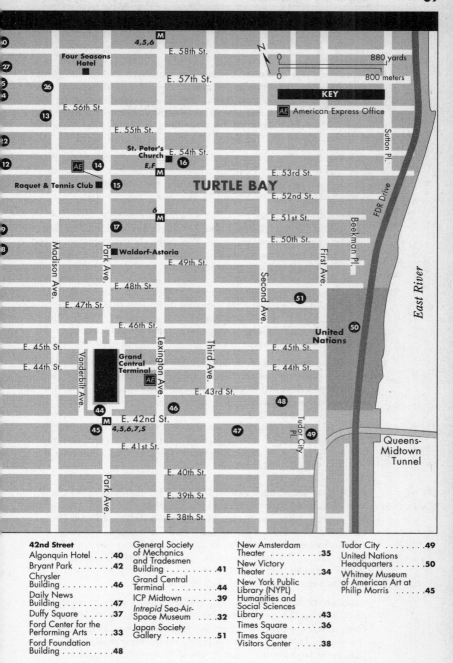

4,5,6 M

E. 58th St.

Four Seasons
Hotel

E. 57th St.

N

0   880 yards
0   800 meters

KEY

AE   American Express Office

E. 56th St.

E. 55th St.

St. Peter's
Church

E. 54th St.

E,F M

TURTLE BAY

Raquet & Tennis Club

E. 53rd St.

E. 52nd St.

E. 51st St.

6 M

E. 50th St.

Waldorf-Astoria

E. 49th St.

E. 48th St.

**United
Nations**

E. 47th St.

E. 46th St.

E. 45th St.

E. 45th St.

E. 44th St.

**Grand
Central
Terminal**

AE

E. 44th St.

E. 43rd St.

44 M

E. 42nd St.

45   **4,5,6,7,S**

E. 41st St.

E. 40th St.

E. 39th St.

E. 38th St.

Madison Ave.
Park Ave.
Vanderbilt Ave.
Lexington Ave.
Third Ave.
Second Ave.
First Ave.
Beekman Pl.
Sutton Pl.
FDR Drive
Tudor City Pl.
Park Ave.

East River

Queens-
Midtown
Tunnel

42nd Street
Algonquin Hotel **40**
Bryant Park **42**
Chrysler
Building **46**
Daily News
Building **47**
Duffy Square **37**
Ford Center for the
Performing Arts **33**
Ford Foundation
Building **48**

General Society
of Mechanics
and Tradesmen
Building **41**
Grand Central
Terminal **44**
ICP Midtown **39**
Intrepid Sea-Air-
Space Museum **32**
Japan Society
Gallery **51**

New Amsterdam
Theater **35**
New Victory
Theater **34**
New York Public
Library (NYPL)
Humanities and
Social Sciences
Library **43**
Times Square **36**
Times Square
Visitors Center **38**

Tudor City **49**
United Nations
Headquarters **50**
Whitney Museum
of American Art at
Philip Morris **45**

Start early in order to arrive at the Museum of Television and Radio when it opens, so you won't have to wait for a TV console on which to watch your shows; break up your MoMA visit with lunch in its café.

Sights to See

⑩ **American Craft Museum.** Distinctions between the terms *craft* and *high art* become irrelevant at this small museum, which showcases works in clay, glass, fabric, wood, metal, paper, and even chocolate by contemporary American and international artisans. ⊠ *40 W. 53rd St., between 5th and 6th Aves.,* ☎ *212/956–3535.* ⌨ *$5.* ☉ *Tues.–Sun. 10–6, Thurs. 10–8.*

❼ **CBS Building.** The only high-rise designed by Eero Saarinen, Black Rock, as this 38-story building is known, was built in 1965. Its dark-gray granite facade actually helps to hold the building up, imparting a sense of towering solidity. ⊠ *51 W. 52nd St., at 6th Ave.*

❷ **Channel Gardens.** This Rockefeller Center promenade, leading from 5th Avenue to the ☞ **Lower Plaza,** has six pools surrounded by flower beds filled with seasonal plantings. The center's horticulturist conceived the gardens and presents around 10 shows a season. This area separates the British building to the north from the French building to the south; above each building's entrance is a national coat of arms. The French building contains, among other shops, the Metropolitan Museum of Art gift shop and the Librairie de France, which sells French-language books, periodicals, tapes, and recordings. The building's surprisingly large basement contains a Spanish bookstore and a foreign-language dictionary store. ⊠ *5th Ave. between 49th and 50th Sts.*

⑯ **Citicorp Center.** The most striking feature of this 1977 design by Hugh Stubbins & Associates is the angled top. The immense solar-energy collector it was designed to carry was never installed, but the building's unique profile changed the New York City skyline. At the base of Citicorp Center is a pleasant atrium mall of restaurants and shops, where occasionally there's music at lunchtime. **St. Peter's Church** (☎ 212/935–2200), whose angled roof is tucked under the Citicorp shadow, is known for its Sunday-afternoon jazz vespers, at 5. ⊠ *Lexington Ave. between 53rd and 54th Sts.*

OFF THE
BEATEN PATH

CORPORATE-SPONSORED EXHIBITS – Though it's not Museum Mile, mid-town does benefit from companies that use part of their space to present free public exhibits. The **Paine Webber Art Gallery** (⊠ 1285 6th Ave., between 51st and 52nd Sts., ☎ 212/713–2885), open weekdays 8–6, hosts four exhibits a year in the base of its building. The **Equitable Center** (⊠ 787 7th Ave., at 51st St., ☎ 212/554–4818) has an enormous Roy Lichtenstein work in its atrium and a gallery with changing exhibits; it is open weekdays 11–6, Saturday noon–5.

DIAMOND DISTRICT – The relatively unglitzy jewelry shops at street level on 47th Street between 5th and 6th avenues are just the tip of the iceberg; upstairs, millions of dollars' worth of gems are traded, and skilled craftsmen cut precious stones. Wheeling and dealing goes on at fever pitch amongst the host of Hasidic Jews in severe black dress, beards, and curled side locks. So thronged with people is this street during the day that it becomes one of the slowest to navigate on foot in Manhattan.

❹ **GE Building.** The backdrop to the ☞ **Channel Gardens, Prometheus,** and the ☞ **Lower Plaza,** this 70-story (850-ft tall) building is the tallest tower in Rockefeller Center. It was known as the RCA Building until GE acquired its namesake company in 1986 (it is also known as 30 Rock): today it is also the headquarters of the NBC television network.

The block-long street called Rockefeller Plaza,
between the GE Building and the Lower Plaza,
the Rockefeller Christmas tree. From 30 Rock em
first TV programs ever, including **the *Today* show**. I
from a ground-floor glass-enclosed studio on the south
49th Street and Rockefeller Plaza, and a small crowd of fes
gathers each day between 7 AM and 9 AM hoping to be caug
era or even interviewed by one of the show's hosts. A one-
of the **NBC Studios** is offered (children under 6 are not permit
30 Rockefeller Plaza, ☎ *212/664–7174.* 🖃 *Tour $10.* ☉ *Tour de
from street level of GE Bldg. every 15 mins Easter–Labor Day, we
days 9:30–6, Sat. 9:30–7, Sun. 9:30–4:45; Thanksgiving–New Year
Day, weekdays 8:30–5, Sat. 9:30–4:30, Sun. 9:30–4:45. Other times
of year, tour departs every ½ hr weekdays 9:30–4:30, every 15 mins
Sat. 9:30–4:30.*

Poised above the GE Building's entrance doors on Rockefeller Plaza
is a striking sculpture of Zeus by Lee Lawrie, the same artist who sculpted
the big Atlas in front of the ☞ **International Building** on 5th Avenue.
Inside, a dramatic mural entitled *Time*, by José María Sert, covers the
ceiling of the foyer. Marble catacombs beneath Rockefeller Center
house restaurants in all price ranges, from the chic American Festival
Café to McDonald's; a post office and clean public rest rooms (scarce
in midtown); and just about every kind of store. To find your way around,
consult the strategically placed directories or obtain the free brochure
"Walking Tour of Rockefeller Center" at the **GE Building information
desk** (☎ 212/332–6868). When you've seen all there is to see, leave
the GE Building from the 6th Avenue side to view the allegorical mosaics above that entrance. ⊠ *Bounded by Rockefeller Plaza, 6th Ave.,
and 49th and 50th Sts.*

NEED A
BREAK?

Dean & DeLuca (⊠ 1 Rockefeller Plaza, at 49th St., ☎ 212/664–
1363), at the foot of the GE Building, serves coffee, tea, and hot chocolate, plus cookies, cakes, and small sandwiches. Restaurateur Pino Lu-
ongo's **Tuscan Square** (⊠ 16 W. 51st St., at Rockefeller Center, ☎
212/977–7777), a restaurant, wine cellar, espresso bar, and house-
wares and accessories market, delivers an old-world Tuscan feel.

❶ **International Building.** A huge statue of Atlas supporting the world stands
sentry before this heavily visited Rockefeller Center structure, which
houses many foreign consulates, international airlines, and a U.S. pass-
port office. The lobby is fitted with Grecian marble. ⊠ *5th Ave. between 50th and 51st Sts.*

⓮ **Lever House.** According to the *AIA Guide to New York City*, this
1952 skyscraper built for the Lever Brothers soap company is "where
the glass curtain wall began." Gordon Bunshaft, of Skidmore, Owings
& Merrill, designed a sheer, slim glass box that rests on the end of a
one-story-thick shelf balanced on square chrome columns. The whole
building seems to float above the street. Because the tower occupies
only half the air space above the lower floors, its side wall reflects a
shimmering image of its neighbors. ⊠ *390 Park Ave., between 53rd
and 54th Sts.*

❸ **Lower Plaza.** Sprawled on his ledge above this Rockefeller Center
plaza, the great gold-leaf statue of the fire-stealing Greek hero **Prometheus**
is one of the most famous sights in the complex, if not in all of New
York. A quotation from Aeschylus—PROMETHEUS, TEACHER IN EVERY
ART, BROUGHT THE FIRE THAT HATH PROVED TO MORTALS A MEANS TO
MIGHTY ENDS—is carved into the red-granite wall behind. The plaza's

...ng rink is open from October through April; the
...omes an open-air café. In December an enormous
...wers above. Most days on the Esplanade above
...United Nations' members alternate with flags
... ⊠ *Between 5th and 6th Aves. and 49th and*
...*654 for the rink.*

...t in 1972, this Rockefeller Center skyscraper
...el plaza with a 50-ft steel sun triangle that
...sions of the sun at noon. ⊠ *6th Ave. between*
...*ts.*

...**seum of Modern Art (MoMA).** Home to many pivotal works of art
of the modern era, MoMA is the city's—and the world's—foremost
showcase of 20th-century art. Opened in 1929 on the heels of the stock
market crash, the museum presented a revolutionary first exhibition—
Cézanne, Gauguin, Seurat, van Gogh. Fortunately, Alfred Barr, the museum's first director, found an enthusiastic audience in New York City,
and he continued to challenge museum goers, not only with avant-garde
painting and sculpture but also by including photography, architecture,
industrial arts, decorative arts, drawings, prints, illustrated books,
and film under the rubric of fine art. MoMA expanded several times
before moving in 1939 into its present six-story building, designed by
Edward Durell Stone and Philip Goodwin. The building has subsequently
lost much of its original detailing, as well as its context—19th-century
town houses and brownstones once sandwiched it on either side—so
it now "appears to be the back end of a back office," as Christopher
Gray has noted in the *New York Times.* Gallery space doubled in
1984, and in 1997 the museum announced plans for a major overhaul,
to be designed by Yoshio Taniguchi. The redesign, incorporating the
site of the former Dorset Hotel at 30 West 54th Street, will reconfig-
ure the museum to a much greater extent than any previous revamp-
ing. Note that because of the renovation (scheduled for completion in
2001), the MoMA plans major changes in the organization and presentation of displays throughout the galleries.

During renovation, starting in the fall of 1999, MoMA presents
MoMA2000, an 18-month series of exhibitions of works drawn from
the museum's own collection. The special exhibitions take the place
of the museum's customary displays while construction is underway.
From a variety of perspectives, three exhibition cycles explore modern art from the periods 1880–1920, 1920–1960, and 1960–2000. At
press time, only information on the first cycle was available. Entitled
Modern Starts, it focuses on the birth of modern art, contrasting early
works with provocative examples from later periods. The exhibition
is split into three sections: People, which treats figurative art from the
likes of Matisse, Rodin, and Munch; Places, which presents rural,
urban, and interior landscapes by Atget, Cézanne, Chirico, Léger, and
others; and Things, which addresses the representation of objects by
artists such as Duchamp, Brancusi, and Picasso.

The second and third exhibitions will use similarly innovative juxta-
positions of old and new, familiar and unfamiliar works to illuminate
modernism and to showcase the museum's incredible collection of
paintings, sculptures, photographs, prints, drawings, architecture, and
design. From early postimpressionism, cubism, dadaism, and surrealism to abstract expressionism, pop art, and contemporary art, MoMA
holds dozens of famous works: van Gogh's *Starry Night* (1889),
Rousseau's *The Sleeping Gypsy* (1897), Picasso's *Les Demoiselles
d'Avignon* (1907), and Matisse's *The Red Studio* (1911) and *Dance*
(1909) are in good company here.

On the ground floor, pause in the serene **Abby Aldrich Rockefeller Sculpture Garden,** on the site of John D. Rockefeller's first New York home. It was designed by architect Philip Johnson as an outdoor "room" with trees, fountains, pools, and sculpture; Juilliard Music School students perform contemporary-music concerts here on weekend evenings in summer. MoMA's two movie theaters are among the finest venues in the city for foreign, independent, and classic films; several series usually run concurrently (☞ Chapter 4). ⊠ *11 W. 53rd St.,* ☎ *212/708–9480; 212/708–9491 for jazz program.* ▣ *$9.50; pay what you wish Fri. 4:30– 8:30.* ⊙ *Sat.–Tues. and Thurs. 10:30–6, Fri. 10:30–8:30.*

⊕ ⑧ **Museum of Television and Radio.** Three galleries of photographs and artifacts document the history of broadcasting in this 1989 limestone building by Philip Johnson and John Burgee. The main attraction is consoles at which you can view a collection of more than 60,000 television shows and radio programs, as well as several thousand commercials. ⊠ *25 W. 52nd St.,* ☎ *212/621–6800 for general information and daily events; 212/621–6600 for other information.* ▣ *$6 (suggested donation).* ⊙ *Tues.–Wed. and Fri.–Sun. noon–6, Thurs. noon–8.*

⊕ ⑫ **Paley Park.** This was the first of New York's vest-pocket parks—small open spaces squeezed between high-rise behemoths—which first sprouted in the '60s. On the site of the former society nightspot the Stork Club ("the New Yorkiest place in New York," said gossip columnist Walter Winchell), Paley Park has a waterfall, which blocks out traffic noise, and feathery honey locust trees to provide shade. A snack bar opens when weather permits. ⊠ *3 E. 53rd St.*

★ ⑤ **Radio City Music Hall.** One of the jewels in the crown of Rockefeller Center, this 6,000-seat Art Deco masterpiece is America's largest indoor theater. Opened in 1932, it astonished the hall's Depression-era patrons with its 60-ft-high foyer, ceiling representing a sunset, and 2-ton chandeliers. The theater originally presented first-run movies in conjunction with live shows featuring the fabled Rockettes chorus line. In 1979 the theater was awarded landmark status. Its year-round schedule now includes major performers, awards presentations, and special events, along with its own Christmas and Easter extravaganzas. A one-hour tour of the theater is offered most days. At press time, plans for a major renovation of the hall were underway, scheduled for completion in September 1999. ⊠ *1260 6th Ave., at 50th St.,* ☎ *212/247– 4777; 212/632–4041 for tour information.* ▣ *Tour $13.75.* ⊙ *Tours usually leave from main lobby every 30 mins Mon.–Sat. 10–5, Sun. 11– 5. Call for current schedules.*

★ ⑰ **St. Bartholomew's Church.** Like the Racquet & Tennis Club two blocks south, this handsome 1919 limestone-and-brick church vividly represents a generation of midtown Park Avenue buildings long since replaced by such modernist landmarks as the ☞ **Seagram** and the ☞ **Lever** buildings. The incongruous juxtaposition plays up the church's finest features—a McKim, Mead & White Romanesque portal from an earlier (1904) church and the intricately tiled Byzantine dome. St. Bart's sponsors music events throughout the year, including the summer's Festival of Sacred Music, which features full-length masses and other choral works; an annual Christmas concert; concerts by L'antica musica, an early-music group; and an organ recital series that showcases the church's 12,422-pipe organ, the largest in the city. ⊠ *Park Ave. between 50th and 51st Sts.,* ☎ *212/378–0200; 212/378–0248 for music program information.* ⊙ *Daily 8–6.*

NEED A
BREAK?

Café St. Bart's (✉ Park Ave. and 50th St., ☎ 212/378–0200), a charming and tranquil outdoor spot for a relatively inexpensive meal or a glass of wine or beer during the summer.

⑮ Seagram Building. Ludwig Mies van der Rohe, a leading interpreter of International Style architecture, built this simple, boxlike bronze-and-glass tower in 1958. The austere facade belies its wit: I-beams, used to hold buildings up, are here attached to the surface, representing the *idea* of support. The Seagram's ground-level plaza, an innovation at the time, has since become a common element in urban skyscraper design. It is a perfect place to contemplate the monumental brick-and-limestone neo-Renaissance **Racquet & Tennis Club** (1916) across the street, which exhibits a complementary restraint and classicism. Inside the Seagram Building is one of New York's most venerated restaurants, the **Four Seasons Grill and Pool Room** (☞ Chapter 5). ✉ *375 Park Ave., between 52nd and 53rd Sts., ☎ 212/572–7404. ☎ Free. ☉ Tours Tues. at 3.*

 ⑬ Sony Building. Commissioned by AT&T, which has since decamped to New Jersey, the Sony Building was designed by Philip Johnson in 1984. Sony's rose-granite columns, its regilded statue of the winged *Golden Boy* in the lobby, and its giant-size Chippendale-style pediment made the skyscraper an instant landmark. The first floor, Sony Plaza, includes a public seating area, a café, a newsstand, a music store, a Sony Electronics store, and the **Sony Wonder Technology Lab,** outfitted with interactive exhibits such as a recording studio, a video-game production studio, and a TV production studio. ✉ *550 Madison Ave., between 55th and 56th Sts., ☎ 212/833–8830 for Sony Wonder Technology Lab. ☎ Free. ☉ Technology Lab: Tues.–Wed. and Fri.–Sat. 10–6, Thurs. 10–8, Sun. noon–6 (last entrance 5:30); Sony Plaza: daily 7 AM–11 PM.*

❾ "21" Club. A trademark row of jockey statuettes parades along the wrought-iron balcony of this landmark restaurant, which has a burnished men's-club atmosphere and a great downstairs bar. After a period of decline in the 1980s, when its menu aged along with its wealthy clientele, "21" reinvented itself in the 1990s. Today the power brokers are back, along with the luster of the past (☞ Chapter 5). ✉ *21 W. 52nd St., ☎ 212/582–7200.*

✂ 5TH AVENUE AND 57TH STREET

For better or for worse, retail and entertainment have converged in the neighborhood just north of Rockefeller Center. This stretch of 5th Avenue is still one of the world's great shopping districts, as evidenced by its many elegant shops and international fashion firms. The rents are even higher along East 57th Street, where there's a parade of exclusive boutiques and fine art galleries. But the area's character has changed as brand-name stores with slick marketing schemes have moved in. Hype aside, these stores can be fun even if you don't want to buy anything, and the many shoppers they attract to the neighborhood bring down the snootiness level in the pricier stores, too. This tour mentions the obvious stores, both new and established, but for more information about these and others, *see* Chapter 9. Theme restaurants dominate 57th Street west of 5th Avenue, though that fad is on the wane.

Numbers in the text correspond to numbers in the margin and on the Midtown map.

A Good Walk

Start right across the street from Rockefeller Center's Channel Gardens (☞ Rockefeller Center and Midtown Skyscrapers, *above*), at the renowned **Saks Fifth Avenue** ⑱, the flagship of the national department store chain. Across 50th Street is the Gothic-style Roman Catholic **St. Patrick's Cathedral** ⑲. From outside, catch one of the city's most photographed views: the ornate white spires of St. Pat's against the black-glass curtain of Olympic Tower, a multiuse building of shops, offices, and luxury apartments at 51st and 5th.

Cartier displays its wares in a jewel-box turn-of-the-century mansion on the southeast corner of 52nd Street and 5th Avenue; similar houses used to line this street, and many of their residents were parishioners of **St. Thomas Church** ⑳, an Episcopal institution that has occupied the site at the northwest corner of 53rd Street and 5th Avenue since 1911. Continuing north, you'll see the imposing bulk of the **University Club** ㉑ at the northwest corner of 5th Avenue and 54th Street; this granite palace was built by New York's leading turn-of-the-century architects, McKim, Mead & White. It shares the block with the **Peninsula,** one of the city's finer hotels (☞ Chapter 6). Across the street is **Takashimaya New York** ㉒, a branch of a Japanese department store chain.

Fifth Avenue Presbyterian Church, a grand brownstone church (1875), sits on the northwest corner of 5th Avenue and 55th Street. On the same block is **Henri Bendel** ㉓, a bustling fashion store organized like a little tower of intimate boutiques. Next door is **Harry Winston** (⊠ 718 5th Ave.), with a spectacular selection of fine jewelry. Across the street, on the northeast corner of 5th Avenue and 55th Street, is the **Disney Store** (⊠ 711 5th Ave.), where you can buy everything Disney, from key chains and clothes to animation stills and even vacations. The **Coca-Cola Store** (⊠ 711 5th Ave.), next door, seems modest by comparison.

Trump Tower ㉔, on the east side of 5th Avenue between 56th and 57th streets, is an exclusive 68-story apartment and office building named for its developer, Donald Trump. To the north, the intersection of **5th Avenue and 57th Street** is ground zero for high-end shopping. And what more fitting resident for this spot than **Tiffany & Co.** ㉕, the renowned jewelers. Around the corner on 57th Street, **NikeTown** (⊠ 6 E. 57th St.) is a shrine to sports; it even has TVs and scoreboards on the first floor, so you can check on how your team is doing. Neighboring **Tourneau TimeMachine** (⊠ 12 E. 57th St.) has four levels of timepieces and the small "Gallery of Time" exhibit hall. It's next to **590 Madison Avenue,** a five-sided, 20-story sheath of dark gray-green granite and glass by Edward Larrabee Barnes. The public is welcome inside to view exhibits at **Newseum/NY** ㉖, a media-monitoring institution. In the building's atrium, you can relax with a snack and enjoy the Alexander Calder sculptures.

Cross 57th Street and head back toward 5th Avenue on the north side of the street, with its stellar lineup of boutiques: the French classics **Chanel** (⊠ 15 E. 57th St.) and **Hermès** (⊠ 11 E. 57th St.), the English shop **Burberrys Ltd.** (⊠ 9 E. 57th St.), and the German **Escada** (⊠ 7 E. 57th St.). Farther west are the watch store **Swatch Timeship** (⊠ 5 E. 57th), the **Original Levi's Store** (⊠ 3 E. 57th St.), and **Warner Brothers Studio Store** (⊠ 1 E. 57th St.), an eight-story extravaganza filled with movie, television, and cartoon paraphernalia as well as interactive displays, movies, and even a café. From outside you can watch a larger-than-life Superman pushing up the store's elevator. Across 5th Avenue stands the elegant **Bergdorf Goodman** ㉗. The extravagant women's boutiques are on the west side of the avenue between 57th and 58th streets, the men's store on the east side at 58th Street. **Van Cleef & Arpels** jewelers is within Bergdorf's West 57th Street corner.

Cross 58th Street to **Grand Army Plaza** ㉘, the open space along 5th Avenue between 58th and 60th streets. Appropriately named **The Plaza** ㉙, the famous hotel at the western edge of this square is a National Historic Landmark, built in 1907. Across the street, on the southeast corner of 58th Street and 5th Avenue, is the legendary **F.A.O. Schwarz** ㉚ toy store, ensconced in the **General Motors Building.**

Now return to 57th Street and head west, where the glamour eases off a bit. The large red NO. 9 on the sidewalk, in front 9 West 57th Street, was designed by Ivan Chermayeff. You'll also pass the excellent **Rizzoli Bookstore** (✉ 31 W. 57th St.), its interior as elegant as many of the art books it carries. Across 6th Avenue (remember, New Yorkers *don't* call it Avenue of the Americas, despite the street signs), you'll know you're in classical-music territory when you peer through the showroom windows at **Steinway and Sons** (✉ 109 W. 57th St.). Presiding over the southeast corner of 7th Avenue and 57th Street, **Carnegie Hall** ㉛ has for decades reigned as a premier international concert hall. Devotees of classical music may want to head from here up to nearby Lincoln Center (☞ The Upper West Side, *below*).

For tourist information, maps, tickets to attractions, souvenirs, and A.T.M.s, stop by the **Visitor Information Center** (✉ 810 7th Ave., between 52nd and 53rd Sts., ☎ 212/484–1222. ☉ 8–6 weekdays, 9–5 weekends).

TIMING
This walk isn't long and can be completed in about 1½ hours. Add at least an hour for basic browsing around stores and several more hours for serious shopping. Make sure the stores are open before you set out. Bear in mind that 5th Avenue is jam-packed with holiday shoppers from Halloween until New Year's. Year-round, if you want to experience one of the theme restaurants plan on waiting up to an hour for a table.

Sights to See

㉗ **Bergdorf Goodman.** Good taste—at a price—defines this understated department store with dependable service. The seventh floor has room after exquisite room of wonderful linens, tabletop items, and gifts. ✉ *Main store: 754 5th Ave., between 57th and 58th Sts.,* ☎ *212/753–7300; men's store: 745 5th Ave., at 58th St.*

★ ㉛ **Carnegie Hall.** Musical headliners have played Carnegie Hall since 1891, when its opening concert series included none other than Tchaikovsky conducting his own works. Designed by William Barnet Tuthill, who was also an amateur cellist, this renowned concert hall was paid for almost entirely by Andrew Carnegie. Outside, the stout, square brown building has a few Moorish-style arches added, almost as an afterthought, to the facade. Inside, however, the simply decorated 2,804-seat auditorium is one of the finest in the world. The hall has attracted the world's leading orchestras and solo and group performers, from Arturo Toscanini and Leonard Bernstein (he made his triumphant debut here in 1943, standing in for New York Philharmonic conductor Bruno Walter) to Duke Ellington, Ella Fitzgerald, Judy Garland, Frank Sinatra, Bob Dylan, the Beatles (playing one of their first U.S. concerts)—and thousands of others.

Carnegie Hall was extensively restored in the 1980s; a subsequent mid-1990s renovation removed concrete from beneath the stage's wooden floor, vastly improving the acoustics. The work also increased the size of the lobby and added the small **Rose Museum** (✉ 154 W. 57th St.,

☎ 212/247–7800), which is free and open Thursday–Tuesday 11–4:30 and through intermission during concerts. Located just east of the main auditorium, it displays mementos from the hall's illustrious history, such as a Benny Goodman clarinet and Arturo Toscanini's baton. You can take a guided 1-hour tour of Carnegie Hall, or even rent it if you've always dreamed of singing from its stage. ✉ *W. 57th St. at 7th Ave.,* ☎ *212/247–7800; for hall rental only 212/903–9710.* 🎫 *$6.* ☺ *Tours Mon.– Tues. and Thurs.–Fri. at 11:30, 2, and 3 (performance schedule permitting).*

OFF THE
BEATEN PATH

DAHESH MUSEUM – Donating his collection of approximately 3,000 works, a Lebanese doctor named Dahesh (1909–84) endowed this small exhibition space dedicated to the European academic tradition. Among the well-known painters represented in changing exhibitions here are Bonheur, Bouguereau, Gérôme, and Troyon—all painters who have since been upstaged by their contemporaries, the Impressionists, but who once claimed greater popularity. ✉ *601 5th Ave.,* ☎ *212/ 759–0606.* 🎫 *Free.* ☺ *Tues.–Sat. 11–6.*

★ ☺ ③⓪ **F.A.O. Schwarz.** A fantastic mechanical clock stands right inside the front doors of this famous toy-o-rama, which offers a vast, wondrously fun selection. Browsing here brings out the child in everyone. If the line to get in looks impossibly long, try walking around the block, past the fanciful window displays, to the Madison Avenue entrance, where the wait may be shorter (☞ Chapters 3 and 9). ✉ *767 5th Ave., at 58th St.,* ☎ *212/644–9400.*

②⑧ **Grand Army Plaza.** At the southeast corner of Central Park is this open space along 5th Avenue between 58th and 60th streets. The **Pulitzer Fountain,** donated by publisher Joseph Pulitzer of Pulitzer Prize fame, dominates the southern portion of the square. Appropriately enough for this prosperous neighborhood, the fountain is crowned by a female figure representing Abundance. To the north prances Augustus Saint-Gaudens's gilded equestrian statue of Civil War general William Tecumseh Sherman. Across 59th street is **Doris C. Freedman Plaza,** which features sculpture exhibits courtesy of the Public Art Fund, at the grand Scholars' Gate entrance to **Central Park** (☞ Central Park, *below*). ☞ **The Plaza,** the internationally famous hotel, stands at the western edge of the square.

②③ **Henri Bendel.** Chic Henri Bendel sells whimsical, expensive clothing in a beautiful store. Inventive displays and sophisticated boutiques are hallmarks. You can view the facade's René Lalique art-glass windows (1912) at close range from balconies ringing the four-story atrium. The second-floor café is particularly charming. ✉ *712 5th Ave., between 55th and 56th Sts.,* ☎ *212/247–1100.*

②⑥ **Newseum/NY.** A sister to the larger Newseum in Arlington, Virginia, the New York Newseum is operated by The Freedom Forum. It offers changing exhibits as well as public roundtables and other programs related to journalism, free speech, and freedom of the press. Exhibits have included a selection of new photographs from 1968, and Pulitzer Prize winner Lucian Perkins's behind-the-scenes shots of runway models. ✉ *580 Madison Ave., between 56th and 57th Sts.,* ☎ *212/317– 7503.* 🎫 *Free.* ☺ *Mon.–Sat. 10–5:30.*

②⑨ **The Plaza.** With Grand Army Plaza, 5th Avenue, *and* Central Park at its doorstep, this world-famous hotel claims one of Manhattan's prize real estate corners. A registered historical landmark built in 1907, The Plaza was designed by Henry Hardenbergh, who also built the Dakota apartment building (☞ The Upper West Side, *below*). Here he concocted a birthday-cake effect of highly ornamented white-glazed brick topped with a copper-and-slate mansard roof. The hotel is home to Eloise, the fictional star of Kay Thompson's children's books, and has been featured in many movies, from Alfred Hitchcock's *North by Northwest* to *Plaza Suite*. Past real-life guests include the Duke and Duchess of Windsor and the Beatles. ⊠ *5th Ave. at 59th St.,* ☎ *212/759–3000.*

★ ⑲ **St. Patrick's Cathedral.** Built in the Gothic style, the Roman Catholic cathedral of New York is one of the city's largest (seating approximately 2,400) and most striking churches. It is dedicated to the patron saint of the Irish, then as now one of New York's principal ethnic groups. The white marble-and-stone structure was begun in 1859 by architect James Renwick and consecrated in 1879. Additions over the years include the archbishop's house and rectory, two 330-ft spires, and the intimate Lady Chapel. The original, predominantly Irish, members of the congregation made a statement when they chose the 5th Avenue location for their church: during the week, most of them came to the neighborhood only as employees of the wealthy. But on Sunday, at least, they could claim a prestigious spot for themselves. Among the statues in the alcoves around the nave is a modern depiction of the first American-born saint, Mother Elizabeth Ann Seton. The steps outside are a convenient, scenic rendezvous spot. ⊠ *5th Ave. at 50th St.,* ☎ *212/753–2261 rectory.* ☉ *Daily 8 AM–8:45 PM.*

⑳ **St. Thomas Church.** This Episcopal institution with a striking French Gothic interior was consecrated on its present site in 1916. The impressive huge stone reredos behind the altar holds the statues of more than 50 apostles, saints, martyrs, missionaries, and other church figures, all designed by Lee Lawrie. The church is also known for its men's and boys' choir; Christmas Eve services here have become a seasonal highlight. ⊠ *5th Ave. at 53rd St.,* ☎ *212/757–7013.* ☉ *Daily 7–6.*

⑱ **Saks Fifth Avenue.** On a breezy day, the 14 American flags fluttering from the block-long facade of Saks' flagship store make for the most patriotic scene in town. In 1926, the department store's move from its original Broadway location solidified midtown 5th Avenue's new status as a prestigious shopping mecca. Saks remains a civilized favorite among New York shoppers. The eighth-floor Café SFA serves delicious snacks and lunches to go with the Rockefeller Center–5th Avenue view. Saks's annual Christmas window displays (on view from late November through the first week of the new year) are among New York's most festive. ⊠ *611 5th Ave., between 49th and 50th Sts.,* ☎ *212/753–4000.*

㉒ **Takashimaya New York.** This elegant yet somewhat austere branch of Japan's largest department store chain features a garden atrium, a two-floor gallery, and a tearoom. It has four floors of men's and women's clothing, gifts, and accessories and also carries household items that combine Eastern and Western styles. ⊠ *693 5th Ave., between 54th and 55th Sts.,* ☎ *212/350–0100.*

★ ㉕ **Tiffany & Co.** One of the most famous jewelers in the world and the quintessential New York store, Tiffany anchors the southeast corner of one of the city's great intersections. The fortress–like Art Deco entrance and dramatic miniature window displays have been a fixture here since 1940, when the store moved from Herald Square. Founded in 1837 at 237 Broadway, Tiffany slowly made its way uptown in five previous moves. The store's signature light blue bags are perennially in style, especially on gift-giving occasions. A New York icon, Tiffany is immortalized in the 1961 Hollywood classic *Breakfast at Tiffany's,* in which a Givenchy-clad Audrey Hepburn emerges from a yellow cab at dawn to window-shop, coffee and Danish in hand. ⊠ *727 5th Ave., at 57th St.,* ☎ *212/755–8000.*

NEED A
BREAK?

Mangia, an Italian and American food shop, is a great place to stop for coffee and a snack, especially if good food is the only theme you want in a restaurant. Desserts are scrumptious, and the salad bar is exceptional. ⊠ *50 W. 57th St.,* ☎ *212/582–5882. Closed Sun.*

㉔ **Trump Tower.** As he has done with other projects, developer Donald Trump named this exclusive 68-story apartment and office building after himself. The grand 5th Avenue entrance leads into a glitzy six-story shopping atrium paneled in pinkish-orange marble and trimmed with lustrous brass. A fountain cascades against one wall, drowning out the clamor of the city, while trees and ivy grow on the setbacks outside. ⊠ *5th Ave. between 56th and 57th Sts.*

㉑ **University Club.** New York's leading turn-of-the-century architects, McKim, Mead & White, designed this 1899 granite palace for an exclusive midtown club of degree-holding men. The club's popularity declined as individual universities built their own clubs and as gentlemen's clubs became less important on the New York social scene, but the seven-story Renaissance Revival building (the facade looks as though it is three stories) is as grand as ever. Critic Paul Goldberger has called it Charles McKim's "best surviving work." The crests of various prestigious universities hang above its windows. ⊠ *1 W. 54th St., at 5th Ave.*

42ND STREET

Few streets in America claim as many landmarks as midtown Manhattan's central axis, from Times Square, Bryant Park, and the main branch of the New York Public Library on its western half to Grand Central Terminal and the United Nations on its eastern flank. Yet as long ago as World War II, 42nd Street began to nosedive, as once-grand theaters around Times Square switched from showing burlesque and legitimate theater to second-run and pornographic movies. With that decline came pickpockets, prostitutes, and the destitute, and the area became synonymous with tawdry blight.

But all that began to change—slowly in the late '80s, and then more rapidly in the 1990s, as first Bryant Park and then the Deuce, as the block between 7th and 8th avenues has long been known (it refers to the 2 in the name), were nurtured back to life. 42nd Street is now poised to reclaim its fame as the metaphorical Broadway, and today each week brings real-estate deals and ground-breakings, theater reopenings, and new stores, hotels, and restaurants, many with entertainment themes, each visually louder than the last. In Times Square itself, the neon lights shine brighter than ever—a local ordinance requires that massive billboard-style ads are included in all new construction. Some critics decry the "Disney-fication" of this part of town, but, really, what New York neighborhood is more appropriate for this over-the-top treatment?

Numbers in the text correspond to numbers in the margin and on the Midtown map.

A Good Walk

Begin at the corner of 42nd Street and 10th Avenue (or for the intrepid, at the *Intrepid* **Sea-Air-Space Museum** ㉜, four blocks north at the Hudson River). The block of 42nd Street stretching toward 9th Avenue is home to a string of thriving off-Broadway playhouses, called **Theatre Row.** Across the street, at 330 West 42nd Street, stands the first **McGraw-Hill Building,** designed in 1931 by Raymond Hood, who later worked on Rockefeller Center (where there is a later McGraw-Hill building (☞ Rockefeller Center and Midtown Skyscrapers, *above*). The lobby is an Art Deco wonder of opaque glass and stainless steel.

The monolithic **Port Authority Bus Terminal,** at the corner of 8th Avenue and 42nd Street, bustles with the millions of travelers arriving and departing the city by bus each year. **The Deuce,** the block of 42nd Street just east of Port Authority, is in the throes of an astonishing, though still incomplete, transformation. Nine theaters once lined the street, and for decades X-rated bookstores and peep shows were their only tenants. Some of those theaters have been immaculately restored or rehabilitated, their facades beaming with high-wattage signs, while others await their turn. The western half of the Deuce, nearest the Port Authority, is still largely under construction. Stretching across the northeast portion of the street, **E Walk,** a huge $300 million hotel, retail, and entertainment complex with 13 movie theaters, is scheduled for completion in 2001. On the Deuce's south side, the former Empire and Liberty theaters are in the process of being transformed into a movie house, food court, and a Madame Tussaud's exhibit.

On the Deuce is the currently dark **Times Square Theater** (✉ 215 W. 42nd St.), where for two decades after its 1920 opening, top hits such as *Gentlemen Prefer Blondes, The Front Page,* and *Strike Up the Band* were staged; Noël Coward's *Private Lives* opened here with Gertrude Lawrence, Laurence Olivier, and the author himself. Moving east toward Times Square, you'll find the **Ford Center for the Performing Arts** ㉝ (which presents only a slim entrance on the Deuce—the main facade is on 43rd Street and well worth a detour) and the **New Victory Theater** ㉞, a reclaimed treasure that mounts theatrical productions for children. Across from the New Victory is the **New Amsterdam Theater** ㉟, brought back to life by the Walt Disney Company.

Times Square ㊱ is one of New York's principal energy centers, not least because of its dazzling billboards. Before continuing east on 42nd Street, head north through Times Square to **Duffy Square** ㊲, a triangle between 46th and 47th streets, the home of the **TKTS** discount ticket booth. On the east side of Broadway, the **Times Square Visitors Center** ㊳ in the historic Embassy Theater is an all-in-one resource for visitors.

At the intersection of 42nd Street and 6th Avenue, look north to see, on the side of a low 43rd Street building, the **National Debt Clock,** an electronic display that tots up the growing national debt of the United States each second. At 6th Avenue and 43rd Street you can visit a branch of the International Center of Photography (☞ Museum Mile, *below*), **ICP Midtown** ㊴.

A block north of that is a rather clubby section of 44th Street that you might want to peek into before returning to 42nd Street. First, you'll see the comfortably understated **Algonquin Hotel** ㊵, an old celebrity haunt (☞ Chapters 6 and 7). Next door is the **Iroquois Hotel** (✉ 49 W. 44th St.), where struggling actor James Dean lived in the early 1950s. Across the street from them is the **Royalton Hotel** (✉ 44 W. 44th St.), a midtown hot spot chicly redone by French designer Philippe Starck (☞ Chapter 6). Its neighbor, at 42 West 44th Street, is the **Association of the Bar of the City of New York,** with an 1896 neoclassical facade resembling the courthouses where its members spend so much of their time. Back on the north side of the street, at 37 West 44th Street, is the **New York Yacht Club** (1900), the former longtime home of the America's Cup trophy. The swelling Beaux Arts windows look just like the sterns of ships, complete with stone-carved water splashing over the sills. Farther east is the redbrick **Harvard Club** (⌧ 27 W. 44th St.); the newer **Penn Club** (⌧ 30 W. 44th St.), with its elegant blue awning, is on the other side of the street. And, yes, something on this block is open to the public: the **General Society of Mechanics and Tradesmen Building** ㊶.

At the southwest corner of 5th Avenue and 44th Street, notice the 19-ft-tall 1907 **sidewalk clock** on a pedestal set in the 5th Avenue sidewalk, a relic of an era when only the wealthy could afford watches.

At 42nd Street and 6th Avenue, steps rise into the shrubbery and trees of the handsomely renovated **Bryant Park** ㊷, a perfect place to relax for a few minutes. The park has been adopted as the backyard of all midtown workers. It's directly behind the magnificent Beaux Arts building that houses the **New York Public Library Humanities and Social Sciences Library** ㊸, the central research branch of the city's library system. The library houses part of its collections under the green lawn.

Continue east on 42nd Street to **Grand Central Terminal** ㊹. This Manhattan landmark was saved from the wrecking ball in a precedent-setting case under New York's landmark-preservation law. On the southwest corner of Park Avenue and 42nd Street, directly opposite Grand Central, the **Whitney Museum of American Art at Philip Morris** ㊺ occupies the ground floor of the Philip Morris Building. The museum abuts **Pershing Square,** the block of Park Avenue east of the viaduct. Attempts to make this area more pleasant have included turning it into a pedestrian zone during the day. Next door is what's known as the **Bowery Savings Bank building** (built in 1923; ⌧ 110 E. 42nd St.), whose massive arches and 70-ft-high marble columns give it a commanding presence; it more closely resembles a church than a bank. At the end of the block is the 1929 **Chanin Building** (⌧ 122 E. 42nd St.), notable for the Art Deco patterns that adorn its facade.

Ask New Yorkers to name their favorite skyscraper, and most will choose the Art Deco **Chrysler Building** ㊻ at 42nd Street and Lexington Avenue. Although the Chrysler Corporation itself moved out long ago, this graceful shaft culminating in a stainless-steel spire still captivates the eye and the imagination. On the south side of 42nd Street and east one block, the **Daily News Building** ㊼, where the newspaper was produced until the spring of 1995, is another Art Deco tower with a lobby worth visiting. The **Ford Foundation Building** ㊽, on the next block, is more modern and encloses a 12-story, ⅓-acre greenhouse.

Climb the steps along 42nd Street between 1st and 2nd avenues to enter **Tudor City** ㊾, a self-contained complex of a dozen buildings featuring half-timbering and stained glass. From here you have a great view of the **United Nations Headquarters** ㊿, which occupies a lushly landscaped 18-acre riverside tract just east of 1st Avenue between 42nd and 48th streets. To end this walk on a quiet note, walk up 1st Avenue and turn left on East 46th Street, where you will find the **Japan Society Gallery,** 51 a lovely oasis of fine and performing arts from Japan.

TIMING

This long walk covers vastly different types of sights, from frenzied Times Square to bucolic Bryant Park, and from the ornate Grand Central Terminal to the sleek United Nations complex. If you start at the *Intrepid,* you could easily eat up most of a day even before you reach 5th Avenue. If you can, time your sightseeing so you visit Times Square at night, perhaps for a meal or a show, to take in the spectacle of bright lights.

Sights to See

40 **Algonquin Hotel.** Considering its history as a haunt of well-known writers and actors, this 1902 hotel is surprisingly unpretentious. Its most famous association is with the Algonquin Round Table, a witty group of literary Manhattanites who gathered in its lobby and dining rooms in the 1920s—a clique that included short-story writer and critic Dorothy Parker, humorist Robert Benchley, playwright George S. Kaufman, journalist and critic Alexander Woolcott, and actress Tallulah Bankhead. One reason they met here was the hotel's proximity to the former offices of the *New Yorker* magazine at 28 West 44th Street (the magazine now operates at 20 West 43rd Street, but is scheduled to move to the new Condé Nast tower on Times Square in 2000). Come here for a cozy drink at the bar or dinner and cabaret performances in the intimate Oak Room (☞ Chapter 7). ✉ *59 W. 44th St., between 5th and 6th Aves.,* ☎ *212/840–6800.*

OFF THE   **BEEKMAN PLACE –** This secluded and exclusive two-block-long East Side
BEATEN PATH   enclave has an aura of unperturbably elegant calm. Residents of its
                 town houses have included the Rockefellers, Alfred Lunt and Lynn
                 Fontanne, Ethel Barrymore, Irving Berlin, and, of course, Auntie Mame,
                 a character in the well-known Patrick Dennis play (and later movie) of
                 the same name. Steps at 51st Street lead to an esplanade along the East
                 River. ✉ *East of 1st Ave. between 49th and 51st Sts.*

★ ☙ **42** **Bryant Park.** Following a dramatic renovation in the early '90s, Bryant Park, midtown's only major green space, has become one of the best-loved and most beautiful small parks in the city. Named for the poet and editor William Cullen Bryant (1794–1878), the 7-acre park was originally known as Reservoir Square (the adjacent main branch of the ☞ **New York Public Library** stands on the former site of the city reservoir). America's first World's Fair, the Crystal Palace Exhibition, was held here in 1853–54. Today, century-old London plane trees and formal flower beds line the perimeter of its grassy central square. In temperate months the park draws thousands of lunching office workers; in summer it hosts live jazz and comedy concerts and sponsors free outdoor film screenings on Monday at dusk (☞ Chapter 4). Each spring and autumn giant white tents spring up in the park for the New York fashion shows. It is also home to the stylish Bryant Park Grill and the open-air Bryant Park Café, which is open April 15–October 14. Kiosks at the west end of the park sell sandwiches and salads. ✉ *6th Ave. between W. 40th and W. 42nd Sts.,* ☎ *212/983–4142.* ☉ *Nov.–Apr., daily 8–7; May and Aug., daily 7 AM–8 PM; June and July, daily 7 AM–9 PM; Sept.–Oct., daily 7–7.*

★ **46** **Chrysler Building.** An Art Deco masterpiece designed by William Van Alen and built between 1928 and 1930, the Chrysler Building is one of New York's most iconic and beloved skyscrapers. It is at its best at dusk, when the setting sun makes the stainless-steel spire glow, and at night, when its illuminated geometric design looks like the backdrop to a Hollywood musical. The Chrysler Corporation moved out in the mid-1950s, but the building retains its name and many automotive details: "gargoyles" shaped like car-hood ornaments sprout from the building's upper stories—wings from the 31st floor, eagle heads from the 61st. At 1,048 ft, the building only briefly held the world's-tallest title—for 40 days before the Empire State Building (☞ Murray Hill, Flatiron District, and Gramercy, *below*) snatched it away. The Chrysler Building has no observation deck, but you can visit its elegant dark lobby faced with African marble and covered with a ceiling mural that salutes transportation and human endeavor. ⊠ *405 Lexington Ave., at 42nd St.*

47 Daily News Building. This Raymond Hood–designed Art Deco tower (1930) has brown-brick spandrels and windows that make it seem loftier than its 37 stories. The newspaper moved to the west side in 1995, but the famous illuminated globe, 12 ft in diameter, is still here. The floor is laid out as a gigantic compass, with bronze lines indicating air mileage from principal world cities to New York. ⊠ *220 E. 42nd St., between 2nd and 3rd Aves.*

37 Duffy Square. This triangle at the north end of ☞ Times Square is named after World War I hero Father Francis P. Duffy (1871–1932), known as "the fighting chaplain," who later was pastor of Holy Cross Church on West 42nd Street. There's also a statue of George M. Cohan (1878–1942), who wrote "Yankee Doodle Dandy." The square is the best place for a panoramic view of Times Square's riotous assemblage of signs. At its north end the **TKTS discount ticket booth** sells discounted tickets to Broadway and off-Broadway shows (☞ Chapter 4). ⊠ *In traffic island between 46th and 47th Sts.*

33 Ford Center for the Performing Arts (☞ Chapter 4). On the site of two classic 42nd Street theaters, the Ford Center incorporates a landmark 43rd Street exterior wall from the Lyric (built in 1903) and architectural elements from the Apollo (1910), including its stage, proscenium, and dome (the other parts of the theaters, which had fallen into disrepair, were demolished). A 1,119-seat orchestra, two 360-seat balconies, and a huge stage make it likely the Ford will continue to be a leading venue for large-scale productions. Such a future is in keeping with the Lyric and Apollo's history: in the early part of this century, the top talents they attracted to their stages included the Marx Brothers, Fred Astaire, Ethel Merman, and W. C. Fields. ⊠ *213–215 W. 42nd St., between 7th and 8th Aves.,* ☎ *212/307–4100 for tickets.*

48 Ford Foundation Building. Home to one of the largest philanthropic organizations in the world, the Ford Foundation Building, built by Kevin Roche, John Dinkeloo & Associates in 1967, is best known for its glass-walled, 130-ft-high atrium, which doubles as a ⅓-acre greenhouse. Its trees, terraced garden, and still-water pool make the atrium a retreat from the crush around ☞ **Grand Central Terminal**. ⊠ *320 E. 43rd St., between 1st and 2nd Aves., with an entrance on 42nd St.* 🎟 *Free.* ☉ *Weekdays 9–5.*

OFF THE
BEATEN PATH

GARMENT DISTRICT – This district, which runs along 7th Avenue between 31st and 41st streets (where it's known as Fashion Avenue), teems with warehouses, workshops, and showrooms that manufacture and finish mostly women's and children's clothing, and countless fabric, button, and notions shops. On weekdays the streets are crowded with trucks and the sidewalks swarm with daredevil deliverymen wheeling garment racks between factories and subcontractors. At the southern edge of the district you'll find New York's Amtrak terminal at **Pennsylvania Station** (⊠ 31st to 34th Sts., between 7th and 8th Aves.); major sporting, entertainment and other events at **Madison Square Garden** (⊠ 31st to 34th Sts., between 7th and 8th Aves.); and the **General Post Office** (⊠ 8th Ave and 33rd St., ☎ 212/967–8585), which is open 24 hours a day, 365 days a year.

41 General Society of Mechanics and Tradesmen Building. A turn-of-the-century prep-school building houses this still-active society, which sponsors a general-membership library. On display in the three-story hall are Colonial-era steamer trunks, Civil War paraphernalia, and locks and keys as old as the United States. ⊠ *20 W. 44th St., between 5th and 6th Aves.,* ☎ *212/840–1840.* ☞ *Free.* ☉ *Weekdays 9–5.*

★ ㊹ **Grand Central Terminal.** Grand Central is not only the world's largest railway station (76 acres) and the nation's busiest (500,000 commuters and subway riders use it daily). It is also one of the world's greatest public spaces, "justly famous," as critic Tony Hiss has said, "as a crossroads, a noble building. . . and an ingenious piece of engineering." A massive four-year renovation completed in October 1998 restored the 1913 landmark to its original splendor—and then some.

The south side of 42nd Street is the best vantage point from which to admire Grand Central's dramatic Beaux Arts facade, which is dominated by three 75-ft-high arched windows separated by pairs of fluted columns. At the top are a beautiful clock and a crowning sculpture, *Transportation,* which depicts a soaring Mercury flanked by Hercules and Minerva. The facade is particularly beautiful at night, when bathed in golden light. Doors on Vanderbilt Avenue and on 42nd Street lead to the cavernous **main concourse.** This majestic space is 200 ft long, 120 ft wide, and 120 ft—roughly 12 stories—high. Overhead, you'll see a massive, robin's egg–blue ceiling covered with a celestial map that gloriously displays the constellations of the zodiac (the major stars actually glow with fiber-optic lights). A new marble staircase modeled after the Garnier stair at the Paris Opera, included in the original terminal plans but never built, has been seamlessly installed onto the concourse's east end. Gold- and nickel-plated chandeliers gleam once more in the passageways.

Dozens of restaurants and shops, many in spaces long closed to the public, now make Grand Central a major destination in its own right. The renovated **dining concourse** has two dozen food vendors, serving everything from caviar to cheesecake. Four restaurants on the balconies, including the mahogany-and-leather Michael Jordan's–The Steak House, offer fine perspectives from which to view this majestic space.

Despite all its grandeur, Grand Central still functions primarily as a railroad station. Underground, more than 60 ingeniously integrated railroad tracks lead trains upstate and to Connecticut via MetroNorth Commuter Rail. The best time to visit is at rush hour, when the concourse crackles with the frenzy of commuters dashing every which way. ⊠ *Main entrance: E. 42nd St. at Park Ave.,* ☎ *212/935–3960 for tour information.* ☞ *Tour free (donations to the Municipal Art Society accepted).* ☉ *Tours Wed. at 12:30 (meet in front of information booth inside terminal on main level).*

OFF THE BEATEN PATH

HELL'S KITCHEN – In an area bordered by 59th Street, the Hudson River, 30th Street, and 8th Avenue, with uninviting landmarks like the Port Authority Bus Terminal and the entrances to the Lincoln Tunnel, Hell's Kitchen has made a neighborhood of itself. As the name suggests, the first waves of immigrants who settled here did not find the living easy. The gritty name came either from a gang that ruled the area in the late 1860s, or a nickname local cops gave it in the 1870s. Today the area is home to dozens of restaurants and take-out eateries, and developers have taken to calling it Clinton.

From 34th to 39th Streets between 11th Avenue and the West Side Highway, the massive **Jacob Javits Convention Center** (⊠ 655 W. 34th Street, ☎ 212/216–2000) brings thousands of visitors to the neighborhood each month for business and entertainment events. Sidewalks are lined with perhaps the world's largest assortment of ethnic cafés and

EVERYTHING YOU ALWAYS WANTED TO KNOW ABOUT THE SUBWAY

NEW YORK CITY has always had a reputation for innovation, so it's not surprising that the world's first elevated railcar ran on tracks between Prince and 14th streets. The fledgling journey took place in 1832, marking the advent of New York City public transit. Necessity was the mother of this invention—the city's population was growing rapidly, fostering the need for affordable and accessible rapid transit. But it would be seven decades before New York's transportation went underground.

By the end of the 19th century New York City was the largest commmercial and industrial metropolis in the world. But while subways had already opened in many other cities worldwide, New York's "public" transportation consisted primarily of horse-drawn streetcars owned and operated by private companies. A few steam-powered elevated trains known as "els" ran above the congested city streets, offering the only alternative to the omnibuses. The omnibuses and els were clearly inadequate for New York, but the proposed subway system spent the last three decades of the nineteenth century on hold, a victim of bureaucratic corruption and incompetence.

The stranglehold finally broke in 1894 when New Yorkers voted overwhemingly for public ownership of the subway. This decision, one of the first major public issues decided by the city's people, gave the city ownership of the yet-to-be-built subway system's physical plant. At the groundbreaking ceremony on March 24, 1900, Mayor Robert A. Van Wyck used a silver spade from Tiffany's. Over the next four years, 12,000 mostly immigrant workers built the first subway routes. These laborers worked ten-hour days for 20 cents an hour. More than fifty men died and thousands were maimed while building the Interborough Rapid Transit (IRT) line. The 9.1 miles of track began at City Hall, continued north to Grand Central, crossed town, and then ran up Broadway to 145th street.

On October 27, 1904, the IRT finally opened. And while New York's subway was not the world's first, it was the first to use electric signals on all its tracks. On opening day, a nickel bought a ticket. Platform attendants watched the "ticket chopper," a collection box made of oak and glass. In the IRT's first year, passengers took more than a billion rides. Many changes were to come. Turnstiles appeared in 1928, but tickets remained, and it would be another twenty years before the fare rose to a dime. In 1953 tokens replaced tickets and the fare rose to fifteen cents.

Those original 9 miles of track have now grown to over 700 miles. The fare has grown too, of course, to $1.50, but the New York City subway is still one of this city's great bargains—and one of its most distinctive features. To learn more, visit ☞ **The New York Transit Museum** in downtown Brooklyn. Boerum Pl. at Schermerhorn St. ☎ 718/243–3060(☞ Chapter 2).

—Heather Lewis

groceries. In an area short on tourist attractions, it is easy to entertain yourself for an afternoon with 9th Avenue's international delicacies.

Start at 38th Street and head north. **Amazonia** (✉ No. 498) does a good Brazilian-inspired lunch. Go to **Los Dos Rancheros Mexicanos** (✉ No. 507) for cooking from Mexico's Puebla region. Tiny **Chantal's Cajun Kitchen** (✉ No. 510) dishes up a mean gumbo. **The Cupcake Café** (✉ No. 522) is an old standby in the 'hood for its pretty cakes and home-made doughnuts. At Nos. 529 and 543, two well-stocked **International Grocery** stores burgeon with Greek and other Mediterranean foods and spices. Rich Senegalese fare cooks at **Gnagna Koty's African Restaurant** (No. 530). The decidedly upscale **Michael London Foods** (✉ No. 542) is a welcome stop for excellent pastries and savories.

Argentine steak and pastais served at the handsome **Chimichurri Grill** (✉ No. 606). Across the avenue, the pastry masters at **Poseidon Bakery** (✉ No. 629) have been rolling out beautiful homemade phyllo dough and putting it to delectable use for over 65 years. Lakuwana (✉ 358 W. 44th, east of 9th Ave.) prepares the food of Sri Lanka, and **Bali Nusa Indah** (✉ No. 651) has a spicy and highly satisfying Indonesian menu. **Amy's Bread** (✉ No. 672) has quickly become a New York institution. At **Rice and Beans** (✉ No. 744), enjoy an excellent plate of the name-sake dish in a walk-in-closet of a Brazilian restaurant.

㊴ ICP Midtown. The midtown branch of the **International Center of Photography** (☞ Museum Mile, *below*) presents several photography shows a year, including selections from its permanent collection. ✉ *1133 6th Ave., at 43rd St.,* ☎ *212/768–4680.* ✆ *$6; Fri. 6–8 pay as you wish.* ◷ *Tues.–Thurs. 10–5, Fri. 10–8, Sat.–Sun 10–6.*

㉜ *Intrepid* Sea-Air-Space Museum. Formerly the USS *Intrepid*, this 900-ft aircraft carrier is serving out its retirement as the centerpiece of Manhattan's only floating museum. An A-12 Blackbird spy plane, lunar landing modules, helicopters, seaplanes, and other aircraft are on deck. Docked alongside, and also part of the museum, are the *Growler*, a strategic-missile submarine; the *Edson*, a Vietnam-era destroyer; and several other battle-scarred naval veterans. Kids will enjoy exploring the ships' skinny hallways and winding staircases, as well as manipulating countless knobs, buttons, and wheels. For an extra thrill (and an extra $5), they can try the Navy Flight Simulator and "land" an aircraft onboard. ✉ *Hudson River, Pier 86 (12th Ave. and W. 46th St.),* ☎ *212/245–0072.* ✆ *$10; free to U.S. military personnel.* ◷ *May–Sept., Mon.–Sat. 10–5, Sun. 10–6; Oct.–Apr., Wed.–Sun. 10–5 (last admission 1 hr before closing).*

㊼ Japan Society Gallery. The wonderfully serene galleries here hold exhibitions from well-known Japanese and American museums, as well as from private collections. Also offered are movies, lectures, classes, concerts, and dramatic performances. ✉ *333 E. 47th St., between 1st and 2nd Aves.,* ☎ *212/832–1155.* ✆ *$5 (suggested donation).* ◷ *Tues.–Sun. 11–6.*

㉟ New Amsterdam Theater (☞ Chapter 4). The Deuce's most glorious theater, neglected for decades, triumphantly returned to life in 1997 following a breathtaking restoration. Built in 1903 by Herts & Tallant, the dazzling theater had an innovative cantilevered balcony and was the original home of the Ziegfeld Follies. Years of decay had left the theater in structural and aesthetic ruins. With the backing of its new tenant, the Walt Disney Company, the 1,814-seat Art Nouveau theater was painstakingly restored by Hardy, Holzman, Pfeiffer, the New York firm that also rehabilitated the ☞ **New Victory Theater** and ☞ **Bryant Park.** Today the theater is "a magical place," architecture critic

Ada Louise Huxtable has said, "from the elaborate peacock prosce-nium arch to the nymphet heads illuminating columns with halos of incandescent lights." Outside, the 1940s-vintage Art Deco facade, in-stalled when the theater became a movie house, was retained in the renovation. The stage version of Disney's *The Lion King*, which opened in 1997 to critical accolades and commercial success, is likely to run at the New Amsterdam for years to come. ⊠ *214 W. 42nd St., between 7th and 8th Aves.,* ☎ *212/282–2900 or 212/282–2907 for informa-tion on theater tours.* ☉ *Tours are offered Mondays 11–5, every hour on the hour. (⊠ Tour admission $10).*

★ ♋ ㉞ **New Victory Theater** (☞ Chapter 4). Since its superb restoration in 1995, the New Victory can make three unique claims: it was the first 42nd Street theater to be renovated as part of the recent revitalization of ☞ **Times Square**, it is the oldest New York theater still in operation, and it is the city's only theater devoted exclusively to productions for chil-dren. Oscar Hammerstein built the theater in 1900 (his more famous grandson, Oscar Hammerstein II, wrote the lyrics to such shows as *Ok-lahoma!* and *Carousel*). Acting legends Lionel Barrymore, Lillian Gish, Mary Pickford, and Tyrone Power strutted its stage, and in the 1930s it was Broadway's most famous burlesque house. Decades of neglect are now a fading memory, as yellow-and-purple signs beckon from its elegant Venetian facade, and a gracious double staircase rises to a sec-ond-floor entry. Inside, garland-bearing putti perch casually on the edge of the theater's dome above gilded deep-red walls, overseeing activity in this theatrical treasure. ⊠ *209 W. 42nd St., between 7th and 8th Aves.,* ☎ *212/382–4000 for tickets.*

★ ㊸ **New York Public Library (NYPL) Humanities and Social Sciences Library.** This 1911 masterpiece of Beaux Arts design (Carrère and Hastings, architects) is one of the great research institutions in the world, with 6 million books, 12 million manuscripts, and 2.8 million pictures. But you don't have to crack a book to make it worth visiting: both inside and out, this stunning building, a National Historic Landmark, will take your breath away with its opulence.

Originally financed in large part by a bequest from former New York governor Samuel J. Tilden, the library combined the resources of two 19th-century libraries: the Lenox Library and the Astor Library. The latter, founded by John Jacob Astor, was housed in a building down-town that has since been turned into the Joseph Papp Public Theater (☞ East Village, *below*). Today, the library anchors a network of close to 200 local branches throughout the city and encompasses a variety of unusual behind-the-scenes collections, ranging from sets of 19th- and early 20th-century menus to the personal library of magician Harry Houdini.

To make a grand entry, walk around to 5th Avenue just south of 42nd Street, where **two marble lions** guard the flagstone plaza in front. Mayor Fiorello La Guardia, who said he visited the facility to "read between the lions," dubbed them "Patience" and "Fortitude." Statues and inscriptions cover the white-marble neoclassical facade; in good weather the block-long grand marble staircase is a perfect spot to peo-ple-watch.

The library's bronze front doors open into the magnificent marble **Astor Hall,** flanked by a sweeping double staircase. Upstairs on the third floor, the magisterial **Rose Main Reading Room**—297 ft long (almost two full north–south city blocks), 78 ft wide, and just over 51 ft high—is one of the world's grandest library interiors. Completely renovated in 1998, it has original chandeliers, oak tables, and bronze reading lamps that gleam as if they were new. Gaze up at the ceiling and you'll see newly repainted murals of blue sky and puffy clouds, inspired by Tiepolo and Tintoretto. Exhibitions on photography, typography, literature, book-making, and maps are held regularly in the **Gottesman Exhibition Hall,** the Edna B. Salomon Room, the **Third Floor Galleries,** and the **Berg Exhibition Room** (exhibit information is available at 212/869–8089). Among the treasures you might see are Gilbert Stuart's portrait of George Washington, Charles Dickens's desk, and Charles Addams cartoons. Free one-hour tours leave Monday–Saturday at 11 and 2 from Astor Hall. ✉ *5th Ave. between 40th and 42nd Sts.,* ☎ *212/930–0800.* ☉ *Mon. and Thurs.–Sat. 10–6, Tues.–Wed. 11–7:30 (exhibitions until 6).*

36 **Times Square.** Love it or hate it, you can't deny that Times Square is one of New York's white-hot energy centers. Hordes of people, mostly tourists, crowd it day and night to walk and gawk. Like many New York City "squares," it's actually two triangles formed by the angle of Broadway slashing across 7th Avenue between 47th and 42nd streets. Times Square (the name also applies to the general area, beyond the intersection of these streets) has been the city's main theater district since the turn of the century: from 44th to 51st streets, the cross streets west of Broadway are lined with some 30 major theaters; film houses joined the fray beginning in the 1920s.

Before the turn of the century, this was New York's horse-trading center, known as Long Acre Square. Substantial change came with the arrival of the subway and the *New York Times,* then a less prestigious paper, which moved here in exchange for having its name grace the square. On December 31, 1904, the *Times* celebrated the opening of its new headquarters, at Times Tower (✉ W. 42nd St. between Broadway and 7th Ave.), with a fireworks show at midnight, thereby starting a New Year's Eve tradition. Now resheathed in marble and called **One Times Square Plaza,** the building is topped with the world's most famous rooftop pole, down which an illuminated 200-pound ball is lowered each December 31 to the wild enthusiasm of revelers below. (In the 1920s the *Times* moved to its present building, a green-copper-roofed neo-Gothic behemoth, at 229 West 43rd Street.)

Times Square is hardly more sedate on the other 364 nights of the year, mesmerizing visitors with its astonishingly high-wattage signage: two-story-high cups of coffee that actually steam, a 42-ft-tall bottle of Coca-Cola, huge billboards of underwear models, a mammoth, superfast digital display offering world news and stock quotes, and countless other technologically sophisticated signs beckoning for attention. The cleanup of Times Square will not turn out the lights, because current zoning *requires* that buildings be decked out with ads, as they have been for nearly a century. ☞ **Duffy Square** occupies the north end of Times Square and is a fine place from which to take it all in. ✉ *42nd–47th Sts. at Broadway and 7th Ave.*

38 **Times Square Visitors Center.** When it opened in 1925, the Embassy Theater showed Metro-Goldwyn-Mayer films for well-heeled patrons. In mid-1998 the landmark theater reopened for everyone, as a one-stop center for general Times Square information, sightseeing and full-price theater tickets, MetroCards, transit memorabilia, and more. Free walking tours are given Friday at noon. Perhaps most important, its rest rooms are the only facilities in the vicinity open to the non-paying public. ✉ *1560 Broadway, between 46th and 47th Sts.,* ☎ *no phone.* ☉ *Daily 8–8.*

④⑨ Tudor City. Built between 1925 and 1928 to attract middle-income residents, this private "city" on a bluff above 1st Avenue occupies 12 buildings containing 3,000 apartments. Two of the buildings originally had no east-side windows, so the tenants wouldn't be forced to gaze at the slaughterhouses, breweries, and glue factories then crowding the shore of the East River. Tudor City now affords great views of the United Nations complex and the East River. The terrace at the end of 43rd Street overlooks the ☞ **United Nations headquarters** and stands at the head of **Sharansky Steps** (named for Natan [Anatoly] Sharansky, the Soviet dissident). The steps run along **Isaiah Wall** (inscribed THEY SHALL BEAT THEIR SWORDS INTO PLOWSHARES); below are **Ralph J. Bunche Park,** named for the African-American former U.N. undersecretary, and **Raoul Wallenberg Walk,** named for the Swedish diplomat and World War II hero who saved many Hungarian Jews from the Nazis. ⊠ *1st and 2nd Aves. from 40th to 43rd Sts.*

★ **⑤⓪ United Nations Headquarters.** Officially an "international zone," not part of the United States, the U.N. Headquarters is a working symbol of global cooperation. The 18-acre riverside tract, now lushly landscaped, was bought and donated by oil magnate John D. Rockefeller Jr. in 1946. The headquarters were built in 1947–53 by an international team led by Wallace Harrison. The slim, 505-ft-tall green-glass **Secretariat Building;** the much smaller, domed **General Assembly Building;** and the **Dag Hammarskjöld Library** (1963) form the complex, before which the flags of member nations, from Afghanistan to Zimbabwe, fly in alphabetical order when the General Assembly is in session (mid-September to mid-December). Architecturally, the U.N. buildings are evocative of Le Corbusier, and their windswept park and plaza remain visionary: there is a beautiful riverside promenade, a rose garden with 1,400 rosebushes, and sculptures donated by member nations.

An hour-long guided tour (given in 20 languages) is the main visitor attraction; it includes the **General Assembly,** the **Security Council Chamber,** the **Trustee Council Chamber,** and the **Economic and Social Council Chamber,** though some rooms may be closed on any given day. Displays on war, nuclear energy, and refugees are also part of the tour; corridors overflow with imaginatively diverse artwork donated by member nations. Free tickets to assemblies are sometimes available on a first-come, first-served basis before sessions begin; pick them up in the General Assembly lobby. The **Delegates Dining Room** (☎ 212/963–7625) is open for a reasonably priced (up to $20) lunch weekdays (jackets required for men; reservations required at least one day in advance). The public concourse, one level down from the visitor entrance, has a coffee shop, gift shops, bookstore, and a post office where you can mail letters with U.N. stamps. ⊠ *Visitor entrance: 1st Ave. and 46th St.,* ☎ *212/963–7713.* ☞ *Tour $7.50.* ⊙ *Tours daily 9:15–4:45; 45-min tours in English leave General Assembly lobby every 30 mins. Children under 5 not admitted.*

④⑤ Whitney Museum of American Art at Philip Morris. An enormous, 42-ft-high sculpture court with outstanding examples of 20th-century sculpture, many of which are simply too big for the Whitney's uptown base, is the centerpiece of the museum's midtown branch. In the adjacent gallery five shows a year cover all aspects of American art. An espresso bar and seating areas make this an agreeable place to rest. ⊠ *120 Park Ave., at E. 42nd St.,* ☎ *917/663–2453.* ☞ *Free.* ⊙ *Sculpture court: Mon.–Sat. 7:30 AM–9:30 PM, Sun. 11–7; gallery: Mon.–Wed. and Fri. 11–6, Thurs. 11–7:30.*

MUSEUM MILE

Once known as Millionaires' Row, the stretch of 5th Avenue between 79th and 104th streets has been fittingly renamed Museum Mile, for it now contains New York's most distinguished cluster of cultural institutions. The connection is more than coincidental: many museums are housed in what used to be the great mansions of merchant princes and wealthy industrialists. A large percentage of these buildings were constructed of limestone (it's cheaper than marble) and reflect the Beaux Arts style, which was very popular among the wealthy at the turn of the century.

Numbers in the text correspond to numbers in the margin and on the Museum Mile, Upper East Side map.

A Good Walk

This tour is a simple, straight walk up 5th Avenue, from 70th Street to 105th, and it covers nearly 2 mi. If you walk up the west side of the street (crossing over to visit museums, of course), you'll be under the canopy of Central Park and have a good view of the mansions and apartments across the street. If you're not sure whether you're interested in a particular museum, stop in its gift store; museum shops are usually good indicators of what's in the rest of the building. Try to catch the annual celebration of "Museum Mile," held annually one evening in early June, when 5th Avenue is closed to traffic, music fills the air, and museums open their doors, free to all, from 6 to 9.

Begin at 5th Avenue and 70th Street (technically not part of Museum Mile) with the **Frick Collection** ①, housed in an ornate, imposing Beaux Arts mansion built in 1913–14 for coke-and-steel baron Henry Clay Frick. It's several blocks north before you get to the next stop. On your way, be sure to admire the former mansions, some of them now converted into multiple-family dwellings, among them the Gothic Revival facade of the Ukrainian Institute of America, on the southeast corner of 5th Avenue at 79th Street. One block north is the **American Irish Historical Society** ②, another fine example of the French-influenced Beaux Arts style that was so popular at the turn of the century.

From here you can't miss the immense and impressive **Metropolitan Museum of Art** ③, one of the world's largest art museums, encroaching on Central Park's turf. The goings on around the steps that sweep you up into the museum merit at least casual observation—it's a favorite spot for performance artists, musicians, and souvenir sellers.

Across from the Met, between 82nd and 83rd streets, one Beaux Arts town house stands amid newer apartment blocks. It now belongs to the Federal Republic of Germany, which has installed a branch of the **Goethe Institut** ④ here. At the corner of 85th Street is 1040 5th Avenue, the former home of Jacqueline Kennedy Onassis, from which she could view Central Park and the reservoir that now bears her name.

Frank Lloyd Wright's **Solomon R. Guggenheim Museum** ⑤, opened in 1959, is the architect's only major New York building. A block north stands the **National Academy** ⑥, an art museum and school (previously known as the National Academy of Design) housed in a stately 19th-century mansion. At 91st Street you'll find the former residence of industrialist Andrew Carnegie, now a museum devoted to contemporary and historic design—the **Cooper-Hewitt National Design Museum** ⑦. Across 91st Street, the **Convent of the Sacred Heart** (⊠ 1 E. 91st St.) is in a huge Italianate limestone mansion, constructed between 1914 and 1918 for financier Otto Kahn and his wife, Addie, noted patrons of the arts.

Museum Mile

American Irish
Historical
Society (AIHS) **2**
Conservatory
Garden **12**
Cooper-Hewitt
National Design
Museum/
Smithsonian
Institution **7**
El Museo del
Barrio **11**
Frick Collection **1**
Goethe Institut **4**
International Center
of Photography
(ICP) **9**
Jewish Museum **8**
Metropolitan
Museum of Art **3**
Museum of
the City of
New York **10**
National
Academy **6**
Solomon R.
Guggenheim
Museum **5**

The Upper East Side

Americas
Society **22**
Asia Society **23**
Asphalt Green **30**
Bloomingdale's **13**
Carl Schurz
Park **28**
Carlyle Hotel **26**
China Institute **19**
Gracie Mansion . . . **29**
Grolier Club **14**
Harmonie Club **15**
Henderson Place
Historic District **27**
Knickerbocker
Club **17**
Lotos Club **20**
Metropolitan
Club **16**
Polo/Ralph
Lauren **24**
Seventh Regiment
Armory **21**
Temple
Emanu-El **18**
Whitney Museum
of American Art . . . **25**

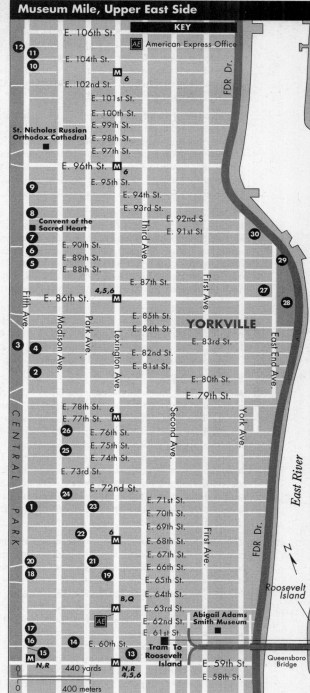

Museum Mile, Upper East Side

KEY

AE American Express Office

E. 106th St.
E. 104th St.
E. 102nd St.
E. 101st St.
E. 100th St.
E. 99th St.
E. 98th St.
St. Nicholas Russian
Orthodox Cathedral   E. 97th St.
E. 96th St.
E. 95th St.
E. 94th St.
E. 93rd St.
E. 92nd S
E. 91st St
Convent of the
Sacred Heart
E. 90th St.
E. 89th St.
E. 88th St.
E. 87th St.
E. 86th St.
E. 85th St.
E. 84th St.
E. 83rd St.
E. 82nd St.
E. 81st St.
E. 80th St.
E. 79th St.
E. 78th St.
E. 77th St.
E. 76th St.
E. 75th St.
E. 74th St.
E. 73rd St.
E. 72nd St.
E. 71st St.
E. 70th St.
E. 69th St.
E. 68th St.
E. 67th St.
E. 66th St.
E. 65th St.
E. 64th St.
E. 63rd St.
E. 62nd St.
E. 61st St.
E. 60th St.
E. 59th St.
E. 58th St.

YORKVILLE

Fifth Ave.
CENTRAL PARK
Madison Ave.
Park Ave.
Lexington Ave.
Third Ave.
Second Ave.
First Ave.
York Ave.
East End Ave.
FDR Dr.
East River

Roosevelt
Island

Abigail Adams
Smith Museum

Tram To
Roosevelt
Island

Queensboro
Bridge

B,Q
AE
N,R
N,R
4,5,6
4,5,6

0   440 yards
0   400 meters

As you continue north, the **Jewish Museum** ⑧, at 92nd Street, is next. The handsome, well-proportioned Georgian-style mansion on the corner of 5th Avenue and 94th Street was built in 1914 for Willard Straight, founder of *The New Republic* magazine. Today it is the home of the **International Center of Photography** ⑨. For some architectural variety, take a short walk east on 97th Street to see the onion-domed cupolas of the baroque-style **St. Nicholas Russian Orthodox Cathedral** (✉ 15 E. 97th St.), built in 1901–02.

The **Museum of the City of New York** ⑩, which has permanent and changing exhibits related to Big Apple history, is one of the homier museums on this tour. Another is **El Museo del Barrio** ⑪, founded in 1969, concentrating on Latin American culture in general, with a particular emphasis on Puerto Rican art. Having completed this long walk, you may want to reward yourself by crossing the street to Central Park's **Conservatory Garden** ⑫, a formal, enclosed tract in the rambling park.

TIMING

It would be impossible to do justice to all these collections in one outing; the Metropolitan Museum alone contains too much to see in a week, much less a day. You may want to select one or two museums or exhibits in which to linger and simply walk past the others, appreciating their exteriors (this in itself constitutes a minicourse in architecture). Save the rest for another day—or for your next trip to New York.

Be sure to pick the right day for this tour: most museums are closed at least one day of the week, usually Monday, and a few have free admission during extended hours on specific days. Others have drinks, snacks, and/or music during late weekend hours. The Jewish Museum is closed Friday and Saturday; the Guggenheim is closed Thursday.

Sights to See

❷ **American Irish Historical Society (AIHS).** U.S. Steel president William Ellis Corey, who scandalized his social class by marrying musical comedy star Mabelle Gilman, once owned this heavily ornamented, mansard-roofed Beaux Arts town house; he died in 1934, and the building remained vacant until it was purchased and renovated by the AIHS (established 1897), which set up shop here in 1940. The society's library holdings chronicle people of Irish descent in the United States. The society hosts talks approximately once a week in the summer; it also puts on exhibitions. Tours of the mansion are usually available on request. ✉ *991 5th Ave., at 80th St.,* ☎ *212/288–2263.* ☞ *Free.* ☉ *Weekdays 10:30–5.*

★ ⑫ **Conservatory Garden.** The most magnificent formal gardens in Central Park occupy 6 acres near the park's northeast corner. The conservatory's entrance leads through elaborate wrought-iron gates that once graced the midtown 5th Avenue mansion of Cornelius Vanderbilt II. The **Central Garden,** in the classic Italian style, has a central lawn bordered by yew hedges and cool crab-apple allées. Across the lawn is the large Conservatory Fountain, beyond which a semicircular wisteria-draped pergola rises into the hillside. The **North Garden,** in the French tradition, marshalls large numbers of bedding plants into elaborate floral patterns. The three spirited girls dancing in the Untermeyer Fountain are at the heart of a great circular bed where 20,000 tulips bloom in spring and 5,000 chrysanthemums herald autumn. The **South Garden** was restored in the early 1980s by celebrated garden designer Lynden B. Miller—she also redesigned Bryant Park and many other public gardens in New York City. This is an exquisite example of the contemporary American mixed border, in this case a highly selective groups of annuals, herbacious perennials, and woody plants in carefully orchestrated beds that provide year-round design interest, with a strong emphasis on colorful foliage and varied textures—and, of course, lots of gorgeous flowers. ⊠ *In Central Park at 104th St.*

❼ Cooper-Hewitt National Design Museum/Smithsonian Institution. Andrew Carnegie sought comfort more than show when he built this 64-room house, designed by Babb, Cook & Williard, on what were the outskirts of town in 1901; he administered his extensive philanthropic projects from the first-floor study. (Note the low doorways—Carnegie was only 5 ft 2 inches tall.) The core of the museum's collection was begun in 1897 by the two Hewitt sisters, granddaughters of inventor and industrialist Peter Cooper; major holdings include drawings, prints, textiles, furniture, metalwork, ceramics, glass, woodwork, and wall coverings. The Smithsonian Institution took over the museum in 1967, and in 1976 the collection moved into the Carnegie mansion. Following a renovation completed in 1998, the museum's three buildings were linked and a Design Resource Center was opened. The changing exhibitions, which focus on various aspects of contemporary or historical design, are invariably enlightening and often amusing. In summer some exhibits make use of the lovely courtyard. In winter 1999 the first-ever *Triennial* design exhibition debuts; it will showcase works in progress by American designers. ⊠ *2 E. 91st St.,* ☎ *212/849–8400.* ⊠ *$5; free Tues. 5–9.* ☉ *Tues. 10–9, Wed.–Sat. 10–5, Sun. noon–5.*

⓫ El Museo del Barrio. *El barrio* is Spanish for "the neighborhood," and the museum is positioned on the edge of East Harlem, a largely Spanish-speaking, Puerto Rican neighborhood. It moved here in 1977, after eight years in various nearby locations. Though the museum focuses on Latin American and Latino culture and has objects from the Caribbean and Central and South America, its collection of Puerto Rican art is particularly strong. The 8,000-object permanent collection includes numerous pre-Columbian artifacts. A new 599-seat theater with floor-to-ceiling murals by Willy Pogany is scheduled to open by summer 2000. ⊠ *1230 5th Ave., at 104th St.,* ☎ *212/831–7272.* ⊠ *$4 (suggested donation).* ☉ *May–Sept., Wed. and Fri.–Sun. 11–5, Thurs. 11–8; Oct.–Apr., Wed.–Sun. 11–5.*

★ ❶ Frick Collection. Coke-and-steel baron Henry Clay Frick found a home for the superb art collection he was amassing far from the soot and smoke of Pittsburgh, where he'd made his fortune. The original mansion was designed by Thomas Hastings and built in 1913–14. Opened as a public museum in 1935 and expanded in 1977, it still resembles a gracious private home, albeit one with bona fide masterpieces in almost every room. The number of famous paintings is astounding; you'll also see sculptures and decorative arts throughout the house. Many treasures bear special mention. Édouard Manet's *The Bullfight* (1864) hangs in the Garden Court. Two of the Frick's three Vermeers—*Officer and Laughing Girl* (circa 1658) and *Girl Interrupted at Her Music* (1660–61)—hang by the front staircase. Fra Filippo Lippi's *The Annunciation* (circa 1440) hangs in the Octagon Room. Gainsborough and Reynolds portraits are in the dining room; canvases by Gainsborough, Constable, Turner, and Gilbert Stuart are in the library; and several Titians (including *Portrait of a Man in a Red Cap*, circa 1516), Holbeins, a Giovanni Bellini (*St. Francis in the Desert*, circa 1480), and an El Greco (*St. Jerome*, circa 1590–1600) are in the living room. Nearly 50 additional paintings, as well as much sculpture, decorative arts and furniture, are in the West and East galleries. Three Rembrandts, including *The Polish Rider* (circa 1655) and *Self-Portrait* (1658), as well as a third Vermeer, *Mistress and Maid* (circa 1667–68), hang in the former; paintings by Whistler, Goya, Van Dyck, Lorrain, David, and Corot in the latter. A free slide presentation introducing the collection runs every half hour in the Music Room. Also recommended it the free "Art-Phone" audio tour, which guides you through the museum at your own pace. When you're through, the tranquil indoor court with a fountain and glass ceiling is a lovely spot for a respite. ⊠ *1 E. 70th St., at 5th Ave.,* ☎ *212/288–0700.* ⊠ *$7. Children under 10 not admitted.* ◷ *Tues.–Sat. 10–6, Sun. 1–6; www.frick.org.*

❹ **Goethe Institut.** This institute, which doubles as a German cultural center, offers art exhibitions as well as lectures, films, and workshops; its extensive library includes current issues of German newspapers and periodicals. ⊠ *1014 5th Ave., at 82nd St.,* ☎ *212/439–8700.* ⊠ *Exhibitions free.* ◷ *Library hours: Tues. and Thurs. noon–7, Wed. and Sat. noon–5; Gallery hours: Tues and Thurs. 10–7, Wed. and Fri. 10–5, Sat. noon–5; www.goethe.de/uk/ney/enindex.htm.*

❾ **International Center of Photography (ICP).** The city's leading photography-only venue, ICP is housed in a 1914 redbrick Georgian Revival mansion that once belonged to one of the founders of *The New Republic.* Founded in 1974 by photojournalist Cornell Capa (photographer Robert Capa's brother), ICP culls from its collection of 45,000 works for its changing exhibitions, both here and at its midtown branch (☞ 42nd Street, *above*). These often focus on the work of a single prominent photographer or one photographic genre (portraits, architecture, etc.). The bookstore carries an impressive array of photography-oriented books, prints, and postcards. ⊠ *1130 5th Ave., at 94th St.,* ☎ *212/860–1777.* ⊠ *$6; Fri. 6–8 pay as you wish.* ◷ *Tues.–Thurs. 10–5, Fri. 10–8, Sat. and Sun. 10–6; www.icp.org.*

❽ **Jewish Museum.** The permanent two-floor exhibition, which complements temporary shows, explores the development and meaning of Jewish identity and culture over the course of 4,000 years. The exhibition draws on the museum's enormous collection of artwork, ceremonial objects, and electronic media. An expansion completed in 1993 preserved the gray-stone Gothic-style 1908 mansion occupied by the museum since 1947 and enlarged the 1963 addition; a café and a larger shop were also added. At the same time, the mansion facade was extended, giving the museum the appearance of a late–French Gothic château. This museum sometimes has a line to get in that extends down the block, so try to arrive early in the day. ⊠ *1109 5th Ave., at 92nd St.,* ☎ *212/423–3200.* ⊠ *$8; Tues. free after 5.* ◷ *Sun., Mon., Wed., and Thurs. 11–5:45, Tues. 11–8.*

★ **❸** **Metropolitan Museum of Art.** The largest art museum in the western hemisphere (spannning 4 blocks, it encompasses 2 million square ft), the Met is one of the city's supreme cultural institutions. Its permanent collection of nearly 3 million works of art from all over the world includes objects from the Paleolithic era to modern times—an assemblage whose quality and range make this one of the world's greatest museums.

Founded in 1870, the Met first opened its doors 10 years later, on March 30, 1880, but the original Victorian Gothic redbrick building by Calvert Vaux has since been encased in other architecture, which in turn has been encased in other architecture. The majestic 5th Avenue facade, designed by Richard Morris Hunt, was built in 1902 of gray Indiana limestone; later additions eventually surrounded the original building on the sides and back. (You can glimpse part of the museum's original redbrick facade in a room to the left of the top of the main staircase and on a side wall of the ground-floor European Sculpture Court.)

The 5th Avenue entrance leads into the **Great Hall,** a soaring neoclassical chamber that has been designated a landmark. Past the admission booths, a vast marble staircase leads up to the **European paintings** galleries, whose 2,500 works include Botticelli's *The Last Communion of St. Jerome,* Pieter Brueghel's *The Harvesters,* El Greco's *View of Toledo,* Johannes Vermeer's *Young Woman with a Water Jug,* Velázquez's *Juan de Pareja,* and Rembrandt's *Aristotle with a Bust of Homer.* The arcaded **European Sculpture Court** includes Auguste Rodin's massive bronze *The Burghers of Calais (1884–95).*

The **American Wing,** in the northwest corner, is best approached from the first floor, where you enter through a refreshingly light and airy garden court graced with Tiffany stained-glass windows, cast-iron staircases by Louis Sullivan, and a marble Federal-style facade taken from the Wall Street branch of the United States Bank. Take the elevator to the third floor and begin working your way down through the rooms decorated in period furniture—everything from a Shaker retiring room to a Federal-era ballroom to the living room of a Frank Lloyd Wright house—and the excellent galleries of American painting.

In the realm of 20th-century art, the Met was a latecomer, allowing the Museum of Modern Art and the Whitney to build their collections with little competition until the Metropolitan's contemporary art department was finally established in 1967. The Met has made up for lost time, however, and in 1987 it opened the three-story **Lila Acheson Wallace Wing,** in the southwest corner. Pablo Picasso's portrait of Gertrude Stein (1906) is the centerpiece of this collection. The **Iris and B. Gerald Cantor Roof Garden,** above this wing and open from May to late October, showcases 20th-century sculptures and provides a refreshing break with its unique view of Central Park and the Manhattan skyline.

There is much more to the Met than paintings, however. Visitors with a taste for classical art should go immediately to the left of the Great Hall on the first floor to see the **Greek and Roman galleries,** including dozens of significant statues and a large collection of rare Roman wall paintings excavated from the lava of Mt. Vesuvius. Directly above these galleries, on the second floor, you'll find room after room of Grecian urns and other classical vases. The Met's awesome **Egyptian collection,** spanning some 3,000 years, is on the first floor, directly to the right of the Great Hall. Its centerpiece is the **Temple of Dendur,** an entire Roman-period temple (circa 15 BC) donated by the Egyptian government in thanks for U.S. help in saving ancient monuments. Placed in a specially built gallery with views of Central Park, the temple faces east, as it did in its original location, and a pool of water has been installed at the same distance from it as the river Nile once stood. Another spot suitable for contemplation is directly above the Egyptian treasures, in the **Asian galleries:** the Astor Court Chinese garden reproduces a Ming dynasty (1368–1644) scholar's courtyard, complete with water splashing over artfully positioned rocks.

The **Amarna galleries** are near the Temple of Dendur, on the first floor past the staircase in the Great Hall. Armana was an Egyptian city founded during the reign of King Akhenaton on the east bank of the Nile, and the galleries contain works from 1353 BC to 1295 BC, including reliefs, sculptures, and paintings. There's also a fine arms-and-armor exhibit on the first floor (go through the medieval tapestries, just behind the main staircase, and turn right). The medieval collection here is lovely, but to see the real medieval treasures, don't miss a trip to the **Cloisters,** the Met's annex in Washington Heights (☞ Morningside Heights, *below*). Keep going straight from the medieval galleries until you enter the cool skylighted white space of the **Lehman Wing,** where the exquisite, mind-bogglingly large personal collection of the late donor, investment banker Robert Lehman, is displayed in rooms resembling those of his West 54th Street town house. The collection's strengths include old-master drawings; Renaissance paintings, including works by Rembrandt, El Greco, Petrus Christus, and Hans Memling; French 18th-century furniture; and 19th-century canvases by Goya, Ingres, and Renoir. Even at peak periods, crowds tend to be sparse here (Lehman's insistence that his collection be exhibited in one place may be one of the reasons, for as great as the collections here are, it feels uncannily like an echo of the Met's main collections). The **Costume Institute,** one level below the main floor's Egyptian Art exhibit, has changing but always extremely well-done displays of clothing and fashion.

Although it exhibits roughly only a quarter of its vast holdings at any one time, the Met offers more than can reasonably be seen in one visit. The best advice for tackling the museum itself is to focus on two to four sections and know that somewhere, there's an empty exhibit that just might be more rewarding than the one you can't see due to the crowds. Walking tours and lectures are free with your admission contribution. Tours covering various sections of the museum begin about every 15 minutes on weekdays, less frequently on weekends; they depart from the tour board in the Great Hall. Self-guided audio tours, which are recorded by Philippe de Montebello, the Met's longtime director, can be rented at a desk in the Great Hall and often at the entrance to major exhibitions. Lectures, often related to temporary exhibitions, are given frequently. ⌧ *1000 5th Ave., at 82nd St.,* ☎ *212/ 535–7710.* ⌧ *$10 (suggested donation); joint admission to the Cloisters, if viewed in the same day.* ☉ *Tues.–Thurs. and Sun. 9:30–5:15, Fri. and Sat. 9:30–8:45; www.metmuseum.org.*

NEED A BREAK?   The first American branch of the very popular Belgian café chain, **Le Pain Quotidien** (⌧ 1131 Madison Ave., between 84th and 85th Sts., ☎ 212/327–4900) attracts Upper East Siders to its large, wide-plank pine communal table for croissants, tarts, brioche, and café au lait or simple meals of soup, open-face sandwiches, or salads. The quintessential Upper East Side café, **E.A.T.** (⌧ 1064 Madison Ave., between 80th and 81st Sts., ☎ 212/772–0022) serves everything from carrot soup and tabbouleh salad to roast lamb sandwiches and fish pâté. Silver-painted columns and a black-and-white checkered floor enliven the light and airy room, which bustles with diners from 7 AM to 10 PM daily.

★ ☞ ❿ **Museum of the City of New York.** One of the best ways to start any visit to this daunting metropolis is with a visit to this museum, set in a massive Georgian mansion built in 1930. From the Dutch settlers of Nieuw Amsterdam to the present day, with period rooms, dioramas, slide shows, films, prints, paintings, sculpture, and clever displays of memorabilia, the museum's got it all. An exhibit on the Port of New York illuminates the role of the harbor in New York's rise to greatness; the noteworthy Toy Gallery has several meticulously detailed dollhouses; maps, Broadway memorabilia, Currier & Ives lithographs, and furniture collections constitute the rest of the museum's vast exhibits. Weekend programs are oriented especially to children. ⌧ *1220 5th Ave., at 103rd St.,* ☎ *212/534–1672.* ⌧ *$5 (suggested donation).* ☉ *Wed.– Sat. 10–5, Sun. noon–5; www.mcny.org.*

❻ The **National Academy** houses a Museum and School of Fine Arts (the oldest art school in New York). The Academy was founded in 1825 and has always required each elected member to donate a representative work of art, producing a strong collection of 19th- and 20th-century

American art. Members have included Mary Cassatt, Samuel F. B. Morse, Winslow Homer, John Singer Sargent, Frank Lloyd Wright, Jacob Lawrence, I. M. Pei, and Robert Rauschenberg. Changing shows of American art and architecture, some curated by member artists, are drawn from the permanent collection. The collection's home is a stately 19th-century mansion donated by members Archer Milton and Anna Hyatt Huntington in 1940. The Academy also schedules loan exhibits. ⊠ *1083 5th Ave., at 89th St.,* ☎ *212/369–4880.* ☜ *$8; free Fri. 5–6.* ☉ *Wed.–Thurs. and weekends noon–5, Fri. 10–6.*

★ ❺ **Solomon R. Guggenheim Museum.** Frank Lloyd Wright's only major New York commission is one of the highlights of the modernist architectural tradition. Opened in 1959, shortly after Wright died, it is a controversial building—even many who love its six-story spiral will admit that it does not result in the best space in which to view art. Wright's attention to detail is everywhere evident—in the circular pattern of the sidewalk outside the museum, for example, the porthole-like windows on its south side, the smoothness of the hand-plastered concrete. Under a 92-ft-high glass dome, a ¼-mi-long ramp spirals down past changing exhibitions of modern art. The museum has especially strong holdings in Wassily Kandinsky, Paul Klee, and Pablo Picasso; the oldest pieces are by the French Impressionists. The Tower Galleries opened in 1992, creating additional gallery space to display the Panza di Buomo collection of minimalist art, among other works. The 10-story annex designed by Gwathmey, Siegel and Associates and based on Wright's original designs offers four spacious galleries that can accommodate the extraordinarily large art pieces that the Guggenheim owns but previously had no room to display. In 1992 the museum received a gift from the Robert Mapplethorpe Foundation of more than 200 of the photographer's works, some of which are on view in the Guggenheim's SoHo branch (☞ SoHo and TriBeCa, *below*). Rumor has it that a new branch on Manhattan's West Side is under consideration. If a visit here whets your appetite for Wright's work, be sure to visit the ☞ **Metropolitan Museum of Art**'s American Wing, which displays a complete living room from one of his finest houses. ⊠ *1071 5th Ave., between 88th and 89th Sts.,* ☎ *212/423–3500.* ☜ *$12, Fri. 6–8 pay as you wish; joint admission to both Guggenheim branches $16.* ☉ *Sun.–Wed. 9–6, Fri.–Sat. 9–8; www.guggenheim.org.*

THE UPPER EAST SIDE

To many New Yorkers, the words *Upper East Side* connote old money, conservative values, and even snobbery. For others, this neighborhood is the epitome of the high-style, high-society way of life often associated with the Big Apple. Between 5th and Lexington avenues, up to about 96th Street or so, the trappings of wealth are everywhere apparent: well-kept buildings, children in private-school uniforms, nannies wheeling grand baby carriages, dog walkers, limousines, doormen in braided livery. This is the territory where Sherman McCoy, protagonist of Tom Wolfe's *Bonfire of the Vanities,* lived in pride before his fall, and where the heroine of Woody Allen's movie *Alice* felt suffocated despite her money.

But like all other New York neighborhoods, this one is diverse, and plenty of local residents live modestly. The northeast section particularly, which is known as Yorkville, is more affordable and ethnic, a jumbled mix of high and low buildings, old and young people. Until the 1830s, when the New York & Harlem Railroad and a stagecoach line began racing through, this was a quiet, remote hamlet with a large German population. Over the years it has also welcomed waves of immigrants from Austria, Hungary, and Czechoslovakia, and local shops and restaurants still bear reminders of this European heritage.

Numbers in the text correspond to numbers in the margin and on the Museum Mile, Upper East Side map.

A Good Walk

A fitting place to begin your exploration of the moneyed Upper East Side is that infamous shrine to conspicuous consumption, **Bloomingdale's** ⑬, at 59th Street between Lexington and 3rd avenues. Leaving Bloomingdale's, head west on 60th Street toward 5th Avenue. As you cross Park Avenue, look for a moment at the wide, neatly planted median strip. Railroad tracks once ran above ground here; they were not completely covered with a roadway until after World War I, and the grand, sweeping street that resulted became a distinguished residential address. Look south toward midtown, and you'll see the Met Life Building; squished up against it, the Helmsley Building looks small and frilly by comparison. Then turn to look uptown, and you'll see a thoroughfare lined with massive buildings that are more like mansions stacked atop one another than apartment complexes. Decorations such as colorful tulips in the spring and lighted pine trees in December in the "park" proclaimed by the street's name are paid for by residents.

On the northwest corner of 60th Street and Park Avenue is **Christ Church United Methodist Church,** built during the Depression but designed to look centuries old, with its random pattern of limestone blocks. Inside, the Byzantine-style sanctuary (open Sunday and holidays) glitters with golden handmade mosaics. Continue west on 60th Street to pass a grouping of clubs, membership-only societies that cater to the privileged. Most were formed in the 1800s, modeled after British gentlemen's clubs. Though the clubs remain exclusive, their admirable architecture is there for all to see. Fanciful grillwork curls over the doorway of the scholarly **Grolier Club,** ⑭ an exception in that it *is* open to the public. On the south side of the block just east of the park is the **Harmonie Club,** ⑮ and across 60th street is the even more lordly **Metropolitan Club** ⑯.

Take a right at 5th Avenue. At 61st Street you'll pass the **Pierre,** a hotel that opened in 1930 (☞ Chapter 6); notice its lovely mansard roof and tower. As you cross East 62nd Street, look at the elegant brick-and-limestone mansion (1915) at 2 East 62nd Street, the home of the **Knickerbocker Club** ⑰, another private social club.

Across 62nd Street is the **Fifth Avenue Synagogue,** a limestone temple built in 1959. Its pointed oval windows are filled with stained glass in striking abstract designs. You may want to detour down this elegant block of town houses; take special note of No. 11, which has elaborate Corinthian pilasters and an impressive wrought-iron entryway. Farther up 5th Avenue, at 65th Street, is another notable Jewish house of worship: **Temple Emanu-El** ⑱, one of the largest synagogues in the world. If you walk east several blocks from 5th Avenue on 65th Street, you'll reach the **China Institute** ⑲, whose museum exhibits Chinese art.

From 5th Avenue, turn right on 66th Street, past the site of the house (✉ 3 E. 66th St.) where Ulysses S. Grant spent his final years, before he moved permanently up to Grant's Tomb (☞ Morningside Heights, *below*). If presidential homes interest you, take a detour over to 65th Street between Madison and Park avenues to 45–47 East 65th Street, a double town house built in 1908 for Sara Delano Roosevelt and her son, Franklin; FDR once lay recovering from polio at No. 47.

Next door to Grant's house, at 5 East 66th Street, is the **Lotos Club** ⑳, a private club whose members are devoted to arts and literature. Continue east across Madison Avenue to Park Avenue. The large apartment building on the northeast corner of Madison Avenue and 66th Street was built from 1906 to 1908 with lovely Gothic-style detail. The red Victorian castle-fortress at 66th Street and Park Avenue is the **Seventh Regiment Armory** ㉑, now often used as an exhibition space.

Though houses have generally been replaced by apartment buildings along Park Avenue, a few surviving mansions give you an idea of how the neighborhood once looked. The grandly simple silvery-limestone palace on the southwest corner of 68th Street and Park Avenue, built in 1919, now houses the prestigious **Council on Foreign Relations** (✉ 58 E. 68th St.). The dark-redbrick town house on the northwest corner was built for Percy Rivington Pyne in 1909–11 by McKim, Mead & White and is now the **Americas Society** ㉒; its art gallery is open to the public. The three houses to the north—built during the following decade and designed by three different architects—carried on the Pyne mansion's Georgian design to create a unified block. Today these buildings hold the **Spanish Institute** (✉ 684 Park Ave.), the **Italian Cultural Institute** (✉ 686 Park Ave.), and the **Italian Consulate** (✉ 690 Park Ave.). Two blocks north, on the east side of Park Avenue, is the **Asia Society** ㉓, a museum and educational center.

At this point, shoppers may want to get down to business back on Madison Avenue. The catchphrase *Madison Avenue* no longer refers to the midtown advertising district (most major agencies have moved away from there) but instead to an exclusive stretch of the avenue between 59th and 79th streets. The area is packed with haute couture designer boutiques, patrician art galleries, and unique stores specializing in fine wares from hair combs to truffles. At Madison Avenue and 76th Street is the **Carlyle Hotel** ㉖, one of the city's most elite and discreet properties. Many of the avenue's shops are small, intimate, expensive—and may be closed on Sunday, but larger brand-name stores such as Calvin Klein (at 60th Street) and the Giorgio Armani Boutique (at 65th Street) have flocked to the prestigious neighborhood. Even if you're just window-shopping, it's fun to step inside the tony digs of **Polo/Ralph Lauren** ㉔, at 72nd Street, which hardly seems like a store at all. The **Whitney Museum of American Art** ㉕, a striking building whose base is smaller than its upper floors, looms on the right at 75th Street; its collection is well worth seeing. For more on Madison Avenue shopping, *see* Chapter 9.

The final leg of this tour is several blocks away. How you get through Yorkville is up to you, but we suggest walking four blocks east on 78th Street, then north on 2nd Avenue, and east again on 86th. The quiet blocks of 78th between Park and 2nd avenues are home to rows of well-maintained Italianate town houses from the late 1800s. Many shops and restaurants line 2nd Avenue, some reflecting the area's Eastern European heritage. At 81st Street, for example, is the **Hungarian Meat Market** (✉ 1560 2nd Ave.), and at 86th Street, the German store **Schaller & Weber** (✉ 1654 2nd Ave.), both recognizable by the array of sausages hanging in their windows. Secondhand stores sell all sorts of odds and ends discarded by the well-to-do (☞ Chapter 9).

On 86th Street at East End Avenue, the **Henderson Place Historic District** ㉗ includes 24 small-scale town houses built in the late 1880s in the Queen Anne style, which was developed in England by Richard Norman Shaw. As if these beautiful dwellings weren't enough, residents here are doubly blessed by the view of and easy access to **Carl Schurz Park** ㉘, across the street and overlooking the East River. **Gracie Man-**

sion ㉙, the mayor's house, sits at its north end. The park comes to a narrow stop at 90th Street, but the greenery continues at **Asphalt Green** ㉚, a concrete parabolic former asphalt plant that's now protected by landmark status and is part of a fitness center.

TIMING

This tour covers a lot of ground, but many sights require looking, not stopping. Allow about three leisurely hours for the walk. The art institutions—the Americas Society, Asia Society, and the Whitney Museum—may take more of your time if you like, so check their hours.

Sights to See

OFF THE
BEATEN PATH

ABIGAIL ADAMS SMITH MUSEUM – Once the carriage house of the home of President John Adams's daughter Abigail and her husband, Colonel William Stephens Smith, this 18th-century treasure is now owned by the Colonial Dames of America and largely restored to its early 19th-century use as a day hotel. Nine rooms display furniture and artifacts of the Federal and Empire periods, and an adjoining garden is designed in 18th-century style. This stone house, complete with a lawn, is hidden among newer, taller structures a few blocks east of Bloomingdale's. ⊠ *421 E. 61st St., at York and 1st Aves.,* ☎ *212/838–6878.* ➮ *$3.* ⊙ *Tues–Sun 11–4; June and July, Tues 11–9, Wed.–Sun. 11–4.*

㉒ **Americas Society.** This McKim, Mead & White–designed neo-Federal town house was among the first on this stretch of Park Avenue (built 1909–11). It was commissioned by Percy Rivington Pyne, the grandson of financier Moses Taylor and a notable financier himself. From 1948 to 1963 the mansion housed the Soviet Mission to the United Nations. In 1965 it was saved from developers by the Marquesa de Cuevas (a Rockefeller descendant), who acquired the property and presented it to the Center for Inter-American Relations, now called the Americas Society, whose mission is to educate U.S. citizens about the rest of the western hemisphere. Its art gallery hosts changing exhibits. ⊠ *680 Park Ave., at 68th St.,* ☎ *212/249–8950.* ➮ *$3 (suggested gallery donation).* ⊙ *Tues.–Sun. 11–6.*

㉓ **Asia Society.** The eight-story red-granite building that houses this museum and educational center complements Park Avenue's older, more traditional architecture. This nonprofit educational society, founded in 1956, offers a regular program of lectures, films, and performances, in addition to changing exhibitions. The permanent holdings comprise Mr. and Mrs. John D. Rockefeller III's collection of Asian art and are used along with pieces from other collections for exhibits that might feature South Asian stone and bronze sculptures; art from India, Nepal, Pakistan, and Afghanistan; bronze vessels, ceramics, sculpture, and paintings from China; Korean ceramics; and paintings, wooden sculptures, and ceramics from Japan. ⊠ *725 Park Ave., at 70th St.,* ☎ *212/288–6400.* ➮ *$4; free Thurs. 6–8.* ⊙ *Tues., Wed., Fri., and Sat. 11–6, Thurs. 11–8, Sun. noon–5; www.asiasociety.org.*

㉚ **Asphalt Green.** When this former asphalt plant was built by Kahn and Jacobs in 1941–44, it was the country's first reinforced concrete arch, and it will be here for the ages thanks to landmark status. The plant is now part of a fitness complex—there are often games on the bright green lawn out front, and the adjoining natatorium (AquaCenter) houses Manhattan's largest pool (☞ Chapter 8). ⊠ *90th St. between York Ave. and FDR Dr.*

⓭ **Bloomingdale's.** A New York institution, this noisy and crowded block-long behemoth sells everything from designer clothes to high-tech teakettles in slick, sophisticated displays. Most selections are high quality, and sale prices on designer goods can be extremely satisfying. In addition to full his, hers, and home sections, Bloomingdale's has four restaurants, a chocolatier, and a coffee shop (☞ Chapter 9). ☒ *59th St. between Lexington and 3rd Aves.,* ☎ *212/705–2000.*

㉘ Carl Schurz Park. During the American Revolution, a house on this promontory was used as a fortification by the Continental Army, then was taken over as a British outpost. In more peaceful times the land became known as East End Park. It was renamed in 1911 to honor Carl Schurz (1829–1906), a famous 19th-century German immigrant who eventually served the United States as a minister to Spain, a major general in the Union Army, and a senator from Missouri. During the Hayes administration, Schurz was secretary of the interior; he later moved back to Yorkville and worked as editor of the *New York Evening Post* and *Harper's Weekly.*

A curved stone staircase leads up to the wrought-iron railings at the edge of John Finley Walk, which overlooks the churning East River— actually just an estuary connecting Long Island Sound with Upper New York Bay. You can see the Triborough, Hell's Gate, and Queensboro bridges, Wards, Randall's, and Roosevelt islands, and on the other side of the river, Astoria, Queens. The view is so tranquil you'd never guess you're directly above the FDR Drive. Behind you along the walk are raised flower beds planted with interesting blooms; there are also a few recreation areas and a playground in the park. Though it doesn't compare in size with the West Side's Riverside Park, this area is a treasure to Upper East Siders.

Stroll to the north end of Carl Schurz Park to reach ☞ **Gracie Mansion,** where the city's mayor resides. The park tapers to an end at 90th Street, where there is a dock from which ferry boats depart to lower Manhattan and up to Yankee Stadium (☞ Chapter 8). ☒ *E. 84th to E. 90th St., between East End Ave. and East River.*

★ ㉖ Carlyle Hotel. The mood here is English manor house. The hotel has the elegant Café Carlyle, where top performers such as Bobby Short, Eartha Kitt, and Woody Allen (the latter on clarinet) appear regularly, and the more relaxed Bemelmans Bar, with murals by Ludwig Bemelmans, the famed illustrator of the Madeline children's books. Stargazers, take note: this hotel's roster of rich-and-famous guests has included Elizabeth Taylor, George C. Scott, Steve Martin, and Warren Beatty and Annette Bening. In the early 1960s President John F. Kennedy frequently stayed here; rumor has it he entertained Marilyn Monroe in his rooms (☞ Chapters 6 and 7). ☒ *35 E. 76th St., at Madison Ave.,* ☎ *212/744–1600.*

⑲ China Institute. A pair of fierce, fat stone lions guards the doorway of this pleasant redbrick town house, which houses a museum and educational center. ☒ *125 E. 65th St., between Lexington and Park Aves.,* ☎ *212/744–8181.* ▦ *$3 (suggested donation); free Thurs. 6–8..* ⊙ *Mon., Wed., Fri, and Sat. 10–5, Tues. and Thurs. 10–8, Sun. 1–5. Closed between exhibitions..*

㉙ Gracie Mansion. Surrounded by a small lawn and flower beds, this Federal-style yellow-frame residence, the official home of the mayor of New York, still feels like a country manor house, which it was when built in 1779 by wealthy merchant Archibald Gracie. The Gracie family entertained many notable guests at the mansion, including Louis Philippe (later king of France), President John Quincy Adams, the Marquis de Lafayette, Alexander Hamilton, James Fenimore Cooper, Washington Irving, and John Jacob Astor. The city purchased Gracie Mansion in 1887, and after a period of use as the Museum of the City of New York,

Mayor Fiorello H. La Guardia made it the official mayor's residence. Rudy Giuliani and his family are the current inhabitants. ✉ *Carl Schurz Park, East End Ave. opposite 88th St.,* ☎ *212/570–4751.* ✉ *$4.* ⊙ *Guided tours late Mar.–mid-Nov., Wed.; all tours by advance reservation only.*

⑭ **Grolier Club.** Founded in 1884, this private club is named after the 16th-century French bibliophile Jean Grolier. Its members are devoted to the bookmaking crafts; one of them, Bertram G. Goodhue, designed this neatly proportioned Georgian-style redbrick building in 1917. The club presents public exhibitions on subjects related to books and has a reference library of more than 100,000 volumes (open by appointment only). ✉ *47 E. 60th St., between Madison and Park Aves.,* ☎ *212/ 838–6690.* ✉ *Free.* ⊙ *Gallery Sept.–May, Mon.–Sat. 10–5; June–August, Mon.–Fri. 10–5. Closed between exhibitions. www.grolierclub.org.*

⑮ **Harmonie Club.** Originally a private club for German Jews, this was the city's first men's club to allow women at dinner. (Stephen Birmingham's *Our Crowd: The Great Jewish Families of New York* profiles the club's original generation.) The building is a pseudo-Renaissance palace built in 1906 by McKim, Mead & White. ✉ *4 E. 60th St.*

㉗ **Henderson Place Historic District.** Originally consisting of 32 small-scale town houses, Henderson Place still has 24 stone-and-brick buildings. They were built in the late 1880s for "people of moderate means" in the Queen Anne style, which was developed in England by Richard Norman Shaw. Designed to be comfortable yet romantic dwellings, they combine elements of the Elizabethan manor house with classic Flemish details. Note especially the lovely bay windows, the turrets marking the corner of each block, and the symmetrical roof gables, pediments, parapets, chimneys, and dormer windows. ✉ *East End Ave. between 86th and 87th Sts.*

NEED A BREAK? | **DTUT** (✉ 1626 2nd Ave., at 84th St., ☎ 212/327–1327), a hip coffee parlor with comfy chairs, sandwiches, s'mores, and pastry. Or try the more traditional **Viand** (✉ 300 E. 86th St., at 2nd Ave., ☎ 212/879–9425), a diner with superlative service and an extensive menu of treats to tide you over on this long walk through the neighborhood.

⑰ **Knickerbocker Club.** Founded in 1871, this serene limestone mansion, the third home of the club, was designed by Delano and Aldrich. ✉ *2 E. 62nd St., between 5th and Madison Aves.*

⑳ **Lotos Club.** Founded in 1870, this private club attracts devotees of the arts and literature. Its current home is a handsomely ornate French Renaissance mansion originally built in 1900 by Richard Howland Hunt for a member of the Vanderbilt family. ✉ *5 E. 66th St.*

⑯ **Metropolitan Club.** A lordly neoclassical edifice, this was built in 1891–94 by the grandest producers of such structures—McKim, Mead & White. Ironically, this exclusive club was established by J. P. Morgan when a friend of his was refused membership in the Union League Club; its members today include leaders of foreign countries and presidents of major corporations. ✉ *1 E. 60th St.*

㉔ **Polo/Ralph Lauren.** Ralph Lauren's flagship New York store, in the landmark, French Renaissance–style Rhinelander mansion, has preserved the grand house's walnut fittings, Oriental rugs, and family portraits as an aristocratic setting in which to display Lauren's to-the-manor-born clothing and home furnishings. (☞ Chapter 9). ✉ *867 Madison Ave., at 72nd St.,* ☎ *212/606–2100.*

ROOSEVELT ISLAND – This 2½-mi-long East River island, which lies parallel to Manhattan from 48th to 85th streets, was taken over by a residential complex in the 1970s and now houses some 2,000 people. The island has a lighthouse designed by James Renwick, Jr. (architect of St. Patrick's Cathedral) and Blackwell House, the fifth oldest wooden house in Manhattan. Some fragments remain of the asylums, hospitals, and jails once clustered here, when it was known as Welfare Island and before that Blackwell's Island (Mae West and William "Boss" Tweed are among those who served time here). Walkways along the edge of the island provide fine river views, and it's surprisingly quiet, considering that the city is so close. The real treat, however, is the 3½-minute ride over on the aerial **Roosevelt Island Tramway** (☎ 212/832–4543); the entrance is at 2nd Avenue and 60th Street, a few blocks east of Bloomingdale's. The one-way fare is $1.50. For more about the island, hit www.rioc.com.

㉑ Seventh Regiment Armory. The term *National Guard* derives from the Seventh Regiment, which has traditionally consisted of select New York men who volunteered for service. (The Seventh Regiment first used the term in 1824 in honor of the Garde National de Paris.) This huge structure, designed by Seventh Regiment veteran Charles W. Clinton in the late 1870s, is still used as an armory, though not exclusively—a homeless shelter, the Seventh Regiment Mess and Bar, and numerous exhibitions use its space. Two posh annual antiques shows take place in the expansive drill hall, for example. Both Louis Comfort Tiffany and Stanford White designed rooms in its surprisingly residential interior; go up the front stairs into the wood-paneled lobby and take a look around. Tours are available by appointment. ⊠ *643 Park Ave.,* ☎ *212/ 744–2968 curator's office.*

⑱ Temple Emanu-El. The world's largest Reform Jewish synagogue seats 2,500 worshipers. Built in 1928–29 of limestone and designed in the Romanesque style with Byzantine influences, the building features Moorish and Art Deco ornamentation; its sanctuary is covered with mosaics. ⊠ *1 E. 65th St., at 5th Ave.,* ☎ *212/744–1400.* ☉ *Sabbath services Fri. 5, Sat. 10:30; weekday services Sun.–Thurs. 5:30; guided group tours of synagogue by appointment. Temple and museum open Mon.–Thurs. 10–4:30, Fri. 10–4, and Sat. 1–4:30.*

★ ㉕ Whitney Museum of American Art. This museum grew out of a gallery in the studio of the sculptor and collector Gertrude Vanderbilt Whitney, whose talent and taste were fortuitously accompanied by the wealth of two prominent families. In 1929 she offered her collection of 20th-century American art to the Met, but they turned it down, so she established an independent museum. The current building, opened in 1966, is a minimalist gray-granite vault separated from Madison Avenue by a dry moat; it was designed by Marcel Breuer, a member of the Bauhaus school (its manifesto called for architects and artists to work toward "the building of the future"). The monolithic exterior is much more forbidding than the interior, where changing exhibitions offer an intelligent survey of 20th-century American works. Following a 1997 renovation, the fifth floor now has eight sleek galleries for permanent exhibitions from the museum's collection; the first, designed to resemble the museum's original, 1931 building (on West 8th Street), includes Carl Walters's original entrance door panels from that location. The Stieglitz circle, urban artists, and abstract art and surrealism are focuses of other galleries. Three feature specific artists: Edward Hopper, including *Early Sunday Morning* and *A Woman in the Sun*; Georgia O'Keeffe, with several of her famous flower paintings; and Alexander Calder, whose *Circus* sculpture has been moved here from the lobby. The famed Whitney Biennial, which showcases the most important developments in 20th-century American art over the past two years, takes place in even-numbered years. In addition, from spring of 1999 to winter of 2000, a massive multimedia exhibit will look back on the century's art and culture. The Whitney also has a branch across from Grand Central Terminal (☞ 42nd Street, *above*). ✉ *945 Madison Ave., at 75th St., ☎ 212/570–3676. ☞ $9; free Thurs. 6–8. ⊙ Wed. and Fri.–Sun. 11–6, Thurs. 1–8. Free tours are available.*

NEED A BREAK?   The soft lighting, tasteful decor, and delicious, if somewhat pricey, pastries, chocolates, and drinks of **Payard Patisserie and Bistro** (✉ 1032 Lexington Ave., between 73rd and 74th Sts., ☎ 212/717–5252) are a perfect complement to a day on the chic Upper East Side. A full restaurant is in back, but you can nibble on sandwiches and desserts at the small café tables up front.

CENTRAL PARK

For many residents, Central Park is the greatest—and most indispensable—part of New York City. Without the park's 843 acres of meandering paths, tranquil lakes, ponds, and open meadows, New Yorkers might be a lot less sane. Every day thousands of joggers, cyclists, inline skaters, and walkers make their daily jaunts around the park's loop, the reservoir, and various other parts of the park. Come summertime the park serves as Manhattan's Riviera, with sun worshipers crowding every available patch of grass. Throughout the year pleasure seekers of all ages come to enjoy horseback riding, softball, ice-skating or roller-skating, rock climbing, croquet, tennis, bird-watching, boating, chess, checkers, theater, concerts, skateboarding, folk dancing, and more—or simply to escape from the rumble of traffic, walk through the trees, and feel—at least for a moment—far from the urban frenzy.

Although it appears to be nothing more than a swath of rolling countryside exempted from urban development, Central Park was in fact the first artificially landscaped park in the United States. The design for the park was conceived in 1857 by park superintendent Frederick Law Olmsted and Calvert Vaux, one of the founders of the landscape architecture profession in the United States. Their design was one of 33 submitted in a contest arranged by the Central Park Commission— the first such contest in the country. The Greensward Plan, as it was called, combined pastoral, picturesque, and formal elements: open rolling meadows complement fanciful landscapes and grand, formal walkways. The southern portion of the park features many formal elements, while the north end is deliberately more rustic. Four transverse roads—at 66th, 79th, 86th, and 96th streets—were designed to carry crosstown traffic beneath the park's hills and tunnels so that park goers would not be disturbed, and 40 bridges were conceived—each with its own unique design and name—to give strollers easy access to various areas.

The job of constructing the park was monumental. Hundreds of residents of shantytowns were displaced, swamps were drained, and great walls of Manhattan schist were blasted. Thousands of workers were employed to move some 5 million cubic yards of soil and plant thousands of trees and shrubs in a project that lasted 16 years and cost $14 million. Today, thanks to the efforts of the Central Park Conservancy, a private, not-for-profit organization that took over the reconstruction and maintenance of the park in 1980, Olmsted and Vaux's green oasis looks better than at any time in its history.

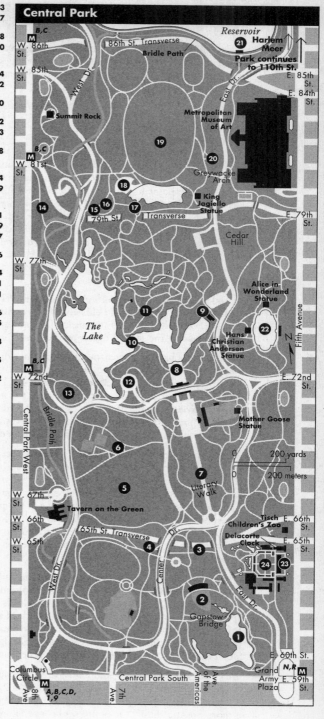

Central Park

In the years following the park's opening in 1857, more than half its visitors arrived by carriage. Today, with a little imagination, you can still experience the park as they did, by hiring a horse-drawn carriage at Grand Army Plaza or any other major intersection of Central Park South at 59th Street between 5th and 8th avenues. Rates, which are regulated, are $34 for the first half hour or $54 per hour for up to four people.

Numbers in the text correspond to numbers in the margin and on the Central Park map.

A Good Walk

If you want to explore the park on foot, begin at the southeast corner, at Grand Army Plaza, at 59th Street. The first path off the main road (East Drive) leads to the **Pond** ①, where Gapstow Bridge provides a great vantage point for the oft-photographed midtown skyscrapers. Heading north on the road, you'll come to **Wollman Memorial Rink** ②, whose popularity is second only to that of the rink at Rockefeller Center. Turn your back to the rink, and you'll see the historic **Dairy** ③, which now serves as the park's visitor center. As you walk up the hill to the Dairy, you'll pass the Chess and Checkers House to your left, where gamesters gather on weekends (playing pieces are available at the Dairy on weekends, 11:30–3).

As you leave the Dairy, to your right (west) is the Playmates Arch, which leads to a large area of ball fields and playgrounds. Coming through the arch, you'll hear the jaunty music of the antique **Friedsam Memorial Carousel** ④, the second oldest on the East Coast.

Turning your back to the carousel, climb the slope to the left of the Playmates Arch and walk beside Center Drive, which veers to the right. Stop for a look at the **Sheep Meadow** ⑤, a 15-acre expanse that was used for grazing sheep until 1934, and the neighboring **Mineral Springs Pavilion** ⑥, one of the park's original refreshment stands. The grand, formal walkway east of the Sheep Meadow is the **Mall** ⑦, which is lined with statuary and magnificent American elms.

As you stroll up the Mall, note the peaceful Sheep Meadow to your left and the buzzing path ahead, where joggers, rollerbladers, and cyclists speed by. This path is the 72nd Street transverse, the only crosstown street that connects with the East, Center, and West drives. The transverse cuts across the park at the north end of the Mall; you can either cross it or pass beneath it through a lovely tiled arcade—elaborately carved birds and fruit trees adorn the upper parts of both staircases—to get to **Bethesda Fountain** ⑧, set on an elaborately patterned paved terrace on the edge of the lake.

If you're in the mood for recreation, take the path east from the terrace to **Loeb Boathouse** ⑨, where in season you can rent rowboats and bicycles. The path to the west of the terrace leads to **Bow Bridge** ⑩, a splendid cast-iron bridge arching over a neck of the lake. Across the bridge is **The Ramble** ⑪, a heavily wooded wild area laced with 37 acres of twisting, climbing paths. Then recross Bow Bridge and continue west along the lakeside path for a view of the lake from **Cherry Hill** ⑫.

Turn your back to the lake and follow the path back to the 72nd Street transverse; on the rocky outcrop across the road, you'll see a statue of a falconer gracefully lofting his bird. Turn to the right, and you'll see a more prosaic statue, the pompous bronze figure of Daniel Webster with his hand thrust into his coat. Cross Center Drive behind Webster, being careful to watch for traffic coming around the corner. Tramp up the winding walk into **Strawberry Fields** ⑬, a verdant 2½-acre land-scape memorializing John Lennon.

At the top of Strawberry Fields' hill, turn right through a rustic wood arbor thickly hung with wisteria vines and follow the path downhill. A view of the lake will open on your right. Start up the road that goes to 77th Street and take the path off the right side down to the southern end of the **Naturalists' Walk** ⑭. After you've explored the varied landscapes of the walk, head back toward the West Drive. Cross the street to the quaint wooden **Swedish Cottage** ⑮, scene of marionette shows.

Rising up behind the Swedish Cottage, the **Shakespeare Garden** ⑯ covers the hillside with flora that has figured in the Bard's work. From the top of the garden, turn east to the steps that lead up to the aptly named Vista Rock, which is dominated by the 1872 **Belvedere Castle** ⑰. The castle building now houses a nature center and a U.S. Weather Bureau measurement station.

Look out from the castle terrace over the rehabilitated Turtle Pond, populated by fish, ducks, and dragonflies, in addition to turtles, of course. To the left you'll see the rear of the **Delacorte Theater** ⑱, where the Joseph Papp Public Theater performs each summer. And stretching out in front of you is the restored **Great Lawn** ⑲.

Walk out the south end of the terrace toward the Weather Bureau's instrument cage, turn left, and make your way downhill along the shaded path above the Turtle Pond. At the east end of the pond curve left past the statue of King Jagiello of Poland, where groups gather on weekends for folk dancing.

Continue around the pond and head uphill to **Cleopatra's Needle** ⑳, an Egyptian obelisk just across the East Drive from the Metropolitan Museum of Art. Vigorous walkers may want to continue north to the **Jacqueline Kennedy Onassis Reservoir** ㉑ for a glimpse of one of the city's most popular and scenic jogging paths. Others can return south from Cleopatra's Needle, following the path through Greywacke Arch under the East Drive. Then angle right (south), around the back corner of the Metropolitan Museum, and take the first right.

After you pass the dog-walking mecca of Cedar Hill on the right, continue south to one of the park's most formal areas: the symmetrical stone basin of the **Conservatory Water** ㉒, which is usually crowded with remote-control model sailboats. Climb the hill at the far end of the water, cross the 72nd Street transverse, and follow the path south to the Tisch Children's Zoo; you'll pass under the Denesmouth Arch to the elaborately designed Delacorte Clock. A path to the left will take you around to the front entrance of the **Arsenal** ㉓, which houses various exhibits and some great WPA-era murals. Just past the clock is the **Central Park Wildlife Center** ㉔, formerly known as the zoo and home to polar bears, sea lions, monkeys, and more.

TIMING

Allow three to four hours for this route so that you can enjoy its pastoral pleasures in an appropriately leisurely mood. Bear in mind that the circular drive through the park is closed to auto traffic on weekdays 10–3 (except for the southeast portion of the road, up to 72nd Street) and 7–10, and on weekends and holidays. Nonautomotive traffic is often heavy and sometimes fast moving, so always be careful when you're crossing the road, and stay toward the inside when you're walking. Weekends are the liveliest time in the park—free entertainment is on tap, and the entire social microcosm is on parade.

Despite its bad reputation, Central Park has the lowest crime rate of any precinct in the city. Just use common sense and stay within sight of other park visitors. Weekend crowds make it safe to go into virtually any area of the park, although even on weekdays you should be safe anywhere along this tour. Take this walk only during the day, since the park is fairly empty after dark.

We've done our best to provide opening hours for the various park attractions, but schedules fluctuate according to the seasons, the weather, and special events schedules. If there's something you don't want to miss, call ahead to confirm the schedule before you set out for the park; you may also want to find out about scheduled events or ranger-led walks and talks. For park information and events, call 212/360–3444. For a recorded schedule of weekend walks and talks led by Urban Park Rangers, call 888/697–2757. Information booths are scattered about the park to help you find your way.

Food for thought: Although there are cafés connected with several attractions, as well as food stands near many entrances, most food choices are limited and predictable; a picnic lunch is usually a good idea. The Boathouse Cafe at the ☞ **Loeb Boathouse**, however, is pleasant.

Sights to See

㉓ The Arsenal. Constructed between 1847 and the early 1850s, the Arsenal, built as a storage facility for munitions, predates the park and is the oldest extant structure within its grounds. Between 1869 and 1877 it was the early home of the American Museum of Natural History (☞ The Upper West Side, *below*), and it now serves as headquarters of the Parks and Recreation Department. The downstairs lobby has some great WPA-era murals, and an upstairs gallery features changing exhibits relating to park and natural environmental design. ⊠ *830 5th Ave. at 64th St.,* ☎ *212/360–8111.* ⊗ *Weekdays 9–5.*

☾ ⑰ Belvedere Castle. Standing regally atop Vista Rock, Belvedere Castle was built in 1872 of the same gray Manhattan schist that thrusts out of the soil in dramatic outcrops throughout the park (you can examine some of this schist, polished and striated by Ice Age glaciers, from the lip of the rock). From here you can also look down directly on the stage of ☞ **Delacorte Theater** and observe the picnickers and softball players on the Great Lawn. The castle itself, a typically 19th-century mishmash of styles—Gothic with Romanesque, Chinese, Moorish, and Egyptian motifs—was deliberately kept small so that when it was viewed from across the lake, the lake would seem bigger. (The Ramble's forest now obscures the lake's castle view.) Since 1919 it has been a U.S. Weather Bureau station; look for twirling meteorological instruments atop the tower. On the ground floor, the Henry Luce Nature Observatory has nature exhibits, children's workshops, and educational programs. ☎ *212/772–0210.* ▨ *Free.* ⊗ *Mid-Apr.–mid-Oct., Tues.–Sun. 10–5; mid-Oct.–mid-Apr., Tues.–Sun. 10–4.*

★ ⑧ Bethesda Fountain. Few New York views are more romantic than the one from the top of the magnificent stone staircase that leads down to the ornate, three-tiered Bethesda Fountain. The fountain itself was dedicated in 1873 to commemorate the soldiers who died at sea during the Civil War. Named for the biblical pool in Jerusalem, which was supposedly given healing powers by an angel, it features the statue of an angel rising from the center. This statue is called *The Angel of the Waters,* and the four figures around the fountain's base symbolize Temperance, Purity, Health, and Peace. Beyond the terrace stretches the lake, filled with drifting swans and amateur rowboat captains.

⑩ Bow Bridge. This splendid cast-iron bridge arches over a neck of the lake to The Ramble. Stand here to take in the picture-postcard view of the water reflecting a quintessentially New York image of vintage apartment buildings peeping above the treetops.

㉔ Central Park Wildlife Center (Zoo). Even a leisurely visit to this small but delightful menagerie, home to about a hundred species, will take only about an hour. The biggest specimens here are the polar bears— go to the Bronx Zoo (☞ Chapter 2) if you need tigers, giraffes, and elephants. Clustered around the central Sea Lion Pool are separate exhibits for each of the earth's major environments; the Polar Circle features a huge penguin tank and polar-bear floe; the open-air Temperate Territory is highlighted by a pit of chattering monkeys; and the Tropic Zone contains the flora and fauna of a miniature rain forest. The **Tisch Children's Zoo,** on the north side of the Denesmouth Arch, has interactive, hands-on exhibits where younglings and older wanna-be farmers can meet and touch such domestic animals as pigs, sheep, goats, and cows. There is also an enchanted forest area, designed to thrill the six and under set. Placed above a redbrick arcade near the Zoo is the **Delacorte Clock,** a delightful glockenspiel that was dedicated to the city by philanthropist George T. Delacorte. Its fanciful bronze face is decorated with a menagerie of mechanical animals, including a dancing bear, a kangaroo, a penguin, and monkeys that rotate and hammer their bells when the clock chimes its tune every half hour. ✉ *Entrance at 5th Ave. and 64th St.,* ☎ *212/439–6500.* 🎫 *$3.50. No children under 16 admitted without adult.* ☉ *Apr.–Oct., weekdays 10– 5, weekends 10:30–5:30; Nov.–Mar., daily 10–4:30.*

⑫ Cherry Hill. Originally a watering area for horses, this circular plaza with a small wrought-iron-and-gilt fountain is a great vantage point for the lake and the West Side skyline.

⑳ Cleopatra's Needle. This exotic, hieroglyphic-covered obelisk began life in Heliopolis, Egypt, around 1600 BC, was eventually carted off to Alexandria by the Romans in 12 BC, and landed here on February 22, 1881, when the khedive of Egypt made it a gift to the city. It stands, appropriately, near the glass-enclosed wing of the Metropolitan Museum (☞ Museum Mile, *above*), which houses the Egyptian Temple of Dendur. Ironically, a century in New York has done more to ravage the Needle than millennia of globe-trotting, and the hieroglyphics have sadly worn away to a *tabula rasa.* The copper crabs supporting the huge stone at each corner almost seem squashed by its weight.

㉒ Conservatory Water. The sophisticated model boats that sail this Renaissance Revival–style stone basin are raced each Saturday morning at 10 from spring through fall. At the north end is one of the park's most beloved statues, José de Creeft's 1960 bronze sculpture of **Alice in Wonderland,** sitting on a giant mushroom with the Mad Hatter, White Rabbit, and leering Cheshire Cat in attendance; kids are free to clamber all over it. On the west side of the pond, a bronze statue of **Hans Christian Andersen,** the Ugly Duckling at his feet, is the site of storytelling hours on summer weekends. A concession in the brick pavilion adjacent to Conservatory Water serves snacks and a fine hot chocolate for a cold day.

❸ The Dairy. When it was built in the 19th century, the Dairy sat amid grazing cows and sold milk by the glass. Today the Dairy's painted, pointed eaves, steeple, and high-pitched slate roof harbor the **Central Park Visitor Center,** which has exhibits and interactive videos on the park's history, maps, and information about park events. ☎ *212/794– 6564.* ☉ *Apr.–Oct., Tues.–Sun. 10–5; Nov.–Mar., Tues.–Sun. 10–4.*

⓲ Delacorte Theater. Some of the best things in New York are, indeed, free—but have *long* lines—including summer performances by the Joseph Papp Shakespeare Theater Company (☞ Chapter 4) at this open-air theater. For free tickets (two per person), plan to arrive by mid-morning or earlier if there have been good reviews; the booth opens at 1 for that evening's performance. Same-day tickets are also given away at the Joseph Papp Public Theater (✉ 425 Lafayette Ave.), also at 1. ☎ 212/539–8750 *(seasonal)*. ☉ *Mid-June–Labor Day, Tues.–Sun. 8 PM.*

★ ☞ ❹ **Friedsam Memorial Carousel.** Remarkable for the size of its hand-carved steeds—all 57 are three-quarters the size of real horses—this carousel was built in 1903 and moved here from Coney Island (☞ Chapter 2) in 1951. Today it's considered one of the finest examples of turn-of-the-century folk art. The organ plays a variety of tunes, new and old. ☎ 212/879–0244. ☎ *90¢.* ☉ *Apr.–Oct., daily 10–6:30; Nov.–Mar., weekends 10–4:30, weather permitting.*

⓳ Great Lawn. After millions of footsteps, thousands of ball games, hundreds of downpours, dozens of concerts, and one papal mass, the Great Lawn had had it. In 1997 the Great Dust Bowl, as it had come to be known, underwent high-tech reconstructive surgery. The central 14-acre oval is now the stuff suburbanites dream—perfectly tended turf (a mix of rye and Kentucky bluegrass), state-of-the-art drainage systems, automatic sprinklers, and careful horticultural monitoring. The area hums with action on weekends and most summer evenings, when its softball fields and picnicking grounds provide a much-needed outlet for city dwellers of all ages.

OFF THE   **HARLEM MEER** – Those who never venture beyond 96th Street miss out on
BEATEN PATH   two of the park's most unusual attractions: the Conservatory Garden (☞ Museum Mile, *above*) and Harlem Meer, where as many as 100 people fish for stocked largemouth bass, catfish, golden shiners, and bluegills every day on a catch-and-release basis. At the north end of the meer is the Victorian-style Charles A. Dana Discovery Center, where you can learn about geography, orienteering, ecology, and the history of the upper park. Within walking distance of the center are fortifications from the American Revolution and other historic sites, as well as woodlands, meadows, rocky bluffs, lakes, and streams. Fishing poles are available with identification from mid-April through October. ✉ *5th Ave. and 110th St.,* ☎ *212/860–1370.* ☉ *Discovery Center: Apr.–Oct., Tues.–Sun. 10–5; Nov.–Mar., Tues.–Sun. 10–4.*

㉑ Jacqueline Kennedy Onassis Reservoir. Named for the former first lady, who frequently jogged in the area, this 106-acre body of water was until recently a holding tank—the city's main reservoirs are upstate. Its future is now under debate. Around its perimeter is a newly renovated 1.58-mi cinder track popular with runners year-round. If you come for some exercise, observe local traffic rules and run counterclockwise. Even if you're not training for the New York Marathon, it's worth visiting for the stellar views of surrounding high-rises and the stirring sunsets; in spring and fall the hundreds of trees around it burst into color, and migrant waterfowl is plentiful. Just remember to look out for the athletes, as they have the right of way.

❾ Loeb Boathouse. At the brick neo-Victorian boathouse, on the east side of the park's 18-acre lake, you can rent a dinghy (or the one authentic Venetian gondola) or pedal off on a rented bicycle. ☎ *212/517–2233 boat rental; 212/861–4137 bicycle rental.* ☎ *Boat rental $10 per hr, $30 deposit; bicycle rental $8–$10 per hr, tandems $14 per hr, de-*

posit required. ☉ *Mar.–Nov., weekdays 10–6, weekends 9–6, weather permitting.*

The **Boathouse Cafe** is a waterside, open-air restaurant and bar that serves lunch and dinner. An adjacent cafeteria dishes up a good cheap breakfast, including freshly made scones, and lunch. Both are open from March through September. Also note the decent public rest rooms on the southeast side of the building. ⊠ *East Park Dr. and E. 72nd St.,* ☎ *212/517–2233.*

★ ❼ **The Mall.** Around the turn of the 20th century, fashionable ladies and gentlemen used to gather to see and be seen on this broad, formal walkway. Today the Mall looks as grand as ever. The south end of its main path, the **Literary Walk,** is covered by the majestic canopy of the largest collection of American elms in North America and lined by statues of famous and not-so-famous men—not all of whom are literary. For statues of the other sex, stretch your imagination and look toward **Alice in Wonderland** (☞ Conservatory Water, *above*) and **Mother Goose,** by East 72nd Street—but, sadly, the female bronze stops there. East of the Mall, behind the Naumburg Bandshell, is the site of **SummerStage,** a free summertime concert series (☞ Outdoor Music *in* Chapter 4).

❻ **Mineral Springs Pavilion.** The Moorish-style palace at the north end of the Sheep Meadow was designed by Calvert Vaux and J. Wrey Mould, who also designed Bethesda Terrace. Built as one of the park's four refreshment stands in the late 1860s, the pavilion still has a snack bar. Behind it are the croquet grounds and lawn-bowling greens. During the season (May–November) you can observe the players, dressed in their crisp whites.

❶❹ **Naturalists' Walk.** Starting at the West 79th Street entrance to the park across from the American Museum of Natural History (☞ Upper West Side, *below*), this recently created nature walk is one of the best places to learn about local wildlife, bird life, flora, fauna, and geology. As you wind your way toward ☞ the **Shakespeare Garden** and **Belvedere Castle,** you'll find the spectacular rock outcrops of Geology Walk, a stream that attracts interesting birdlife, a woodland area with various native trees, stepping-stone trails that lead over rocky bluffs, and benches.

❶ **The Pond.** Swans and ducks can sometimes be spotted on the calm waters of the Pond. For an unbeatable view of the city skyline, walk along the shore to **Gapstow Bridge.** From left to right, you'll see the peak-roofed brown Sherry-Netherland Hotel, the black-and-white General Motors Building, the rose-color Chippendale-style top of the Sony Building, the black-glass shaft of Trump Tower, and in front, the green gables of The Plaza hotel.

❶❶ **The Ramble.** Across the ☞ **Bow Bridge** from the lake, the Ramble is a heavily wooded, wild 37-acre area laced with twisting, climbing paths, designed to resemble upstate New York's Adirondack Mountain region. This is prime bird-watching territory; a rest stop along a major migratory route, it shelters many of the more than 260 species of birds that have been sighted in the park. The Urban Park Rangers lead **bird-watching tours** here; call ☎ 212/988–4952 for details. Because the Ramble is so dense and isolated, however, it is not a good place to wander alone.

★ ❶❻ **Shakespeare Garden.** Inspired by the flora mentioned in the playwright's work, and nestled between Belvedere Castle and the Swedish Cottage, this somewhat hidden garden is a true find. Under the dedicated care of the gardener something is always in flower on the terraced hillside of lush beds. Of particular note are the fantastic spring bulb display beginning in March and June's peak bloom of antique roses. The curving paths of the lower garden and the upper lawn leading to Belvedere Castle are furnished with handsome rustic benches that in this park-designated Quiet Zone make a superb spot for a good read or contemplative thought.

⑤ Sheep Meadow. A sheep grazing area until 1934, this grassy 15-acre meadow is now a favorite of picnickers and sunbathers. It's an officially designated quiet zone; the most vigorous sports allowed are kite flying and Frisbee tossing. Just west of the meadow, the famous **Tavern on the Green,** originally the sheepfold, was erected by Boss Tweed in 1870 and is now an overpriced Manhattan tourist destination (☞ Chapter 5).

★ ⑬ **Strawberry Fields.** This memorial to John Lennon, who wrote the song "Strawberry Fields Forever" in 1967, is sometimes called the "international garden of peace." Its curving paths, shrubs, trees, and flower beds donated by many countries, creates a deliberately informal pastoral landscape reminiscent of the English parks of Lennon's homeland. Every year on December 8, Beatles fans mark the anniversary of Lennon's death by gathering around the star-shape, black-and-white tiled IMAGINE mosaic set into the sidewalk. Lennon's 1980 murder took place across the street at the Dakota (☞ The Upper West Side, *below*), where he lived.

🖑 ⑮ **Swedish Cottage.** Yet another newly renovated park feature, this traditional Swedish school house was imported in 1876 for the Philadelphia Exhibition and brought to Central Park soon thereafter. Marionette theater is performed regularly to the delight of young park visitors. ☏ 212/988–9093. ▣ $5. ☉ Shows Tues.–Fri. 10:30 and noon; Sat. 11 and 1; call for reservations.

🖑 ❷ **Wollman Memorial Rink.** Its music blaring out into the tranquillity of the park can be a bit of a intrusion, but you can't deny that the lower park makes a great setting for a spin on the ice. Even if you don't want to join in, you can stand on the terrace here to watch ice-skaters throughout the winter and roller skaters and dancers in the summer (☞ Dance with Me! *in* Chapter 7). ☏ 212/396–1010. ▣ $7, skate rentals and lockers extra. ☉ Mid-Oct.–Mar., Mon. 10–3, Tues. 10–9:30, Wed.–Thurs. 10–5:30, Fri. 10 AM–11 PM, Sat. 10 AM–11 PM; Sun. 10–9 for ice-skating; late Apr.–Sept., hrs are approximately the same for in-line skating. Call to confirm prices and hrs, as dates are subject to change due to weather.

THE UPPER WEST SIDE

The Upper West Side—never as exclusive as the tony East Side—has always had an earthier appeal. Although real-estate prices keep going up (its restored brownstones and co-op apartments are among the city's most coveted residences), the Upper West Side is still a haven for families—albeit increasingly well-heeled ones—who give the area a pleasant, neighborhood feel. On weekends parents cram the sidewalks as they push babies around in their imported strollers, and shoppers jam the fantastic gourmet food stores and fashion emporiums that line Broadway, the Upper West Side's main drag. In the evenings, however, the action moves inside, where singles from the city and suburbs mingle in bars and restaurants. Columbus Avenue is one such boutique-and-restaurant strip; Amsterdam Avenue is quickly following suit, its shop fronts a mix of bodegas, new restaurants, and boutiques. These lively avenues, the Upper West Side's many quiet tree- and brownstone-lined side streets, its two flanking parks—Central on its east flank, Riverside on its west, as well as such leading cultural complexes as the American Museum of Natural History and Lincoln Center, are all perennial attractions and make for a great variety of things to do in one relatively compact area.

Numbers in the text correspond to numbers in the margin and on the Upper West Side, Morningside Heights map.

A Good Walk

The West Side story begins at **Columbus Circle** ①, the bustling intersection of Broadway, 8th Avenue, Central Park West, and Central Park South. Cars enter this enormous circle from any one of seven directions (use caution and cross only at marked intersections). On the leafy southwest corner of **Central Park,** a line of horse-drawn carriages awaits fares. If you're in the mood for an ecclesiastical outing, stop in at the nearby **American Bible Society Gallery and Library** ②, home of the largest Bible collection in the United States.

With its parade of elegant, monumental apartment buildings on one side and Central Park on the other, **Central Park West** is one of the city's grandest avenues and the ideal place to begin a walk of the area. In the 1930s it was quite the rage to have your home address at the block-long **Century** (⊠ 25 Central Park W, between 62nd and 63rd Sts.), which went up in 1931, taking with it one of the last large lots below 96th Street—only two buildings have gone up on this stretch since then. Continue past the solid brick-and-limestone **New York Society for Ethical Culture** buildings (⊠ 33 Central Park W, at 63rd St.), built in 1903–10, where lectures and concerts are held periodically, to 64th Street. The view up the avenue from here is particularly handsome. Turn west on 64th Street; on your left is the back of the **West Side YMCA** (⊠ 10 W. 64th St., between Central Park W and Columbus Ave.), which has a neo-Moorish portal that sports tiny carved figures representing the worlds of sport (golfers, tennis players) *and* religion (St. George slaying the dragon). As you approach Broadway, **Lincoln Center** ③, New York's premier performing arts venue, widens into view. On summer nights the fountain in the central plaza with the **Metropolitan Opera House** behind is a lovely sight.

On the east side of Columbus Avenue just below 66th Street, stands the **Museum of American Folk Art** ④. Around the corner on 66th Street is the headquarters of the ABC television network; ABC owns several buildings along Columbus Avenue as well, including some studios where news shows and soap operas are filmed, so keep an eye out for your favorite daytime doctors, tycoons, and temptresses. Up Columbus Avenue one block, turn right onto West 67th Street and head toward Central Park West, where on the corner you'll encounter the Elizabethan front of the **Hotel des Artistes** ⑤. Across the street, just inside Central Park, is **Tavern on the Green** (☞ Chapter 5).

Walk north on the east (park) side of Central Park West for the best view of the stately apartment buildings that line the avenue. Mixed among them is the **Spanish & Portuguese Synagogue, Shearith Israel** ⑥ at 70th Street, thought to be the first synagogue built in the classical style of the Second Temple in Jerusalem. At 72nd Street cross back over Central Park West to get a close-up view of **The Dakota** ⑦, the château-like apartment building that presides over the block. Its neighbors to the north include several other famous apartment buildings and their

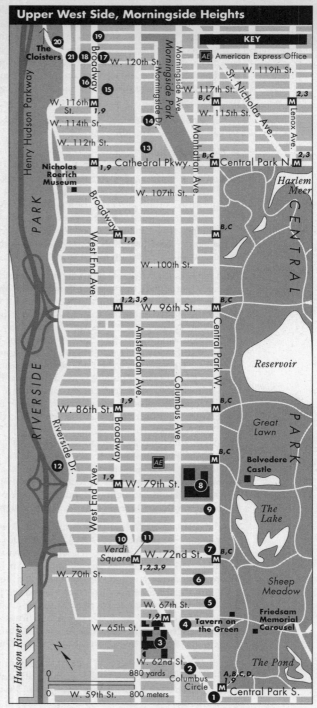

famous residents: the **Langham** (✉ 135 Central Park W, at 73rd St.), an Italian Renaissance–style high-rise designed by leading apartment architect Emery Roth in 1929–30; the twin-tower **San Remo** (✉ 145– 146 Central Park W, at 74th St.), also designed by Roth in 1930 and over the years home to Rita Hayworth, Dustin Hoffman, Raquel Welch, Paul Simon, Barry Manilow, Tony Randall, and Diane Keaton; and the **Kenilworth** (built in 1908, ✉ 151 Central Park W, at 75th St.), with its immense pair of ornate front columns, once the address of Basil Rathbone (Hollywood's quintessential Sherlock Holmes) and Michael Douglas. The final beauty is the cubic **Beresford** (built in 1929, ✉ 211 Central Park W, at 81st St.), also by Emery Roth, whose lighted towers romantically haunt the night sky.

The row of massive buildings along Central Park West breaks between 77th and 81st streets to make room for the **American Museum of Natural History** ⑧, where past and present inhabitants of the entire world are on display. Before dashing off to fight the crowds there, however, consider a stop at the **New-York Historical Society** ⑨ for a quick history lesson on the city itself.

At this point you've covered the mandatory itinerary for the neighborhood. If you've had enough sightseeing, you could forsake the rest of this tour for shopping along Columbus Avenue (☞ Chapter 9), which is directly behind the museum. If you're here on a Sunday, check out the **flea market** at the southwest corner of 77th Street and Columbus Avenue. Food lovers should continue on to the four foodie shrines along the west side of Broadway: **Zabar's** (✉ 2245 Broadway, between 80th and 81st Sts.), where shoppers battle it out for exquisite delicatessen items, prepared foods, gourmet groceries, coffee, and cheeses as well as cookware, dishes, and small appliances; **H & H Bagels** (✉ 2239 Broadway, at 80th St.), which sells (and ships around the world) a dozen varieties of chewy bagels hot from the oven; **Citarella** (✉ 2135 Broadway, at 75th St.), with its intricate arrangements of seafood on shaved ice in the front window; and the bountiful but unpretentious **Fairway Market** (✉ 2127 Broadway, at 74th St.), where snack food, cheeses, and produce practically burst onto the street.

At 73rd Street and Broadway stand the white facade and fairy-castle turrets of the **Ansonia Hotel** ⑩, a turn-of-the-century luxury building. At 72nd Street, where Broadway cuts across Amsterdam Avenue, is triangular **Verdi Square** (named for Italian opera composer Giuseppe Verdi); here a marble statue of the composer is flanked by figures from Verdi's operas: *Aida, Otello,* and *Falstaff.* The triangle south of 72nd Street is **Sherman Square** (named for Union Civil War general William Tecumseh Sherman); the **subway kiosk** ⑪ here is an official city landmark.

Blocks like West 71st Street or West 74th Street between Broadway and Central Park West are perfect for casual strolling; Riverside Drive to 116th Street and Columbia University in Morningside Heights makes another fine walk. The latter leads past **Riverside Park** ⑫, which many neighborhood residents consider their private backyard. A long, slender green space along the Hudson River, Riverside, like Central Park, was landscaped by architects Frederick Law Olmsted and Calvert Vaux; its finest stretches are between 79th Street and Grant's Tomb (☞ Morningside Heights, *below*), at 122nd Street.

TIMING

Tree- and brownstone-lined park blocks are a main charm of this tour, which would easily take two or three hours at a relaxed clip. The exhibits at the Museum of American Folk Art and the New-York Historical Society shouldn't take more than an hour or so to view, but the mammoth and often crowded American Museum of Natural History can eat up most of a day. In bad weather you might want to limit your itinerary to what's covered between Lincoln Center and the Museum of Natural History.

Sights to See

② American Bible Society Gallery and Library. With nearly 50,000 scriptural items in 2,000 languages, this is the largest Bible collection in the world outside the Vatican. The library, which can be toured by appointment, houses Helen Keller's massive 10-volume Braille Bible, leaves from a first edition Gutenberg Bible, and a Torah from China. The public gallery features changing exhibitions of sacred art, ranging from stained glass to sculpture. ✉ *1865 Broadway, at 61st St.,* ☎ *212/408–1200.* ☉ *Bookstore and gallery: Mon.–Wed. and Fri. 10–6, Thurs. 10–7, Sat. 10–5; library: by appointment only..*

★ ☙ ⑧ American Museum of Natural History. With more than 36 million artifacts and specimens, including its awe-inspiring collection of dinosaur skeletons, this wonderland is the world's largest and most important museum of natural history. Forty-two exhibition halls display something for everyone. Dinosaur-mania begins in the massive, barrel-vaulted **Theodore Roosevelt Rotunda,** where a 50-ft-tall skeleton of a barosaurus rears on its hind legs, protecting its fossilized baby from an enormous marauding allosaurus. Three spectacular $34 million dinosaur halls on the fourth floor—the **Hall of Saurischian Dinosaurs,** the **Hall of Ornithischian Dinosaurs,** and the **Hall of Vertebrate Origins**—use real fossils and interactive computer stations to present the most recent interpretations of how dinosaurs and pterodactyls might have behaved. The **Hall of Fossil Mammals** has interactive video monitors featuring museum curators explaining what caused the woolly mammoth to vanish from the earth and why mammals don't have to lay eggs to have babies. The new **Hall of Biodiversity** focuses on Earth's wealth of plants and animals; its main attraction is the walk-through "Dzanga-Sangha Rainforest," a life-size diorama complete with the sounds of the African tropics—from bird calls to chain saws. The **Hall of Human Biology and Evolution**'s wondrously detailed dioramas trace human origins back to Lucy and feature a computerized archaeological dig and an electronic newspaper about human evolution. The **Hall of Meteorites** displays the 4-billion-year-old *Ahnighito,* the largest meteorite ever retrieved from the Earth's surface. The **Hall of Minerals and Gems** shows off the glittering 563-carat Star of India sapphire. On Friday and Saturday evenings, when the museum stays open late, the **Hall of Ocean Life,** where a fiberglass replica of a 94-ft blue whale hangs from the ceiling, doubles as a cocktail lounge.

Films on the **IMAX Theater's** (☎ 212/769–5034 for show times) 40-ft-high, 66-ft-wide screen are usually about nature (a jaunt through the Grand Canyon, a safari in the Serengeti, or a journey to the bottom of the sea to the wreck of the *Titanic*), and cost $9. Slated to open early in 2000, the new high-tech **Hayden Planetarium** is housed in a 90-foot, glass-walled sphere; inside, visitors will witness a re-creation of the Big Bang before they ascend a spiral walkway that tracks the next 15 billion years of the universe's evolution. At the top of the sphere is the new Sky Theater, which—using "all-dome video"—transports viewers from galaxy to galaxy, as if they were actually traveling through space. Part of the new **Rose Center for Earth and Space,** the Hayden Planetarium will be accompanied by two new major exhibits, the **Hall of the Universe** and the **Hall of Planet Earth.** The latter, scheduled to open in the summer of 1999, explains the climate, geology, and evolution of *our* world with the help of over 100 giant rocks from such spots as the ocean floor, glaciers, and active volcanoes. ✉ *Central Park W at W. 79th St.,* ☎ *212/769–5200 for museum tickets and programs; 212/769–5100 for museum general information.* 🎟 *Museum $8 (suggested donation); museum and IMAX Theater combination tickets available.* ☉ *Sun.–Thurs. 10–5:45; Fri.–Sat. 10–8:45.*

NEED A BREAK?   For a diner-style cheeseburger or just a banana split, stop by **EJ's Luncheonette** (✉ 447 Amsterdam Ave., between 81st and 82nd Sts., ☎ 212/873–3444).

---

⑩ Ansonia Hotel. This 1904 Beaux Arts masterpiece designed by Paul M. Duboy commands its corner of Broadway with as much architectural detail as good taste can stand. Inspiration for the Ansonia's turrets, mansard roof, and filigreed-iron balconies came from turn-of-the-century Paris. Now a condominium apartment building, it was originally built as an apartment hotel, with suites without kitchens (and separate quarters for a staff that took care of the food). Designed to be fireproof, it has thick, soundproof walls that make it attractive to musicians; famous denizens of the past include Enrico Caruso, Igor Stravinsky, Arturo Toscanini, Florenz Ziegfeld, Theodore Dreiser, and Babe Ruth. ✉ *2109 Broadway, between 73rd and 74th Sts.*

❶ Columbus Circle. This confusing intersection—where Broadway, 8th Avenue, Central Park West, and Central Park South all meet—has never had the grandeur or the definition of Broadway's major intersections to the south, but it does have a 700-ton granite monument capped by a marble statue of Columbus himself in the middle of a traffic island. (The monument had to be elaborately supported when the land underneath was torn up during the construction of the Columbus Circle subway station in the early 1900s.) On the southwest quadrant of the circle is the **New York Coliseum,** a functional-looking white-brick building that served as the city's chief convention and trade-show venue before the Jacob Javits Center opened farther south on 11th Avenue. A multi-towered office/hotel/apartment/entertainment complex will soon replace it.

On the northeast corner of the circle, opposite the impending Coliseum development and standing guard over the entrance to Central Park, is the **Maine Monument,** whose gleaming equestrian figures perch atop a formidable limestone pedestal. At the monument's foot, horse-drawn cabs await fares through Central Park, and a Victorian-style gazebo houses a 24-hour newsstand. The Trump International Hotel and Tower (☞ Chapter 6) fills the wedge of land between Central Park West and Broadway; Donald Trump spent $250 million to gut this once marble-clad tower and rewrap it in a lamentable brown-glass curtain wall. Happily, it's also home to Jean George (☞ Chapter 5), where celebrity chef Jean George Vongerichten works his foodie magic. You can sometimes see his white-clad assistants furiously stirring and chopping in the window as you walk past on Broadway.

★ ❼ The Dakota. The most famous of all the apartment buildings lining Central Park West, the Dakota set a high standard for the many that followed it. Designed by Henry Hardenbergh, who also built The Plaza (☞ 5th Avenue and 57th Street, *above*), the Dakota was so far uptown when it was completed in 1884 that it was jokingly described as being "out in the Dakotas." Indeed, this buff-color château, with picturesque gables and copper turrets, housed some of the West Side's first residents. The Dakota is often depicted in scenes of old New York, and it was by looking out of a window here that Si Morley was able to travel back in time in Jack Finney's *Time and Again.* Its slightly spooky appearance was played up in the movie *Rosemary's Baby,* which was filmed here. The building's entrance is on 72nd Street; the spacious, lovely courtyard is visible beyond the guard's station. At the Dakota's gate, in December 1980, a deranged fan shot John Lennon as he came home from a recording session. Other celebrity tenants have included Boris Karloff, Rudolf Nureyev, José Ferrer and Rosemary Clooney, Lauren Bacall, Rex Reed, Leonard Bernstein, and Gilda Radner. ⊠ *1 W. 72nd St., at Central Park W.*

❺ **Hotel des Artistes** Built in 1918 with an elaborate, mock-Elizabethan lobby, this "studio building," like several others on West 67th Street, was designed with high ceilings and immense windows, making it ideal for artists. Its tenants have included Isadora Duncan, Rudolph Valentino, Norman Rockwell, Noël Coward, Fannie Hurst, and contemporary actors Joel Grey and Richard Thomas; another tenant, Howard Chandler Christy, designed the lush, soft-toned murals in the ground-floor restaurant, Café des Artistes (☞ Chapter 5). ⊠ *1 W. 67th St., at Central Park W.*

★ ❸ **Lincoln Center** (☞ Chapter 4). A unified complex of pale travertine, Lincoln Center (built 1962–1968) is the largest performing arts center in the world—so large it can seat nearly 18,000 spectators at one time in its various halls. Here Kurt Masur conducts Schubert and Mahler, the American Ballet Theater performs *Swan Lake,* and Luciano Pavoratti sings arias and duets—and that's just an average day. The complex's three principal venues are grouped around the central Fountain Plaza: to the left, as you face west, is Philip Johnson's **New York State Theater,** home to the New York City Ballet and the New York City Opera. In the center, Wallace Harrison's **Metropolitan Opera House,** with its brilliantly colored Chagall murals visible through the arched lobby windows, is home not only to the Metropolitan Opera but to the American Ballet Theatre. And to the north is Max Abramovitz's **Avery Fisher Hall,** host to the New York Philharmonic Orchestra. A great time to visit the complex is on summer evenings, when thousands of dancers trot and swing around the plaza during the Midsummer Night Swing. One-hour guided "Introduction to Lincoln Center" tours, given daily, cover the center's history and wealth of artwork and usually visit these three theaters, performance schedules permitting.

Lincoln Center encompasses much more than its three core theaters. Its major outdoor venue is **Damrosch Park,** on the south flank of the Met, where summer open-air festivals are often accompanied by free concerts at the **Guggenheim Bandshell.** Accessible via the walk between the Metropolitan and Avery Fisher is the North Plaza—the best of Lincoln Center's spaces—with a massive Henry Moore sculpture reclining in a reflecting pool. The long lines and glass wall of Eero Saarinen's **Vivian Beaumont Theater** stand behind the pool. It is officially considered a Broadway house, despite its distance from the theater district. Below it is the smaller **Mitzi E. Newhouse Theater,** where many award-winning plays originate. To the rear is the **New York Public Library for the Performing Arts** (☎ 212/870–1600), a research and circulating library with an extensive collection of books, records, videos, and scores on music, theater, and dance; now undergoing a two-year renovation, the library is slated to reopen in the fall of 2000. An overpass leads from this plaza across 65th Street to the world-renowned **Juilliard School** (☎ 212/769–7406) for music and theater; actors Kevin Kline, Robin Williams, and Patti LuPone studied here. An elevator leads down to street level and **Alice Tully Hall,** home of the Chamber Music Society of Lincoln Center and the New York Film Festival. Or turn left from the overpass and follow the walkway west to Lincoln Center's **Walter Reade Theater,** one of the finest places in the city to watch films. ⊠ *W. 62nd to 66th Sts. between Broadway and Amsterdam Ave.,* ☏ *212/546–2656 for general information; 212/875–5350 for tour schedule and reservations.* ▨ *Tour $9.50.*

NEED A
BREAK?

Before or after a Lincoln Center performance, the pleasant **Cafe Mozart** (⊠ 154 W. 70th St., ☏ 212/595–9797) is the closest place to stop for conversation with a friend. The operatic atmosphere and espresso at **Cafe La Fortuna** (⊠ 69 W. 71st St., ☏ 212/724–5846) are just right.

④ Museum of American Folk Art. The collection of this small museum includes arts and crafts from all over the Americas: native paintings, quilts, carvings, dolls, trade signs, painted-wood carousel horses, and a giant Indian-chief copper weather vane. Changing exhibits are often worth seeing. The gift shop has intriguing craft items, books, and great cards. ⊠ *2 Lincoln Sq. (Columbus Ave. between 65th and 66th Sts.),* ☏ *212/595–9533.* ▨ *$3 (suggested donation).* ☉ *Tues.–Sun. 11:30–7:30.*

★ **⑨ New-York Historical Society.** Founded in 1804, the New-York Historical Society is the city's oldest museum and one of its finest research libraries, with a collection of 6 million pieces of art, literature, and memorabilia. Exhibitions shed light on New York's—and America's—history, everyday life, art, and architecture. Highlights of the collection include George Washington's inaugural chair, 500,000 photographs from the 1850s to the present, original watercolors for John James Audubon's *Birds of America,* the architectural files of McKim, Mead & White, and the largest U.S. collection of Louis Comfort Tiffany's lamps. In fall 2000, 40,000 of the society's most treasured pieces are slated to go on long-awaited, permanent display in a new wing, the Henry Luce III Center for the Study of American Culture. Among them will be the society's impressive collection of paintings by Hudson River School artists Thomas Cole, Asher Durant, and Frederic Church. ⊠ *2 W. 77th St., at Central Park W,* ☏ *212/873–3400.* ▨ *Museum $5 (suggested donation).* ☉ *Museum: Tues.–Sun. 11–5, library: Tues.–Sat. 11–5.*

☝ **⑫ Riverside Park.** Long and narrow, tree-lined Riverside Park—laid out by Central Park's designers Olmsted and Vaux between 1873 and 1888—runs along the Hudson from 72nd Street to 159th Street. More manageable than Central Park—which can feel overwhelming—Riverside Park is best visited on weekends, when Upper West Side residents and their children throng its walkways. A **statue of Eleanor Roosevelt** stands at the 72nd Street entrance. Locals gravitate to the **Promenade,** a broad formal walkway, extending a few blocks north from 80th Street, with a stone parapet looking out over the river. The steps that descend here lead to an underpass beneath Riverside Drive and the **79th Street Boat Basin,** a rare spot in Manhattan where you can walk right along the river's edge, smell the salt air, and watch a flotilla of houseboats bobbing in the water. These boats must sail at least once a year to prove their seaworthiness. Behind the boat basin, the **Rotunda** occupies a wonderful circular space punctuated by a fountain.

At the end of the Promenade, a patch of its median strip explodes with flowers tended by nearby residents. To the right, cresting a hill along Riverside Drive at 89th Street, stands the Civil War **Soldiers' and Sailors' Monument** (1902, designed by Paul M. Duboy), an imposing 96-ft-high circle of white-marble columns. From its base is a refreshing view of Riverside Park, the Hudson River, and the New Jersey waterfront. *See also* Grant's Tomb *in* Morningside Heights, *below.* ⊠ *72nd to 159th Sts. between Riverside Dr. and the Hudson River.*

6 Spanish & Portuguese Synagogue, Shearith Israel. Built in 1897, this is the fifth home of the oldest Jewish congregation in the United States, founded in 1654. The adjoining "Little Synagogue" is a replica of Shearith Israel's Georgian-style first synagogue. ⊠ *2 W. 70th St., at Central Park W,* ☎ *212/873–0300.*

11 Subway kiosk. This brick and terra-cotta building with rounded neo-Dutch molding is one of two remaining control houses from the original subway line (the other is at Bowling Green in lower Manhattan [☞ Wall Street and the Battery, *below*]). Built 1904–05, it was the first express station north of 42nd Street. ⊠ *W. 72nd St. and Broadway.*

MORNINGSIDE HEIGHTS

On the high ridge just north and west of Central Park, a cultural outpost grew up at the end of the 19th century, spearheaded by a triad of institutions: the relocated Columbia University, which developed the mind; St. Luke's Hospital, which cared for the body; and the Cathedral of St. John the Divine, which tended the soul. Idealistically conceived as an American Acropolis, the cluster of academic and religious institutions that developed here managed to keep these blocks stable during years when neighborhoods on all sides were collapsing. More recently, West Side gentrification has reclaimed the area to the south, while the areas north and east of here haven't changed as much. Yet within the gates of the Columbia or Barnard campuses or inside the hushed St. John the Divine or Riverside Church, the character of the city changes. This is an *uptown* student neighborhood—less hip than the Village, but friendly, fun, and intellectual.

Numbers in the text correspond to numbers in the margin and on the Upper West Side, Morningside Heights map.

A Good Walk

Broadway is the heartbeat of Morningside Heights, but many of the most remarkable sights will take you east and west of the main thoroughfare. Walk east from Broadway on grungy 112th Street and the massive **Cathedral of St. John the Divine** ⑬ will gradually loom up before you. You could easily spend an hour wandering through the church, gawking at its monumental architecture, inspecting its stained-glass windows, looking at its tapestries and art, and browsing in its gift store. Don't miss a stroll on the driveway just south of the nave. It doesn't look like much, but it leads back past a neoclassical building to the delightful Biblical Garden—an utter escape from the urban crush. Just south of the upper drive, the Peace Fountain sits in a circular plaza off Amsterdam Avenue at 111th Street.

From here swing east on 113th Street to secluded Morningside Drive. You'll pass the Beaux Arts–baroque 1896 core of **St. Luke's Hospital,** which has sprouted an awkward jumble of newer buildings. On Morningside Drive at 114th Street, the **Church of Notre Dame** ⑭ nestles into its corner with as much personality but far less bulk than the other churches on this tour. At 116th Street, catercorner from Columbia University's President's House, pause at the overlook on the right to gaze out at the skyline and down into **Morningside Park,** tumbling precipitously into a wooded gorge. Designed by Olmsted and Vaux of Central Park fame, the park has a lovely landscape, but since it is bordered by some rough blocks of Harlem, it would be safest not to get any closer.

Turn back toward Amsterdam Avenue on 116th Street, and walk past the Law School's streamlined Greene Hall to the eastern gates of **Columbia University** ⑮. Its quadrangle is hardly a respite from the urban activity around it, but it does have its share of collegiate grandeur. The university's renowned journalism school, founded by Joseph Pulitzer (hence Columbia's relationship to the Pulitzer Prize), holds classes in the building just south of the campus's west gates. A new bookstore is slated to open in May of 1999 at 115th Street and Broadway—in the campus's brand-new student center. Across Broadway from Columbia proper is its sister institution, **Barnard College** ⑯.

Institutes of higher learning abound as you follow Broadway on the east side of the street north to 120th Street—on the right is **Teachers College** ⑰, a part of Columbia, and on the left, on the west side of the street, is the interdenominational **Union Theological Seminary** ⑱. At the northeast corner of 122nd Street and Broadway, behind a large blank-walled redbrick tower that fronts the intersection at an angle, is the **Jewish Theological Seminary** ⑲. Walk west on 122nd Street; between Claremont Avenue and Broadway the prestigious **Manhattan School of Music** is on your right, with musical instruments carved into the stone beneath its upper-story windows. Between Claremont and Riverside Drive is **Sakura Park,** a quiet formal garden.

Cross Riverside Drive at West 122nd Street into Riverside Park (☞ The Upper West Side, *above*). The handsome white-marble **Grant's Tomb** ⑳ was one of the city's most popular sights around the last turn of the century. Finish the walk at **Riverside Church** ㉑, at Riverside Drive and 120th Street—any afternoon but Monday you can climb the tower for a view up the palisades across the Hudson River. Then, stroll back along Riverside Drive; you'll be able to admire Riverside Park and the Hudson to your right, and a long row of magnificent stone apartment buildings to your left.

TIMING

Allow yourself about two hours to leisurely walk the tour. To get the true flavor of the neighborhood, which is often student dominated, come during the week, when classes are in session. You'll be able to visit campus buildings, sample café life, and because the major churches on the tour are active weeklong, you won't miss seeing them in action. If you visit on a Sunday, you could attend church services.

Sights to See

⑯ **Barnard College.** Established in 1889 and one of the former Seven Sisters women's colleges, Barnard has steadfastly remained single-sex and independent from Columbia, although its students can take classes there (and vice versa). Note the bear (the college's mascot) on the shield above the main gates at 117th Street. Through the gates is **Barnard Hall,** which houses classrooms, offices, a pool, and dance studios. Its brick-and-limestone design echoes the design of Columbia University's buildings. To the right of Barnard Hall, a path leads through the narrow but neatly landscaped campus; to the left from the main gate is a quiet residential quadrangle. ☎ 212/854–2014. ☉ *Student-led tours Mon.–Fri. 10:30 and 2:30.*

★ ⑬ **Cathedral of St. John the Divine.** Everything about the Episcopal Cathedral of St. John the Divine is colossal, from its cavernous 601-ft-long nave, which can hold some 6,000 worshipers, to its 155-ft-tall domed crossing, which could comfortably contain the Statue of Liberty. When this Gothic behemoth is finished—the transepts and facade are the most noticeably uncompleted elements—it will be the largest cathedral in the world. To get the full effect of the building's mammoth size, approach it from Broadway on 112th Street. On the wide steps climbing to the Amsterdam Avenue entrance, five portals arch over the entrance doors. The central portal depicts St. John having his vision of the Lord. The bronze doors he presides over open only twice a year—on Easter and in October for the Feast of St. Francis, when animals as large as elephants and camels are brought in, along with cats and dogs, to be blessed. The doors have relief castings of scenes from the Old Testament on the left and the New Testament on the right.

The cathedral's first cornerstone was laid in 1892, and in 1911 a major change in architectural vision came at the hands of Ralph Adams Cram, a Gothic Revival purist who insisted on a French Gothic style for the edifice. The granite of the original Romanesque-Byzantine design is visible inside at the crossing, where it has yet to be finished with the Gothic limestone facing. Note that the finished arches are pointed—Gothic—while the uncovered two are in the rounded Byzantine style. The one-two punch of the Great Depression and World War II brought construction to a halt.

Inside, along the cathedral's side aisles, some chapels are dedicated to contemporary issues such as sports, poetry, and AIDS. The **Saint Saviour Chapel** contains a three-panel plaster altar with religious scenes by artist Keith Haring (this was his last work before he died of AIDS in 1990). The more conventional **baptistry,** to the left of the altar, is an exquisite octagonal chapel with a 15-ft-high marble font and a polychrome sculpted frieze commemorating New York's Dutch heritage. The altar area itself expresses the cathedral's interfaith tradition and international mission—with menorahs, Shinto vases, golden chests presented by the king of (then) Siam, and in the ring of chapels behind the altar, dedications to various ethnic groups.

A peaceful precinct of châteaulike Gothic-style buildings, known as the **Cathedral Close,** is behind the cathedral on the south side. In a corner by the Cathedral School is the delightful **Biblical Garden.** Perennials, roses, herbs, and an arbor are planted in and around the stone border of a Greek cross, bounded on the outside by the cathedral, a low stone wall, and a hedge. Around the bend from this garden, a small rose garden will thrill your nose with its spicy scents. Back at Amsterdam Avenue, the **Peace Fountain** depicts the struggle of good and evil. The forces of good, embodied in the figure of the archangel Michael, triumph by decapitating Satan, whose head hangs from one side. The fountain is encircled by small, whimsical animal figures cast in bronze from pieces sculpted by children.

Along with Sunday services (8, 9, 9:30, 11, and 1 and 7), the cathedral operates a score of community outreach programs, has changing museum and art gallery displays, supports artists-in-residence and an early music consortium, and presents a full calendar of nonreligious (classical, folk, solstice) concerts. Christmastime programs are especially worth looking into. ✉ *1047 Amsterdam Ave., at 112th St.,* ☎ *212/316–7540; 212/662–2133 box office; 212/932–7347 to arrange tours.* ⌨ *Tours $3 (suggested donation), vertical tours $10 (suggested donation).* ☉ *Mon.–Sat. 7–6, Sun. 7 AM–8 PM; tours Tues.–Sat. at 11, Sun. at 1; vertical tours 1st and 3rd Sat. of month at noon and 2 (reservations required).*

NEED A BREAK?   If St. John has filled your soul but your stomach is crying out for its share, head for the **Hungarian Pastry Shop** (✉ 1030 Amsterdam Ave., at 110th St., ☎ 212/866–4230) for tasty desserts and coffee.

⓮ Church of Notre Dame. A French neoclassical landmark building, this Roman Catholic church has a replica of the French grotto of Lourdes behind its altar. It once served a predominantly French community of immigrants, but like the neighborhood, today's congregation is more diverse ethnically, with Irish, German, Italian, African-American, Hispanic, and Filipino members. The building is open 30 minutes before masses, which are held weekdays at 8, 12:05, and 5:30; Saturdays at 12:05 and 5:30; and Sundays at 8:30, 10 (in Spanish), 11:30, and 5:30. ✉ *405 W. 114th St., at Morningside Dr.,* ☎ *212/866–1500.*

OFF THE BEATEN PATH	**THE CLOISTERS –** Perched atop a wooded hill in Fort Tryon Park, near Manhattan's northernmost tip, the Cloisters houses the medieval collection of the Metropolitan Museum of Art in an appropriately medieval monastery-like setting. Colonnaded walks connect authentic French and Spanish monastic cloisters, a French Romanesque chapel, a 12th-century chapter house, and a Romanesque apse. An entire room is devoted to the richly woven and extraordinarily detailed 15th- and 16th-century Unicorn Tapestries—a must-see. Three enchanting gardens shelter more than 250 species of plants similar to those grown during the Middle Ages, including herbs and medicinals; the Unicorn Garden blooms with flowers and plants depicted in the tapestries. The Cloisters frequently hosts concerts of medieval music (☞ Chapter 4). The Cloisters is easily accessible by public transportation: the M4 Cloisters–Fort Tryon Park bus provides a lengthy but scenic ride; catch it along Broadway, or take the A train to 190th Street. If you're traveling from below 110th Street, the M4 bus runs along Madison Avenue. ✉ *Fort Tryon Park,* ☎ *212/ 923–3700.* 🎟 *$8 (suggested donation).* ☉ *Mar.–Oct., Tues.–Sun. 9:30–5:15; Nov.–Feb., 9:30–4:45.*

Also worthy of a detour uptown are two of the city's oldest houses: Harlem Heights' **Morris–Jumel Mansion** is an elegant 1765 Palladian-style mansion with twelve period rooms. *65 Jumel Terr., at 160th St.,* ☎ *212/923–8008.* 🎟 *$3.* ☉ *Wed.–Sun. 10–4.*

Inwood's homelier **Dyckman Farmhouse Museum** is a Dutch Colonial farmhouse from the 18th century. ✉ *4881 Broadway, at 204th St.,* ☎ *212/304–9422.* 🎟 *Free.* ☉ *Tues.–Sun. 11–4.*

⑮ Columbia University. This wealthy, private, coed Ivy League school was New York's first college when it was founded in 1754. Back then, before American independence, it was called King's College—note the gilded crowns on the black wrought-iron gates at the Amsterdam Avenue entrance. The herringbone-pattern brick paths of College Walk lead into the refreshingly open main quadrangle, dominated by neoclassical **Butler Library** to the south and the rotunda-topped **Low Memorial Library** to the north. Butler, built in 1934, holds the bulk of the university's 7 million books. Low was built in 1895–97 by McKim, Mead & White, which laid out the general campus plan when the college moved here in 1897. Modeled on the Roman Pantheon, Low is now mostly offices, but on weekdays you can go inside to see its domed, templelike former Reading Room. Low Library also houses the visitor center, where you can pick up a campus guide or arrange a tour. The steps of Low Library, presided over by Daniel Chester French's statue *Alma Mater,* have been a focal point for campus life, not least during the student riots of 1968. The southwest corner of the quad is the site of a new **student center,** scheduled to open in September 1999. ✉ *Visitor Center, north of W. 116th St. between Amsterdam Ave. and Broadway,* ☎ *212/854–4900.* ☉ *Weekdays 9–5. Tours begin 11 and 2 weekdays from Room 213, Low Library.*

Before Columbia moved here, this land was occupied by the Bloomingdale Insane Asylum; the sole survivor of those days is **Buell Hall,** the gabled orange-red brick house, east of Low Library. North of Buell Hall is the interdenominational **St. Paul's Chapel** (1907), an exquisite little Byzantine-style domed church laid out in the shape of a cross, with fine tiled vaulting inside. ☎ 212/854–6246. ☉ *Sept.–May, Mon.– Sat. 10AM–11PM, Sun. 10:30 AM–11 PM (with services for different denominations and religions held throughout the day on Sunday—call for schedule). Greatly reduced hrs June–Aug. and during winter intercession, so call ahead for Sun. schedule..*

NEED A   The exterior of **Tom's Restaurant** (✉ 2880 Broadway, at 112th St., ☎
BREAK?   212/864–6137) made frequent appearances on the TV show *Seinfeld*.
               Whether or not you care about its claim to fame, this diner is still a
               good place for a New York bite.

⑳ Grant's Tomb. This commanding position along the Hudson River, within Riverside Park, is Civil War general and two-term president Ulysses S. Grant and wife Julia Dent Grant's final resting place. Opened in 1897, almost 12 years after Grant's death, it was a more popular sight than the Statue of Liberty until the end of World War I. An architectural mishmash outside, the towering granite mausoleum is engraved with the words LET US HAVE PEACE, which recall Grant's speech to the Republican convention upon his presidential nomination. Under a small white dome, the Grants' twin black-marble sarcophagi are sunk into a deep circular chamber visible from above; minigalleries to the sides display photographs and Grant memorabilia. The surrounding plaza's benches, finished with 1960s-era mosaic designs by local schoolchildren, are a colorful counterpoint to the monument's Victorian bulk. ✉ *Riverside Dr. and 122nd St.,* ☎ *212/666–1640.* ▨ *Free.* ☉ *Daily 9–5, 20-min tours run on the hr.*

⑲ Jewish Theological Seminary. The seminary was founded in 1887 as a training ground for rabbis, cantors, and scholars of Conservative Judaism, but this complex wasn't built until 1930. The tower, gutted by fire in 1966, underwent restoration in 1999. Visit the seminary's excellent library, which holds frequent exhibits. ✉ *3080 Broadway, at 122nd St.,* ☎ *212/678–8000, 212/678–8002 for library.* ▨ *Free.* ☉ *Call for library hours.*

OFF THE   **NICHOLAS ROERICH MUSEUM –** An 1898 Upper West Side town house is
BEATEN PATH   the site of this small, eccentric museum dedicated to the work of Russian
               artist Nicholas Roerich, who emigrated to New York in the 1920s and
               quickly developed an ardent following. Some 200 of his paintings hang
               here—notably some vast canvases of the Himalayas. He also designed
               sets for Diaghilev ballets, such as *Rite of Spring*, photographs of which
               are also on view. ✉ *319 W. 107th St.,* ☎ *212/864–7752.* ▨ *Free.*
               ☉ *Tues.–Sun. 2–5.*

★ **㉑ Riverside Church.** In this modern (1930) Gothic-style edifice, the smooth, pale limestone walls seem the antithesis of the rougher hulk of the Cathedral of St. John the Divine. Most of the building is refined and restrained, but the main entrance, on Riverside Drive, explodes with elaborate stone carvings modeled on the French cathedral of Chartres (as are many other details here). Inside, look at the handsomely ornamented main sanctuary and take the elevator to the top of the 22-story, 356-ft tower (▨ $1, ☉ Tues.–Sat. 11–4, Sun. noon–6), with its 74-bell carillon, the largest in the world. Although affiliated with the American Baptist church and the United Church of Christ, Riverside is interdenominational, interracial, international, extremely aware politically, and socially conscious. Its calendar includes political and community events, dance and theater programs, and concerts, along with regular Sunday services. ✉ *Riverside Dr. and 120nd St.,* ☎ *212/870–*

6700. ✉ *Church free; tower $2.* ⊙ *Mon.–Sat. 9–5, Sun. noon–4; service each Sun. 10:45.*

⓱ Teachers College. Redbrick Victorian buildings house Columbia University's Teachers College, founded in 1887 and still the world's largest graduate school in the field of education. Names of famous teachers throughout history line the frieze along the Broadway facade. ✉ *525 W. 120th St.*

⓲ Union Theological Seminary. Founded in 1836, the seminary moved here, to its rough, gray, collegiate Gothic quadrangle, in 1910; it has one of the world's finest theological libraries. Step inside the main entrance, on Broadway at 121st Street, and ask to look around the serene central quadrangle. ✉ *W. 120th to W. 122nd Sts., between Broadway and Claremont Ave.*

HARLEM

Harlem has been the mecca for African-American culture and life for nearly a century. Originally called Nieuw Haarlem and settled by Dutch farmers, Harlem became a well-to-do suburb by the 19th century; many Jews moved here from the Lower East Side in the late 1800s, and black New Yorkers began settling here in large numbers in about 1900, moving into a surplus of fine apartment buildings and town houses built by real estate developers for a middle-class white market that never materialized. By the 1920s Harlem had become the most famous black community in the United States, perhaps in the world.

In an astonishing confluence of talent known as the Harlem Renaissance, black novelists, playwrights, musicians, and artists—many of them seeking to escape discrimination and persecution in other parts of the country—gathered here. Black performers starred in chic Harlem jazz clubs—which, ironically, only whites could attend. Throughout the Roaring '20s, while whites flocked here for the infamous parties and nightlife, blacks settled in for the opportunity this self-sustaining community represented. But the Depression hit Harlem hard. By the late 1930s it was no longer a popular social spot for downtown New Yorkers, and many African-American families began moving out to houses in the suburbs of Queens and New Jersey.

By the 1960s Harlem's population had dropped dramatically, and many of those who remained were disillusioned enough to join in civil rights riots. A vicious cycle of crowded housing, poverty, and crime turned the neighborhood into a simmering ghetto. Today, however, Harlem is restoring itself. Deserted buildings, burned-out shop fronts, and yards of rubble still scar certain parts, but shining amidst these seedy remains of the past are old jewels such as the refurbished Apollo Theatre and newer attractions like the Studio Museum. Black professionals and young families are restoring many of Harlem's classic brownstone and limestone buildings, bringing new life to the community.

Harlemites are accustomed to seeing tourists; only common traveler's caution is necessary during daytime excursions to any of the places highlighted. For nighttime outings it's smart to take a taxi. Bus tours may be a good option because they cover more areas than the central Harlem walk outlined below (☞ Sightseeing *in* Smart Travel Tips).

Note that the city's north–south avenues acquire different names up here, commemorating heroes of black history: 6th Avenue becomes Lenox Avenue or Malcolm X Boulevard, 7th Avenue is Adam Clayton Powell Jr. Boulevard, and 8th Avenue is Frederick Douglass Boulevard; 125th Street, the major east–west street, is Martin Luther King Jr. Boulevard. Many people still use the streets' former names, but the street signs use the new ones.

Numbers in the text correspond to numbers in the margin and on the Harlem map.

A Good Walk

Beginning on West 115th Street and Adam Clayton Powell Jr. Boulevard, head west on the north side of the block to admire the facade of this branch of the **New York Public Library** ①. It's sufficiently interesting for you to make the trip even on Sunday, when the library is closed. The next two stops, however, are most worthwhile on Sunday, because church is in session and gospel singers fill the sanctuaries with soulful, moving, often joyous gospel music. **Memorial Baptist Church** (✉ 141 W. 115th St., ☎ 212/663–8830) welcomes visitors at its two-hour service, which begins at 10:45. Gospel fans and visitors are also welcome at the 10:45 Sunday service at **Canaan Baptist Church of Christ** (✉ 132 W. 116th St., ☎ 212/866–0301).

On the southwest corner of 116th Street and Lenox Avenue, an aluminum onion dome tops the **Malcolm Shabazz Mosque** (✉ 102 W. 116th St.), a former casino that was converted in the mid-1960s to a black Muslim temple (Malcolm X once preached here). Several Muslim stores are nearby. Continuing north along Lenox Avenue and then east on 120th Street brings you to **Marcus Garvey Park** ②, which interrupts 5th Avenue between 120th and 124th streets. Stay outside the park, but be sure to notice its watchtower and the pretty row houses as you skirt its west side. At the north end of the park, walk east to 5th Avenue and then north one block to 125th Street.

Harlem's main thoroughfare is 125th Street (also known as Martin Luther King Jr. Boulevard), the chief artery of its cultural, retail, and economic life. Real estate values here have never come close to those downtown along 5th Avenue or even Broadway, and many commercial buildings rise only a few stories. But never fear—Harlem isn't missing out on the malling of America, as new businesses, many of them branches of national chains, have moved in of late, bringing new shop fronts along a retail row that used to see many FOR RENT signs. There's even a bona fide mall planned for the street—Harlem USA. Above the street-level stores is the home of the **National Black Theatre** (✉ 2033 5th Ave., between 125th and 126th Sts., ☎ 212/722–3800), which produces new works by contemporary African-American writers. A literary landmark, the **Langston Hughes House** ③ is a quick detour away. Walking west along 125th Street you'll pass a number of African-themed stores. On Lenox Avenue between 126th and 127th streets is **Sylvia's Soul Food Restaurant** ④, owned by Sylvia Woods, New York's self-proclaimed "queen of soul food."

Continuing along 125th Street, you can't help but notice the lovely **Theresa Towers** ⑤ office building, formerly the Hotel Theresa, at the southwest corner of Adam Clayton Powell Jr. Boulevard. Another community showplace is also on the block between Lenox Avenue and Adam Clayton Powell Jr. Boulevard, the **Studio Museum in Harlem** ⑥, and on the next block across the street, the famous **Apollo Theatre** ⑦. One of Harlem's greatest landmarks, the Apollo was fantastically restored and brought back to life in the 1980s.

Return to Adam Clayton Powell Jr. Boulevard and continue north. Between 131st and 132nd streets you'll pass what is today the **Williams Institutional (Christian Methodist Episcopal) Church.** From 1912 to 1939 this was the Lafayette Theatre, which presented black revues in

Harlem

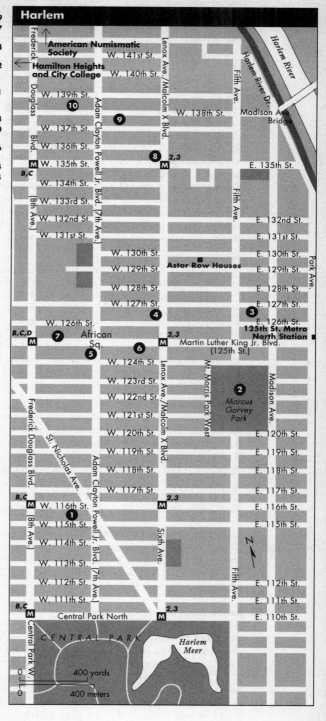

the 1920s and housed the WPA's Federal Negro Theater in the 1930s. A tree outside the theater was considered a lucky charm for black actors to touch, and it eventually became known as the Tree of Hope; though the original tree and then its live replacement were both cut down, it has been replaced by the colorful, abstract metal "tree" on the traffic island in the center of the street. A stump from the second tree is now a lucky charm for performers at the Apollo.

At 135th Street cross back east to Lenox Avenue. Notice the branch of the **YMCA** at 180 West 135th Street; writers Langston Hughes, Claude McKay, and Ralph Ellison all rented rooms here. At the corner of Lenox Avenue you'll find the **Schomburg Center for Research in Black Culture** ⑧, a research branch of the New York Public Library that also functions as a community center of sorts. Three blocks north is another neighborhood landmark, the **Abyssinian Baptist Church** ⑨, one of the first black institutions to settle in Harlem when it moved here in the 1920s; it was founded downtown in 1808. Across Adam Clayton Powell Jr. Boulevard from the church is **St. Nicholas Historic District,** a handsome set of town houses known as **Strivers' Row** ⑩.

TIMING

The walk takes about four hours, including stops at the Studio Museum and the Schomburg Center. Sunday is a good time to tour Harlem if you'd like to listen to gospel music at one of the area's many churches, and weekends in general are the liveliest time for walking around the neighborhood. If you do attend a church service, remember that most other people are there to worship and that they probably don't think of themselves or their church as tourist attractions. Be respectful of ushers, who may ask you to sit in a special section; don't take pictures; make a contribution when the collection comes around; and stay for the full service.

Sights to See

⑨ **Abyssinian Baptist Church.** A famous family of ministers—Adam Clayton Powell Sr. and his son, Adam Clayton Powell Jr., the first black U.S. congressman—have presided over this Gothic-style bluestone church, which moved here in the 1920s. Stop in on Sunday to hear the gospel choir and the fiery sermon of its present activist minister, Reverend Calvin Butts. The baptismal font's Coptic Cross was a gift from Haile Selassie, then the emperor of Ethiopia. ⊠ *132 Odell Clark Pl. W, at 138th St.,* ☎ *212/862–7474.* ⊙ *Sun. services 9 and 11.*

OFF THE BEATEN PATH **AMERICAN NUMISMATIC SOCIETY** – The society, founded in 1858, displays its vast collection of coins and medals, including many that date from ancient civilizations, in one of several museums in the Audubon Terrace complex. ⊠ *Broadway at 155th St.,* ☎ *212/234–3130.* ▪ *Free (donations accepted).* ⊙ *Tues.–Sat. 9–4:30, Sun. 1–4.*

★ ⑦ **Apollo Theatre.** When it opened in 1913, it was a burlesque hall for white audiences only, but after 1934 music greats such as Billie Holiday, Ella Fitzgerald, Duke Ellington, Count Basie, and Aretha Franklin performed at the Apollo. The theater fell on hard times and closed for a while in the early 1970s but has been renovated and in use again since 1983. The current Apollo's roster of stars isn't as consistent as it was in the past, but its regular Wednesday-night amateur performances at 7:30 are as wild and raucous as they were in the theater's heyday. The Wall of Fame, in the lobby, is a giant collage of Apollo entertainers. Included in an hour-long guided tour is a spirited, audience-participation-encouraged oral history of the theater, with many inside stories about past performers, as well as a chance to perform in a no-boos-allowed

"Amateur Night" show. Tour goers also get to touch what's left of the Tree of Hope as they walk across the stage. A gift shop sells Apollo clothing, gift items, jewelry, and recordings. ⊠ *253 W. 125th St., between 7th and 8th Aves.,* ☎ *212/749–5838 for performance schedules; 212/222–0992 for tours.* ⊠ *Tours $8.*

NEED A BREAK? | If you smell a sweet aroma, it's probably doughnuts frying at **Krispy Kreme** (⊠ 280 W. 125th St., at Frederick Douglass Blvd., ☎ 212/ 531–0111), which has quickly become New York's favorite chain of doughnut shops.

OFF THE BEATEN PATH | **HAMILTON HEIGHTS AND CITY COLLEGE** – From Strivers' Row, you can see the beautiful neo-Gothic stone towers of City College along the ridge of Hamilton Heights (City College's center is 138th Street and Convent Avenue), and it's a short walk up the hill, on 141st Street past St. Nicholas Park, to this quiet neighborhood. City College's arched schist gates, green lawns, and white terra-cotta trim could easily be part of an Ivy League campus, but this has always been a public institution (tuition was free until the mid-1970s). The pretty row houses and churches that comprise Hamilton Heights were built around the turn of the century on land once owned by Alexander Hamilton. His Federal-style house, known as Hamilton Grange, is at 287 Convent Avenue (about 100 yards south of its original location). Wide sidewalks, quiet streets, green plantings, and well-maintained houses make this neighborhood a real charmer. ⊠ *St. Nicholas Ave. to Hudson River, approx. 135th St. to 155th Sts.*

❸ Langston Hughes House. From his top-floor apartment here, Harlem Renaissance master Langston Hughes (1902–1967) penned many of his Jesse B. Semple, or "Simple," columns about Harlem life, in addition to numerous plays, stories, and poems. Hughes lived in this Italianate brownstone from 1948 until his death in 1967. ⊠ *20 E. 127th St., between 5th and Madison Aves.,* ☎ *212/534–5992.* ⊙ *By appointment only.*

❷ Marcus Garvey Park. Originally Mount Morris Square, this rocky plot of land was renamed in 1973 after Marcus Garvey (1887–1940), who preached from nearby street corners and led the back-to-Africa movement. It's not known for being safe, so you should stay outside the park itself. From the street on its south side, however, you can see its three-tiered, cast-iron fire **watchtower** (Julius Kroel, 1856), the only remaining part of a now defunct citywide network useful in the days before the telephone. The handsome neoclassical row houses of the **Mount Morris Park Historic District** front the west side of the park and line side streets. ⊠ *Interrupts 5th Ave. between 120th and 124th Sts., Madison Ave. to Mt. Morris Park W.*

❶ New York Public Library 115th Street Branch. This bubbly Italian Renaissance–style row house was designed by McKim, Mead & White in 1908. The money for the construction of this and more than 60 other branch libraries was donated by Andrew Carnegie in 1901, and almost all of these were narrow, midblock structures—because Manhattan real estate was and still is so expensive. ⊠ *203 W. 115th St., between 7th and 8th Aves.,* ☎ *212/666–9393.* ⊙ *Mon. and Wed. 10–6, Tues. noon–8, Thurs.–Fri. noon–6, Sat. 1–5.*

★ **❽ Schomburg Center for Research in Black Culture.** The New York Public Library's Division of Negro History bought the vast collection of Arturo Alfonso Schomburg, a scholar of black and Puerto Rican descent, in 1926. In 1940, after Schomburg died, this collection of more than 10,000 books, documents, paintings, and photographs recording black history was named after him. Later designated a research library, the ever-growing collection moved in 1980 into this modern redbrick building from the handsome Victorian one next door (designed by McKim, Mead & White and paid for by Andrew Carnegie), which is now an exhibit hall that's part of the Schomburg. Today more than 5 million items compose the collection. The expansion and renovation of the Schomburg building was completed in 1991 and includes the refurbished **American Negro Theatre** and increased gallery space. Just past the main entrance is an airy lobby, also the entrance to the **Langston Hughes Auditorium.** Inlaid in the floor is the artistic work *Rivers,* a memorial tribute to Hughes. The center's resources include rare manuscripts, art and artifacts, motion pictures, records, and videotapes. Regular exhibits in two halls, performing arts programs, and lectures continue to contribute to Harlem culture. ✉ *515 Lenox Ave., at 135th St.,* ☎ *212/491–2200.* ☑ *Free.* ☉ *Mon.–Wed. noon–8, Thurs.–Sat. 10–6; exhibits: Mon.–Wed. noon–6, Fri.–Sat. 10–6, Sun. 1–5.*

NEED A BREAK?   A good place for coffee and maybe a bite to eat, whether it's grits, a delicious dessert, or fried chicken, is **Pan Pan Restaurant** (✉ 500 Lenox Ave., at 135th St., ☎ 212/926–4900), catercorner from the Schomburg Center.

★ ⑩ **Strivers' Row.** Since 1919, African-American doctors, lawyers, and other middle-class professionals have owned these elegant homes designed by such notable architects as Stanford White (his neo-Renaissance creations stand on the north side of 139th Street). Behind each row are service alleys, a rare luxury in Manhattan. Musicians W. C. Handy ("The St. Louis Blues") and Eubie Blake ("I'm Just Wild About Harry") were among the residents here. The area, now officially known as the **St. Nicholas Historic District,** got its nickname because less affluent Harlemites felt that its residents were "striving" to become well-to-do. These quiet, tree-lined streets are a remarkable reminder of the Harlem that used to be. ✉ *W. 138th and W. 139th Sts. between 7th and 8th Aves..*

⑥ **Studio Museum in Harlem.** One of the community's showplaces, this small art museum houses a large collection of paintings, sculpture (there is a small, light-filled sculpture garden), and photographs (including historic photographs of Harlem by James Van Der Zee, popular in the 1930s, and works by Jacob Lawrence and Romare Bearden). The museum offers changing exhibitions, special lectures and programs, and its gift shop is full of black American and African-inspired books, posters, and jewelry. ✉ *144 W. 125th St., between 6th and 7th Aves.,* ☎ *212/864–4500.* ☑ *$5, free 1st Sat. of month.* ☉ *Wed.–Fri. 10–5, weekends 1–6.*

④ **Sylvia's Soul Food Restaurant.** Although there have been rumors about her retiring, personable Sylvia Woods still stays late most nights chatting with her customers. Southern specialties and cordiality are the rule here. Sylvia's own line of foods is now available at the restaurant and in neighborhood supermarkets. ✉ *328 Lenox Ave., between 126th and 127th Sts.,* ☎ *212/996–0660.*

⑤ **Theresa Towers.** Its former incarnation as Harlem's poshest place to stay, the Hotel Theresa, is still evident from the HT crests under some windows and a sign painted on its west side, which towers over the neighboring buildings. Fidel Castro left his midtown accommodations to stay here during his 1960 visit to the United Nations. Now an office building, Theresa Towers is home to several community organizations. ⊠ *2090 Adam Clayton Powell Jr. Blvd., at 125th St..*

MURRAY HILL, FLATIRON DISTRICT, AND GRAMERCY

Numbers in the text correspond to numbers in the margin and on the Murray Hill, Flatiron District, and Gramercy map.

A Good Walk

Begin on East 36th Street, between Madison and Park avenues, at the **Morgan Library** ①, where old-master drawings, medieval manuscripts, illuminated books, and original music scores are on opulent display. As you proceed south on Madison Avenue, at 35th Street you'll pass the **Church of the Incarnation** ②, a broodingly dark brownstone version of a Gothic chapel. Across the street and taking up the entire next block is the landmark **B. Altman Building** ③, home of the famous department store from 1906 to 1989 and now the site of the New York Public Library's most high-tech research center: the **Science, Industry, and Business Library.**

At 5th Avenue and 34th Street, you can't miss the **Empire State Building** ④, one of the world's best-loved skyscrapers. South of the Empire State, at 5th Avenue and 29th Street, is **Marble Collegiate Church** ⑤. Cross the street and head east on 29th Street to **Church of the Transfiguration** ⑥, known as the Little Church Around the Corner. Continuing south along Madison Avenue, you'll come to the **New York Life Insurance Building** ⑦, which occupies the block between 26th and 27th streets on the east side of Madison, its distinctive gold top visible from afar. The limestone Beaux Arts courthouse, one block down at 25th Street, is the **Appellate Division, New York State Supreme Court** ⑧. The **Metropolitan Life Insurance Tower** ⑨, between 23rd and 24th streets, is another lovely, classically inspired insurance-company tower.

Across from these latter two sites, on the west side of Madison Avenue, is **Madison Square** ⑩, one of Manhattan's nicest green pockets and locus of a burgeoning new restaurant neighborhood. A walk through the square leads to one of New York's most photographed buildings—the Renaissance-style **Flatiron Building** ⑪, by architect Daniel Burnham. This distinguished building has lent its name to the now trendy **Flatiron District,** which lies to the south between 6th Avenue and Park Avenue South. The neighborhood's massive buildings, the last of the pre-skyscraper era and remnants of New York's Gilded Age, have had their ornate Romanesque facades gleamingly restored; hip boutiques and some of the city's best restaurants occupy their street levels, while advertising agencies, publishing houses, architects' offices, graphic design firms, residential lofts, and new media companies fill the upper stories.

Continue south on Broadway and turn east on 20th Street to the **Theodore Roosevelt Birthplace** ⑫, a reconstruction of the Victorian brownstone where Teddy lived until he was 15 years old. The prettiest part of this residential district, **Gramercy Park** ⑬, lies a block farther east, at the top of Irving Place between 20th and 21st streets. Alas, this picture-perfect park, with its flower beds, bird feeders, sundials, and cozy-looking benches, is accessible only to area residents who have keys. But you can still enjoy the beautiful 19th-century row houses fronting the park by taking a turn around its perimeter.

Jutting off Gramercy Park to the south is **Irving Place,** a short street lined with charming row houses, some of them occupied by restaurants.

Murray Hill, Flatiron District, and Gramercy

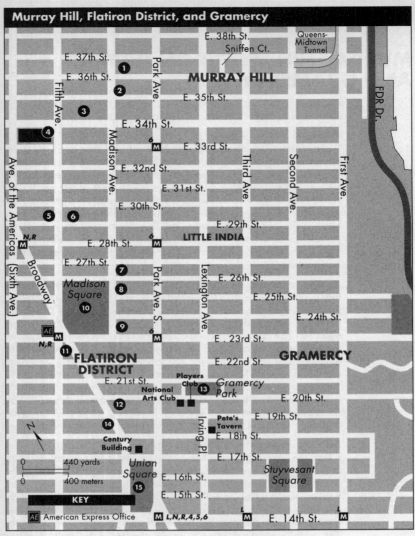

Local legend has it that O. Henry (pseudonym of William Sidney Porter) wrote "The Gift of the Magi" while sitting in the second booth to the right of the door at **Pete's Tavern** (⊠ 129 E. 18th St., at Irving Pl.), which also claims to be the oldest saloon in New York (1864, ☞ Chapter 7) both assertions are disputed, but it's still a good spot for a drink in a Gaslight Era atmosphere. O. Henry lived at 55 Irving Place in a building long ago demolished.

Wander up to Lexington Avenue in the high 20s, a neighborhood affectionately known as **Little India,** which has a concentration of Indian restaurants, spice shops, imported-video stores, and clothing emporiums; Middle Eastern, Indonesian, and Vietnamese restaurants also dot the area, which has a strong multicultural flavor. Now turn around, head back to Broadway, and turn left. Once again lined with stores— such as Fishs Eddy (⊠ 889 Broadway at 19th St.), a china shop specializing in American "diner"-ware, and ABC Carpet and Home (⊠ 888 Broadway at 18th Street ☞ Chapter 9), a potpourri-scented home-decor extravaganza—this section of Broadway was part of *the* most fashionable shopping area in the city during the late 19th century. Thanks to the Union Square/Flatiron District renaissance, its incredible emporium-style buildings have finally been re-occupied. The old **Arnold Constable Dry Goods Store Building** ⑭, which takes up almost an entire city block, has been taken over by such retailers as 9 West and Victoria's Secret. If you continue down Broadway, it leads to **Union Square** ⑮. The square itself bustles with the **Greenmarket,** a farmers' market, four days a week, but fashionable restaurants, cafés, theaters, and stores make the area a great destination anytime.

TIMING

Half a day should suffice for this tour. Allow 1½ hours each for the Empire State Building and the Morgan Library. Keep in mind that some office buildings included in the walk are open only during the week. The Union Square Greenmarket, a must-visit, is open all day every Monday, Wednesday, Friday, and Saturday. Before traipsing to the top of the Empire State Building, consider the weather and how it is likely to affect visibility. Sunsets from the observation deck are spectacular, so you may want to end your day there (but be sure to factor in the time you'll spend waiting on line).

Sights to See

⑧ **Appellate Division, New York State Supreme Court.** Figures representing "Wisdom" and "Justice" flank the main portal of this imposing Corinthian courthouse, built in 1900, on the east side of Madison Square. Statues of great lawmakers of the past line the roof balustrade, including Moses, Justinian, Confucius, although a statue of Muhammad was removed in the 1950s at the request of local Islamic groups, as Islamic law forbids the representation of humans in sculpture or painting. Inside are exhibitions of New York historical ephemera, murals, and furniture by the Herter Brothers. ⊠ *27 Madison Ave., at 25th St. (entrance on 25th St.),* ☎ 212/340–0400. ⊙ *Weekdays 9–5.*

⑭ **Arnold Constable Dry Goods Store Building.** Imagine yourself riding in a shining black carriage drawn by a set of four trotters, and you'll travel back in time to when this section of Broadway was the most fashionable strip of stores in New York. Arnold Constable was the Bloomingdale's of its era. Built 1869–1877 and designed by architect Griffith Thomas, this elegant five-story dry-goods building spans 19th Street with entrances on both Broadway and 5th Avenue. A double-story mansard roof tops it, white marble covers the Broadway side, and a cast-iron facade hovers over 5th Avenue. Re-occupied by several high-end clothing stores on the street level, this historic building now crackles with business again. ⊠ *881–887 Broadway, at 19th St.*

🖐 ❸ **B. Altman Building/New York Public Library Science, Industry, and Business Library (SIBL).** In 1906, department-store magnate Benjamin Altman gambled that the fashionable shoppers who patronized his store at 6th Avenue and 18th Street would follow him uptown to large new quarters on 5th Avenue and 34th Street, then a strictly residential street. They indeed came, and other stores followed, but then moved uptown again, to the 50s, leaving this trailblazer behind. Green canopies reminiscent of old subway kiosks grace the building's elaborate entrances. In the wake of the B. Altman chain's 1989 bankruptcy, the landmark sat vacant for several years. In 1996 the New York Public Library transferred all scientific, technology, and business materials from its main 42nd Street building to a new state-of-the-art facility here, the **Science, Industry, and Business Library (SIBL).** In the entrance area, a wall of TVs tuned to business-news stations and an electronic ticker tape reporting the latest stock market prices set SIBL's high-tech tone, while electronic signs beam instructions to patrons. Hundreds of computers wired to the Internet and research databases are the library's hottest tickets. ⊠ *188 Madison Ave., at 34th St.,* ☎ *212/592–7000.* ☉ *Mon. and Fri.–Sat. 10–6, Tues.–Thurs. 11–7.*

❷ **Church of the Incarnation.** A broodingly dark brownstone version of a Gothic chapel on the outside, this 1864 Episcopal church boasts jewel-like stained glass inside that counteracts the building's dour effect. The north aisle's 23rd Psalm Window is by the Tiffany Glass works; the south aisle's two Angel windows, dedicated to infants, are by the 19th-century English writer-designer William Morris. ⊠ *205 Madison Ave., at 35th St.* ☎ *212/689–6350*

❻ **Church of the Transfiguration.** Known as the Little Church Around the Corner, this Gothic Revival church complex (1849–1861) is set back in a shrub-filled New York version of an old English churchyard. It won its memorable appellation in 1870 when other area churches refused to bury actor George Holland, a colleague of well-known thespian Joseph Jefferson. Jefferson was directed to the "little church around the corner" to accomplish the burial, and the Episcopal institution has welcomed literary and theater types ever since. The south transept's stained-glass window, by John LaFarge, depicts 19th-century superstar actor Edwin Booth as Hamlet, his most famous role. ⊠ *1 E. 29th St., between 5th and Madison Aves.,* ☎ *212/684–6770.* ☉ *Sun. after 11 AM mass.*

★ 🖐 ❹ **Empire State Building.** It may no longer be the world's tallest building (it currently ranks seventh), but it is certainly one of the world's best-loved skyscrapers, its pencil-slim silhouette a symbol for New York City. The Art Deco playground for King Kong opened in April 1931 after only about a year of construction; the framework rose at a rate of 4½ stories per week, making the Empire State Building the fastest-rising major skyscraper ever built. Many floors were left completely unfinished, however, so tenants could have them custom-designed. The depression delayed this process, and critics deemed it the "Empty State Building." The crowning spire was originally designed as a mooring mast for dirigibles, but none ever docked here; in 1951 a TV transmittal tower was added to the top, raising the total height to 1,472 ft (its signals reach 8 million television sets in four states). Ever since the 1976 American bicentennial celebration, the top 30 stories have been spotlighted at night with seasonal colors. Today some of the holidays celebrated in lights include: Martin Luther King Jr. Day (red, black, and green); Valentine's Day (red and white); the Fourth of July (red, white, and blue); Columbus Day (red, white, and green); Hanukkah (blue and white); and Christmas (red and green). The building has appeared in more than 100 movies, among them 1933's unforgettable *King Kong* and 1957's *An Affair to Remember,* in which Cary Grant waited impatiently at the top for his rendezvous with Deborah Kerr.

Today about 20,000 people work in the Empire State Building, and more than 3.8 million people visit its 86th- and 102nd-floor observation decks annually. Tickets are sold on the concourse level; on your way up admire the illuminated panels depicting the Seven Wonders of the World—with the Empire State brazenly appended as number eight—in the three-story-high marble lobby. If you choose one observatory, make it the 86th (1,050 feet high), which is open to the air; on clear days you can see up to 80 mi. The 102nd-floor spot (1,250 feet high) is smaller, cramped, and glassed in (but if you have time for both, it's fun to compare the views from the different heights). It's worth timing your visit for early or late in the day, when the sun is low on the horizon and the shadows are deep across the city. Morning is the least crowded time, while at night the views of the city's lights are dazzling. ⊠ *350 5th Ave., at 34th St.,* ☎ *212/736–3100.* ☞ *$6.* ☉ *Daily 9:30* AM*–midnight; last elevator up leaves at 11:30* PM.

The Empire State Building's other major tourist attraction is the **New York Skyride.** A three-minute Comedy Central video presentation on the virtues of New York precedes a 17-minute motion-simulator ride above and around some of the city's top attractions, which are projected on a two-story-tall screen. The show, which leaves you feeling a little dizzy and disoriented, is not recommended for anyone who has trouble with motion sickness, and pregnant women are not admitted. ☎ *212/279–9777.* ☞ *$11.50; $14 for Skyride and Observatory.* ☉ *Daily 10–10.*

★ ⑪ **Flatiron Building.** When it opened in 1902, the Fuller Building, as it was originally known, was the tallest building in the world. Architect Daniel Burnham made ingenious use of the triangular wedge of land and employed a revolutionary steel frame, which allowed for its unprecedented 20-story, 286-ft height. Covered with a limestone and terracotta skin in the Italian Renaissance style, the ship's-bow-like structure, appearing to sail intrepidly up the avenue, was the most popular subject of picture postcards at the turn of the century. Winds invariably swooped down at its 23rd Street tip, billowing up the skirts of women pedestrians on 23rd Street, and local traffic cops had to shoo away male gawkers—coining the phrase "23 skiddoo." It was immediately noticed that the building resembled the then-popular flatirons, and the popular nickname eventually became official. ⊠ *175 5th Ave., bordered by 22nd and 23rd Sts., 5th Ave., and Broadway.*

NEED A
BREAK?
A good stop for coffee, hearty soups, salads, or sandwiches on thick, crusty bread is **La Boulangère** (⊠ 49 E. 21st St., between Park Avenue S. and Broadway, ☎ 212/475–8772), just 2½ blocks from the Flatiron Building. Or try **Henry's Gourmet Foods** (⊠ 186 5th Ave., at 23rd St., ☎ 212/924–2050) for hot blueberry oatmeal, grilled vegetable sandwiches, and fresh fruit-and-yogurt smoothies. Madison or Union squares are both nearby take-out destinations.

⑬ **Gramercy Park.** New York's only surviving private square occupies what was originally swamp. In 1831 real estate developer Samuel B. Ruggles bought and drained the land and created a park, inspired by London's residential squares, for the exclusive use of those who would buy the surrounding lots. Sixty-six of the city's fashionable elite did just that, and no less than golden keys were provided for them to penetrate the park's 8-ft-high cast-iron fence. Although no longer golden, keys are still given only to residents. The park's pristine flower beds, bird feeders, sundials, and benches may not be accessible, but its charms are apparent even to passersby.

Original 19th-century row houses in Greek Revival, Italianate, Gothic Revival, and Victorian Gothic styles still surround the south and west sides of the park. On the south side of the square stands a statue of actor Edwin Booth playing Hamlet; Booth lived at No. 16, which he remodeled in the early 1880s to serve as an actors' association, the **Players Club**. Stanford White, the architect for the renovation, was a member of the club, as were many other nonactors. Members over the years have included Mark Twain, Booth Tarkington, John and Lionel Barrymore, Irving Berlin, Winston Churchill, Sir Laurence Olivier, Frank Sinatra, Walter Cronkite, Jack Lemmon, and Richard Gere.

The **National Arts Club** (✉ 15 Gramercy Park S) was once the home of Samuel Tilden, a governor of New York and the 1876 Democratic presidential candidate. Calvert Vaux, codesigner of Central Park, remodeled this building in 1884, conjoining two houses and creating a 40-room mansion. Among its Victorian Gothic decorations are medallions portraying Goethe, Dante, Milton, and Benjamin Franklin. The club, founded in 1898 to bring together "art lovers and art workers," moved into the mansion in 1906. Early members included Woodrow Wilson and Theodore Roosevelt; Robert Redford and Martin Scorsese are more recent members. The Club now houses the Poetry Society of America, which sponsors poetry readings (☞ Chapter 4).

The austere gray-brown Friends Meeting House at 28 Gramercy Park South (1859) became the **Brotherhood Synagogue** in 1974, and a narrow plaza just east of the synagogue contains a Holocaust memorial. No. **19 Gramercy Park South** (1845) was the home in the 1880s of society doyenne Mrs. Stuyvesant Fish, a fearless iconoclast who shocked Mrs. Astor and Mrs. Vanderbilt when she reduced the time of formal dinner parties from several hours to 50 minutes, thus ushering in the modern social era. ✉ *Lexington Ave. between 20th and 21st Sts.*

❿ Madison Square. With a picturesque view of some of the city's oldest and most charming skyscrapers (the Flatiron Building, Met Life Insurance Tower, and New York Life Insurance Building), this tree-filled 7-acre park mainly attracts dog owners and office workers, but it's a fine spot for people- or squirrel-watching, relaxing, and picnicking, too. Baseball was invented across the Hudson in Hoboken, New Jersey, but the city's first baseball games were played here circa 1845. On the north end an imposing 1881 statue by Augustus Saint-Gaudens memorializes Civil War naval hero Admiral Farragut. An 1876 statue of Secretary of State William Henry Seward (the Seward of the phrase "Seward's folly"—as Alaska was originally known) sits in the park's southwest corner, though it's rumored the sculptor placed a reproduction of the statesman's head on a likeness of Abraham Lincoln's body. ✉ *23rd to 26th Sts., between 5th and Madison Aves.*

❺ Marble Collegiate Church. Built in 1854 for the Reformed Protestant Dutch Congregation first organized in 1628 by Peter Minuit, the canny Dutchman who bought Manhattan from the Native Americans for the equivalent of $24, this impressive Romanesque Revival church takes its name from the Tuckahoe marble that covers it. Dr. Norman Vincent Peale (*The Power of Positive Thinking*) was pastor here from 1932 to 1984. ✉ *1 W. 29th St., at 5th Ave.,* ☎ *212/686–2770.*

9 **Metropolitan Life Insurance Tower.** When it was added in 1909, the 700-ft tower, which re-creates the campanile of St. Mark's in Venice, made this 1893 building the world's tallest. Its clock's four dials are each three stories high, and their minute hands weigh half a ton each; it chimes on the quarter hour. A skywalk connects Met Life's North Building, between 24th and 25th streets. Its Art Deco loggias have attracted many film crews—the building has appeared in such films as *After Hours, Radio Days,* and *The Fisher King.* ✉ *1 Madison Ave., between 23rd and 24th Sts.*

★ **1** **Morgan Library.** One of New York's most patrician museums, the Morgan is a world-class treasury of medieval and Renaissance illuminated manuscripts, old-master drawings and prints, rare books, and autographed literary and musical manuscripts. Many of the crowning achievements produced on paper, from the Middle Ages to the 20th century, are here: letters penned by John Keats and Thomas Jefferson; a summary of the theory of relativity in Einstein's own elegant handwriting; three Gutenberg Bibles; drawings by Dürer, da Vinci, Rubens, Blake, and Rembrandt; the only known manuscript fragment of Milton's "Paradise Lost"; Thoreau's journals; and original manuscripts and letters by Charlotte Brontë, Jane Austen, Thomas Pynchon, and many others. Originally built for the collections of Wall Street baron J. Pierpont (J. P.) Morgan (1837–1913), the museum has at its core a Renaissance-style palazzo, completed in 1906 by McKim, Mead & White, which houses the opulent period rooms of Morgan's original library. The **East Room** (the main library) has dizzying tiers of handsomely bound rare books, letters, and illuminated manuscripts. The **West Room,** Morgan's personal study, contains a remarkable selection of mostly Italian Renaissance furniture, paintings, and other marvels within its red-damask-lined walls.

Changing exhibitions, drawn from the permanent collection, are often highly distinguished. In January through April 2000 the Library will mount an exhibition of books made by William Caxton (ca. 1422–ca. 1491), renowned as England's first printer. Among the works on display will be a complete copy of Mallory's *Le Morte D'Arthur.* The library shop is within an 1852 Italianate brownstone, once the home of Morgan's son, J. P. "Jack" Morgan Jr., which is connected to the rest of the library by a graceful glass-roof garden court where lunch and afternoon tea are served. Outside on 36th Street, the sphinx in the right-hand sculptured panel of the original library's facade was rumored to wear the face of architect Charles McKim. Exhibition tours are offered free with admission Tuesday–Friday at noon. ✉ *29 E. 36th St., at Madison Ave.,* ☎ *212/685–0008.* ✆ *$6 (suggested donation).* ☉ *Tues.–Fri. 10:30–5, Sat. 10:30–6, Sun. noon–6.*

7 **New York Life Insurance Building.** Cass Gilbert, better known for the Woolworth Building (☞ The Seaport and the Courts, *below*), capped this 1928 building with a gilded pyramid that is stunning when lighted at night. The soaring lobby's coffered ceilings and ornate bronze doors are equally sumptuous. P. T. Barnum's Hippodrome formerly occupied this site, and after that (1890–1925) Madison Square Garden, designed by architect and playboy Stanford White. White was shot in the Garden's roof garden by Harry K. Thaw, a partner in White's firm and the jealous husband of actress Evelyn Nesbit, with whom White was purportedly having an affair—a lurid episode more or less accurately depicted in E. L. Doctorow's book *Ragtime.* ✉ *51 Madison Ave., between 26th and 27th Sts.*

OFF THE BEATEN PATH	**SNIFFEN COURT –** Just two blocks from the Morgan Library, the 10 Romanesque Revival former brick carriage houses that line this easily overlooked cul-de-sac are equal parts Old London and New Orleans. Peer through the locked gate to admire the lovely buildings. ⊠ *150–158 E. 36th St., between Lexington and 3rd Aves.*

⑫ Theodore Roosevelt Birthplace National Historic Site. The 26th U.S. president—the only one from New York City—was born on this site in 1858. The original 1848 brownstone was demolished in 1916, but this Gothic Revival replica, built in 1923, is a near-perfect reconstruction of the house where Teddy lived until he was 15 years old. Now administered by the National Park Service, the house has a fascinating collection of Teddyana in five Victorian period rooms. Saturday-afternoon chamber music concerts are offered each fall, winter, and spring. ⊠ *28 E. 20th St., between Broadway and Park Ave. S,* ☎ *212/260–1616.* ☎ *$2.* ☉ *Wed.–Sun. 9–5; guided tours every hr until 4.*

NEED A BREAK?	A vegetarian restaurant in the style of a Japanese tea house, the **Zen Palate Gourmet Shop** (⊠ 34 E. Union Square, at 16th St., ☎ 212/614–9291) serves up an innovative culinary experience at moderate prices. Try the sweet yam fries, kale and seaweed salad, or steamed vegetable bun. Table service is fast-paced; consider carrying out and picnicking in neighboring Union Square.

⑮ Union Square. A park, meeting place, and outdoor shopping area, this pocket of green space is the focus of a bustling residential and shopping neighborhood. Its name—"Union"—originally signified that two main roads—Broadway and 4th Avenue—crossed here, but it took on a different meaning in the late 19th and early 20th centuries, when the square became a rallying spot for labor protests and mass demonstrations; many unions, as well as fringe political parties, moved their headquarters nearby. In fact, the square is full of the statues of former politicians: George Washington (1856, Henry Kirke Brown), Abraham Lincoln (1866, Henry Kirke Brown), the Marquis de Lafayette (1875, Frederic Auguste Bartholdi, who also sculpted the Statue of Liberty), and Gandhi (1986, Kantilal B. Patel), whose likeness stands in the southwest corner of the park.

Union Square is at its best on Monday, Wednesday, Friday, and Saturday (8–5), when the largest of the city's two dozen **Greenmarkets** brings farmers and food purveyors from all over the Northeast to its western and northern edges. Crowds of neighborhood residents and workers browse among the stands of fresh produce, flowers and plants, homemade bakery goods, cheeses, cider, New York State wines, and fish and meat. On the north end, the park's 1932 **Pavilion** is flanked by playgrounds and **Luna Park** (☎ 212/475–8464), an open-air café open mid-May through October. The **Green Arc** sells funky books and postcards on the western edge of the park.

Movie theaters and retail superstores occupy the handsome, restored 19th-century commercial buildings that surround the park. Foremost among these is the redbrick and white-stone **Century Building** (built in 1881, ⊠ 33 E. 17th St.), now a Barnes & Noble bookstore, which has preserved the building's original cast-iron columns and other architectural details. The building at 17th Street and Union Square East, now housing the New York Film Academy and the Union Square Theatre (☞ Chapter 4), was the final home of **Tammany Hall**. This organization, famous in its day as a fairly corrupt yet effective political machine, moved here just at the height of its power in 1929, but by

1943 it went bankrupt and had to sell the building. ⊠ *14th to 17th Sts. between Broadway and Park Ave. S.*

CHELSEA

Like the London district of the same name, New York's Chelsea has preserved its villagelike personality. Both have their quiet nooks where the 19th century seems to live on; both have been havens for artists, writers, and bohemians—New York's notables include Louise Bourgeois and Susan Sontag. New York's Chelsea is catching up to London's as upscale real estate, with town house renovations reclaiming side-street blocks. Restored historic cast-iron buildings on 6th Avenue house America's ubiquitous superstore tenants, who have nonetheless revitalized the area. Seventh, 8th, and 9th avenues may never equal the shopping mecca of King's Road in London's Chelsea, but they have one-of-a-kind boutiques sprinkled among unassuming grocery stores and other remnants of the neighborhood's immigrant past.

Actually, the New York neighborhood was named not after Chelsea itself but after London's Chelsea Royal Hospital, an old soldiers' home. Until the 1830s one family's country estate occupied the area from 19th to 28th Street and from 8th Avenue west. Then the owner, Clement Clarke Moore, realized the city was moving north and decided to divide his land into lots. With an instinctive gift for urban planning, he dictated a pattern of development that ensured street after street of graceful row houses. A clergyman and classics professor, Moore is probably best known for his 1822 poem "A Visit from St. Nicholas"—"'Twas the night before Christmas. . . ." He composed it while bringing a sleigh full of Christmas treats from lower Manhattan to his Chelsea home.

Today's Chelsea extends west of 5th Avenue from 14th Street to 29th Street. Eighth Avenue now rivals Christopher Street in the West Village as New York's gay Main Street: shops, fitness clubs, and restaurants cater to a largely gay clientele. Yet the thriving neighborhood also accommodates a multicultural population that has lived here for decades, as well as a burgeoning arts community west of 10th Avenue.

Numbers in the text correspond to numbers in the margin and on the Chelsea map.

A Good Walk

Begin on the corner of 6th Avenue and 18th Street. Sixth Avenue was once known as Ladies' Mile for its concentration of major department stores (also in the late 19th century, elevated tracks cast their shadow along this street). After the stores moved uptown in the early 1900s, the neighborhood declined, and the grand old store buildings stood empty and dilapidated. The 1990s, however, brought a renaissance to the Flatiron district to the east (☞ Murray Hill, Flatiron District, and Gramercy, *above*), and 6th Avenue's grandest buildings once again purvey wares of all kinds. On the east side of the avenue, between 18th and 19th streets, stands the former **Siegel-Cooper Dry Goods Store** ①.

Between 18th and 19th streets on the west side of the avenue is the 1877 cast-iron **B. Altman Dry Goods Store** ②, now occupied by Today's Man. Continue walking north to 20th Street. The Gothic-style Church of the Holy Communion, an Episcopal house of worship dating from 1846, is on the northeast corner of the avenue. To the horror of some preservationists, it was converted into the Limelight nightclub. On the west side of the avenue between 20th and 21st streets stands another former cast-iron retail palace, the **Hugh O'Neill Dry Goods Store** ③.

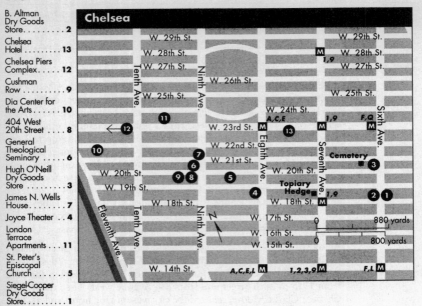

Chelsea

On weekends, 6th Avenue between 24th and 27th streets is the site of the city's longest-running outdoor flea market (☞ Chapter 9). But if you turn left from 6th Avenue onto 21st Street you'll come upon **Third Cemetery of the Spanish & Portuguese Synagogue, Shearith Israel** on the south side of the street. These days it is a rather neglected spot with upset marble gravestones, adjacent to a parking lot. In use from 1829 to 1851, it is one of three graveyards created in Manhattan by this congregation (☞ Greenwich Village *and* Little Italy and Chinatown, *below*).

At 7th Avenue cross the street and detour down to Chadwin House, No. 140, between 18th and 19th streets. In front of this very ordinary Chelsea apartment building, stands a fabulous, Edward Scissorhands–like display of fanciful **topiary** maintained by New York City gardener Lynn Torgerson.

Back up on 21st Street, continue west to 8th Avenue, where the Chelsea Historic District officially begins. Its residential heart is between 19th and 23rd streets, from 8th to 10th avenues. To get a quick feel for 8th Avenue, head down to 19th Street to the Art Deco **Joyce Theater** ④, primarily a dance venue. Its presence, along with the burgeoning lesbian and gay community here, helped attract many good moderately priced restaurants to 8th Avenue.

On 20th Street between 8th and 9th avenues, you'll find the brick parish house, fieldstone church, and rectory of 19th-century **St. Peter's Episcopal Church** ⑤, which houses the well-known Atlantic Theater Company (☞ Chapter 4). Next, head west on 20th Street to 9th Avenue; on the west side of the avenue between 20th and 21st streets is the **General Theological Seminary** ⑥, the oldest Episcopal seminary in the United States. A block north at 21st street on the northwest corner is the **James N. Wells House** ⑦, once the home of the man who planned Chelsea. The café on its first floor is great for a neighborhood break.

Across the street from the seminary, **404 West 20th Street** ⑧ is the oldest house in the historic district. The residences next door, from 406 to 418 West 20th Street, are called **Cushman Row** ⑨ and are excellent examples of Greek Revival town houses. Farther down West 20th Street, stop to look at the fine Italianate houses from Nos. 446 to 450. The arched windows and doorways are hallmarks of this style, which prized circular forms—not least because the expense required to build them showed off the owner's wealth. West 22nd Street has a string of handsome old row houses just east of 10th Avenue.

Between 10th and 11th avenues, from 20th to 29th Street, you can explore the Chelsea galleries. A good place to begin is 22nd Street, home to **Dia Center for the Arts** ⑩, the anchor of Chelsea's renaissance as an art community. Besides 22nd Street, 21st and 24th streets also have an ever-growing contingent of galleries large and small, including many relocated from SoHo. Several of the neighborhood's most recent additions are large, upscale places. East of Dia on 22nd Street are quite a few galleries, including **Matthew Marks Gallery** and **Pat Hearn Gallery.** One block down, on 21st Street, is the major SoHo transplant, **Paula Cooper Gallery.** Because each gallery keeps its own hours, it's best to call ahead about openings and closings. See ☞ Chapter 4 for a complete listing of Chelsea galleries, with addresses and phone numbers.

From the gallery zone return to 10th Avenue and walk to 23rd Street. Occupying the entire block between 10th and 9th avenues and 23rd and 24th streets, the **London Terrace Apartments** ⑪ is a vast 1930 complex containing 1,670 apartments. As you walk along 23rd Street, notice the lions on the arched entrances; from the side they look as if they're snarling, but from the front they have wide grins.

If you walk west on 23rd Street as far as you can go, you'll come to the mammoth new **Chelsea Piers Sports and Entertainment Complex** ⑫, where you can take a breath of sea air and look at Chelsea's slice of the Hudson River waterfront. The entrance is at 23rd Street. If you don't head to the river, continue east on 23rd Street. During the 1880s and Gay '90s, the street was the heart of the entertainment district, lined with theaters, music halls, and beer gardens. Today it is an undistinguished commercial thoroughfare. Among the relics of its proud past is the **Chelsea Hotel** ⑬.

TIMING

Allow yourself at least three to four hours to explore Chelsea. If your schedule permits, plan to spend the day so you have ample time to browse the stores and galleries and have a leisurely lunch.

Sights to See

❷ **B. Altman Dry Goods Store.** Built in 1877 with additions in 1887 and 1910, this ornate cast-iron giant originally housed B. Altman Dry Goods until the business moved in 1906 to its imposing quarters at 5th Avenue and 34th Street (☞ Murray Hill, Flatiron District, and Gramercy, *above*). ✉ *621 6th Ave., between 18th and 19th Sts.*

⑬ **Chelsea Hotel.** Constructed of red brick with lacy wrought-iron balconies and a mansard roof, this 11-story neighborhood landmark opened in 1884 as a cooperative apartment house. It became a hotel in 1905, although it has always catered to long-term tenants, with a tradition of broad-mindedness that has attracted many creative types. Its literary roll call of former live-ins includes Mark Twain, Eugene O'Neill, O. Henry, Thomas Wolfe, Tennessee Williams, Vladimir Nabokov, Mary McCarthy, Brendan Behan, Arthur Miller, Dylan Thomas, William S. Burroughs, and Arthur C. Clarke (who wrote the script for *2001: A Space Odyssey* while living here). In 1966 Andy Warhol filmed artist Brigid Polk in her Chelsea Hotel room, which eventually became *The Chelsea Girls*. More recently, the hotel was seen on screen in *I Shot Andy Warhol* (1996) and *Sid and Nancy* (1986), a dramatization of the true-life Chelsea Hotel murder of Nancy Spungen, who was stabbed to death here, allegedly by her boyfriend, drugged punk rocker Sid Vicious. The shabby aura of the Chelsea Hotel is part of its allure. Read the commemorative plaques outside and then step into the lobby to see the 10-floor-high, skylighted open stairwell and the artwork, some of it donated in lieu of rent by residents down on their luck. ⊠ *222 W. 23rd St., between 7th and 8th Aves.,* ☎ *212/243–3700.*

☾ ⑫ **Chelsea Piers Sports and Entertainment Complex.** Beginning in 1910, the Chelsea Piers were the launching point for a new generation of big ocean liners; they were also the destination of the *Titanic,* which never arrived, and the departure point for the last sailing of the *Lusitania,* the British liner sunk by a German submarine in 1915. Decades-long neglect ended with the transformation of the four piers' old buildings along the Hudson River into a 1.7-million-square-ft state-of-the-art facility, providing a huge variety of activities (☞ Chapter 8 for details). The complex has a wall of historical photographs, sporting goods shops, and several restaurants with river views, including the Crab House and the Chelsea Brewing Company. ⊠ *Piers 59–62 on the Hudson River from 17th to 23rd Sts.; entrance at 23rd St.,* ☎ *212/336–6666.*

⑨ **Cushman Row.** Built by dry-goods merchant Don Alonzo Cushman, a friend of Clement Clarke Moore, who made a fortune developing Chelsea, this string of homes between 9th and 10th avenues represents some of the country's most perfect examples of Greek Revival town houses. The residences retain such original details as small wreath-encircled attic windows, deeply recessed doorways with brownstone frames, and striking iron balustrades and fences. Pineapples, a traditional symbol of welcome, perch atop the newels in front of Nos. 416 and 418. ⊠ *406–418 W. 20th St., between 9th and 10th Aves.*

★ ⑩ **Dia Center for the Arts.** This facility provides contemporary artists with the chance to develop new work or to mount an organized exhibit on a full floor for extended time periods, usually an entire year. Besides installations by diverse artists, you might find an exhibit from Dia's permanent collection, which includes creations by Joseph Beuys, Walter De Maria, Dan Flavin, Blinky Palermo, Cy Twombly, Richard Serra, and Andy Warhol. Installed outside on the roof is a fascinating exhibition designed by Dan Graham, which consists of a two-way mirror glass cylinder inside a cube. ⊠ *548 W. 22nd St., between 10th and 11th Aves.,* ☎ *212/989–5566.* ▣ *$6.* ◷ *Wed.–Sun. noon–6.*

NEED A   **Wild Lily Tearoom** (511A W. 22 St., between 10th and 11th Aves., ☎
BREAK?   212/691–2258). This tiny Japanese art-cum-food shop, complete with a
            koi (carp) pool, serves teas with poetic names like Buddha's Finger and
            Pink Infusion alongside salads, sandwiches, and desserts. For burgers
            and shakes, stop at **Empire Diner** (210 10th Ave., at 22nd St.,
            212/243–2736), a gleaming stainless steel hash house.

⑧ **404 West 20th Street.** The oldest house in the historic district was built between 1829 and 1830 in the Federal style. It still has one clapboard side wall; over the years it acquired a Greek Revival doorway and Italianate windows on the parlor floor, and the roof was raised one story. *404 W. 20th St. at 9th Ave.*

6 General Theological Seminary. When Chelsea developer Clement Clarke Moore divided his estate, he deeded a large section to this Episcopal seminary, where he had taught Hebrew and Greek; the religious oasis still occupies a block-long stretch. The stoutly fenced campus is accessible through the clunky modern building on 9th Avenue; during off-hours you can view the grounds from West 20th Street. The 1836 **West Building** is a fine early example of Gothic Revival architecture. Most of the rest of the complex was completed in 1883–1902, when the school hired architect Charles Coolidge Haight to design, in the style known as English Collegiate Gothic, which Haight had pioneered, a campus that would rival those of most other American colleges of the day. Today the quiet interior gardens are a welcome green spot in park-poor Chelsea. The aforementioned 1960s-era building facing 9th Avenue houses administrative offices, a bookstore, and the 210,000-volume **St. Mark's Library,** generally considered the nation's greatest ecclesiastical library; it has the world's largest collection of Latin Bibles. ⊠ *175 9th Ave., at W. 20th St.,* ☎ *212/243–5150.* ☉ *Grounds weekdays noon–3; call for information on using the library.*

3 Hugh O'Neill Dry Goods Store. Constructed in 1875, this cast-iron building, originally an emporium, features Corinthian columns and pilasters; its corner towers were once topped with huge bulbous domes. The name of the original tenant is proudly displayed on the pediment. ⊠ *655–671 6th Ave., between 20th and 21st Sts.*

7 James N. Wells House. This 1833 2½-story brick house was the home of Clement Clarke Moore's property manager, the man who planned Chelsea. Wells was responsible for the strict housing codes that created the elegant residential neighborhood by prohibiting stables and manure piles and requiring tree planting. ⊠ *401 W. 21st St.*

NEED A BREAK? At **Le Gamin** (⊠ 183 9th Ave., at 21st St., ☎ 212/243–8864), a rustic French café where soup-bowl size café au lait, crepes, and salads are de rigueur, you can sit for hours without being disturbed.

4 Joyce Theater. The former Elgin movie house, built in 1942, was gutted and in 1982 transformed into this sleek modern theater that pays tribute to its Art Deco origins. It is one of the city's leading modern-dance venues (☞ Chapter 4). ⊠ *175 8th Ave., at W. 19th St.,* ☎ *212/ 242–0800.*

11 London Terrace Apartments. When this vast block-long brick complex first opened in 1930, the doormen dressed as London bobbies. Today, the desirable real estate is home to the fashion glitterati who work just up 7th Avenue in the garment district. ⊠ *W. 23rd to W. 24th Sts. between 9th and 10th Aves.*

5 St. Peter's Episcopal Church. Built in 1836 to 1838 on a rising tide of enthusiasm for Gothic Revival architecture, the modest fieldstone St. Peter's is one of New York's first examples of early Gothic Revival, though retaining elements of Greek Revival style. To the left of the church, the brick **parish hall** is now the home of the Atlantic Theater Company, founded by playwright David Mamet (☞ Chapter 4). ⊠ *344 W. 20th St., between 8th and 9th Aves.,* ☎ *212/929–2390.*

1 Siegel-Cooper Dry Goods Store. Built in 1896, much later than its neighbors, this impressive building adorned with glazed terra-cotta encompasses 15½ acres of space, yet it was built in only five months. In its retail heyday, the store's main floor featured an immense fountain— a circular marble terrace with an enormous white-marble-and-brass replica of *The Republic,* the statue Daniel Chester French displayed at the 1883 Chicago World's Fair—which became a favorite rendezvous point for New Yorkers. During World War I the building was a military hospital. The building's splendid exterior ornamentation contrasts with its otherwise unremarkable brick facade. Today its principal tenants are Bed, Bath & Beyond, Filene's Basement, and T. J. Maxx. ⊠ *620 6th Ave., between 18th and 19th Sts.*

NEED A BREAK?	**La Petite Abeille** (⊠ 107 W. 18th St., ☎ 212/604–9350), just west of 6th Avenue, serves tasty café standards in addition to traditional Belgian waffles, chocolates, and cookies. Decorated with painted tiles, **O Padiero** (641 6th Ave, between 19th and 20th Sts., ☎ 212/414–9661) is a handsome Portuguese bakery/café—a warm welcome amid the merchandising giants of 6th Avenue. Surrounded by rustic loaves of freshly baked bread, sit at one of the tiny tables and enjoy Portuguese salads, sandwiches, and beer, wine, or coffee.

GREENWICH VILLAGE

Greenwich Village, which New Yorkers invariably speak of simply as "the Village," enjoyed a raffish reputation for years. Originally a rural outpost of the city—a haven for New Yorkers during early 19th-century smallpox and yellow fever epidemics—many of its blocks still look somewhat pastoral, with brick town houses and low-rises, tiny green parks and hidden courtyards, and a crazy-quilt pattern of narrow, tree-lined streets (some of which follow long-ago cow paths). In the mid-19th century, however, as the city spread north of 14th Street, the Village became the province of immigrants, bohemians, and students (New York University [NYU], today the nation's largest private university, was planted next to Washington Square in 1831). Its politics were radical and its attitudes tolerant, which is one reason it remains a home to such a large lesbian and gay community.

Several generations of writers and artists have lived and worked here: in the 19th century, Henry James, Edgar Allan Poe, Mark Twain, Walt Whitman, and Stephen Crane; at the turn of the century, O. Henry, Edith Wharton, Theodore Dreiser, and Hart Crane; and during the 1920s and '30s, John Dos Passos, Norman Rockwell, Sinclair Lewis, John Reed, Eugene O'Neill, Edward Hopper, and Edna St. Vincent Millay. In the late 1940s and early 1950s, the Abstract Expressionist painters Franz Kline, Jackson Pollock, Mark Rothko, and Willem de Kooning congregated here, as did the Beat writers Jack Kerouac, Allen Ginsberg, and Lawrence Ferlinghetti. The 1960s brought folk musicians and poets, notably Bob Dylan and Peter, Paul, and Mary.

Today, block for block, the Village is still one of the most vibrant parts of the city. Well-heeled professionals occupy high-rent apartments and town houses side by side with bohemian, longtime residents, who pay cheap rents thanks to rent-control laws, as well as NYU students. Locals and tourists rub elbows at dozens of small restaurants, cafés spill out onto sidewalks, and an endless variety of small shops pleases everyone. Except for a few pockets of adult-entertainment shops and divey bars, the Village is as scrubbed as posher neighborhoods.

Numbers in the text correspond to numbers in the margin and on the Greenwich Village, the East Village, and the Lower East Side map.

A Good Walk

Begin your tour of Greenwich Village at the foot of 5th Avenue at Washington Arch in **Washington Square** ①, a hugely popular 9½-acre park that provides a neighborhood oasis for locals and tourists alike. Most

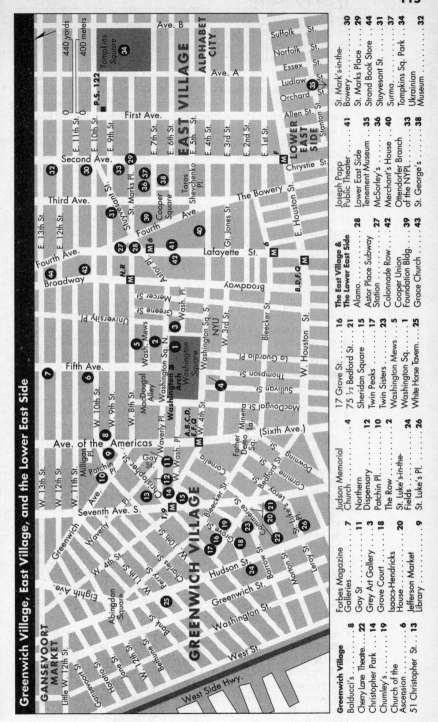

Greenwich Village, East Village, and the Lower East Side

buildings bordering Washington Square belong to NYU. On Washington Square North, between University Place and MacDougal Street, stretches **The Row** ②, composed of two blocks of lovingly preserved Greek Revival and Federal-style town houses.

On the east side of the square, you can take in a contemporary art exhibit at **Grey Art Gallery** ③, housed in NYU's main building. If you walk to the south side of the square, a trio of red sandstone hulks represents an abortive 1960s attempt to create a unified campus look for NYU, as envisioned by architects Philip Johnson and Richard Foster. At one time plans called for all the Washington Square buildings to be refaced in this red stone; fortunately, the cost proved prohibitive. At La Guardia Place and Washington Square South, the undistinguished modern Loeb Student Center stands on the site of a famous boardinghouse that had been nicknamed the House of Genius for the talented writers who lived there over the years: Theodore Dreiser, John Dos Passos, and Eugene O'Neill, among others. A block west of the student center, at the corner of Washington Square South and Thompson Street, is the square-towered **Judson Memorial Church** ④.

From Washington Square Arch and the park, cross Washington Square North to the east side of 5th Avenue. On your right, at the northeast corner of Washington Square North and 5th Avenue, is the portico entrance to 7–13 Washington Square North. Beyond the white columns of this entrance is the small, attractive **Willy's Garden.** A statue of Miguel de Cervantes, the author of *Don Quixote,* stands at the far end. The likeness, cast in 1724, was a gift from the mayor of Madrid.

Another half a block north, on the east side of 5th Avenue, is **Washington Mews,** ⑤ a cobblestone private street. A similar Village mews, MacDougal Alley, can be found between 8th Street and the square just off MacDougal Street, one block west. Continue up the west side of 5th Avenue; you'll pass the **Church of the Ascension** ⑥, a Gothic Revival brownstone building. At 5th Avenue and 12th Street you can stop in the **Forbes Magazine Galleries** ⑦, which house the late publisher Malcolm Forbes's unusual personal collection.

Backtrack on 5th Avenue to West 11th Street and turn right to see one of the best examples of a Village town-house block. One exception to the general 19th-century redbrick look is the modern, angled front window of 18 West 11th Street, usually occupied by a stuffed bear whose outfit changes from day to day. This house was built after the original was destroyed in a 1970 explosion of a basement bomb factory, which had been started by members of the radical Weather Underground faction. At the end of the block, behind a low gray-stone wall on the south side of the street, is the **Second Shearith Israel graveyard,** used by the country's oldest Jewish congregation after the original cemetery in Chinatown (☞ Little Italy and Chinatown, *below*) and before the one in Chelsea (☞ Chelsea, *above*).

On Avenue of the Americas (6th Avenue), turn left to sample the wares at **Balducci's** ⑧, a high-end gourmet food store. Directly opposite, the triangle formed by West 10th Street, 6th Avenue, and Greenwich Avenue originally held a market, a jail, and the magnificent towered courthouse that is now the **Jefferson Market Library** ⑨. Just west of 6th Avenue on 10th Street is the wrought-iron gateway to a tiny courtyard called **Patchin Place** ⑩; around the corner, on 6th Avenue just north of 10th Street, is a similar cul-de-sac, Milligan Place.

Next, proceed to Christopher Street, which veers off from the south end of the library triangle. Christopher Street has long been the symbolic heart of New York's gay and lesbian community. Before you proceed just a few steps, you'll see **Gay Street** ⑪ on your left. This quiet curved thoroughfare of early 19th-century row houses was immortalized in Ruth McKinney's book *My Sister Eileen*. Continuing west on Christopher Street, cross Waverly Place, where on your left you'll pass the 1831 brick **Northern Dispensary** ⑫ building, which at one time provided health care to poor neighborhood residents. Across the street is **51 Christopher Street** ⑬, where the historic Stonewall riots marked the beginning of the gay rights movement. Across the street is a green triangle named **Christopher Park** ⑭, not to be confused with **Sheridan Square** ⑮, another landscaped triangle to the south.

Across the busy intersection of 7th Avenue South, Christopher Street has many bars and stores; several cater to a gay clientele, but all kinds of people traverse the busy sidewalks. Two shops worth a visit are **Mc-Nulty's Tea and Coffee Co.** (⊠ 109 Christopher St.), with a large variety of tea and coffee blends, and **Li-Lac Chocolate Shop** (⊠ 120 Christopher St.), a longtime favorite in the area for its homemade chocolate and butter crunch. West of 7th Avenue South, the Village turns into a picture-book town of twisting tree-lined streets, quaint houses, and tiny restaurants. Starting from Sheridan Square west, follow Grove Street past the house where Thomas Paine died (⊠ 59 Grove St.)—now the site of Marie's Crisis Cafe—and the boyhood home of poet Hart Crane (⊠ 45 Grove St.). At this point you'll be close to the intersection of Grove and Bleecker streets. You may now choose to take a leisurely stroll along the portion of Bleecker Street that extends west of 7th Avenue South from Grove to Bank Street, heading northwest toward Abingdon Square. This section of Bleecker Street is full of crafts and antiques shops, coffeehouses, and small restaurants.

If you forego Bleecker Street, continue your walk west on Grove Street. The secluded intersection of Grove and Bedford streets seems to have fallen through a time warp into the 19th century. On the northeast corner stands **17 Grove Street** ⑯, one of the few remaining clapboard structures in Manhattan. Behind it, at 102 Bedford Street, is **Twin Peaks** ⑰, an early 19th-century house that resembles a Swiss chalet. Heading west, Grove Street curves in front of the iron gate of **Grove Court** ⑱, a group of mid-19th-century brick-front residences.

Return to Bedford Street, turn right and walk down until you get to No. 86. Behind the unmarked door is **Chumley's** ⑲, a former speakeasy. Walk a couple of blocks farther down to the oldest house in the Village, the **Isaacs-Hendricks House** ⑳, at 77 Bedford Street,. The place next door, **75½ Bedford Street** ㉑, at 9½ ft wide, is New York's narrowest house. Bedford Street intersects Commerce Street, one of the Village's most romantic untrod lanes, and home to the historic **Cherry Lane Theater** ㉒. Across the street, past the bend in the road, stand two nearly identical brick houses separated by a garden and popularly known as the **Twin Sisters** ㉓.

Turn left from Commerce Street onto Barrow Street, which next intersects with Hudson Street, so named because this was originally the bank of the Hudson River. The block to the northwest is owned by **St. Luke's-in-the-Fields** ㉔, built in 1822 as a country chapel for downtown's Trinity Church. Writer Bret Harte once lived at 487 Hudson Street, at the end of the row. If your feet are getting tired, you can head north on Hudson Street for four blocks and take a rest at the legendary **White Horse Tavern** ㉕, at 11th Street.

If you choose to continue, head south on Hudson Street for two blocks until you reach Leroy Street. On your left, to the east of Hudson Street, Leroy Street becomes **St. Luke's Place** ㉖, a one-block row of classic 1860s town houses shaded by graceful gingko trees. Across 7th Avenue South, St. Luke's Place becomes Leroy Street again, which terminates in an old Italian neighborhood at Bleecker Street. Because of all the touristy shops and crowds, Bleecker Street between 6th and 7th avenues seems more vital these days than Little Italy does. For authentic Italian ambience, stop into one of the fragrant Italian bakeries, such as **A. Zito & Sons** (⊠ 259 Bleecker St.) and **Rocco's** (⊠ 243 Bleecker St.), or look inside the old-style butcher shops, such as **Ottomanelli & Sons** (⊠ 285 Bleecker St.) and **Faicco's** (⊠ 260 Bleecker St.). In a town that's fierce about its pizza, some New Yorkers swear by **John's Pizzeria** (⊠ 278 Bleecker St.), the original of what are now four branches citywide. Be forewarned, however: no slices; whole pies only.

Head east on Bleecker. At the corner of Bleeker and Carmine you'll see the **Church of Our Lady of Pompeii,** where Mother Cabrini, a naturalized Italian immigrant who became the first American saint, often prayed. When you reach **Father Demo Square** (at Bleecker Street and 6th Avenue), head up 6th Avenue to 3rd Street and check out the playground caged there within a chain-link fence. NBA stars of tomorrow learn their moves on this patch of asphalt, where city-style basketball is played all afternoon and evening in all but the very coldest weather. Return along West 4th Street to MacDougal Street and turn right. The **Provincetown Playhouse** (⊠ 133 MacDougal St.) premiered many of Eugene O'Neill's plays. Louisa May Alcott wrote *Little Women* while living at 130–132 MacDougal Street. The two houses at 127 and 129 MacDougal Street were built for Aaron Burr in 1829; notice the pineapple newel posts, a symbol of hospitality.

At **Minetta Tavern** (⊠ 113 MacDougal St.), a venerable Village watering hole, turn right onto Minetta Lane, which leads to narrow Minetta Street, another former speakeasy alley. Both streets follow the course of Minetta Brook, which once flowed through this neighborhood and still bubbles deep beneath the pavement. The foot of Minetta Street returns you to the corner of 6th Avenue and Bleecker Street, where you will have reached the stomping grounds of 1960s-era folksingers (many performed at the now-defunct Folk City, one block north on West 3rd Street). This area still attracts a young crowd—partly because of the proximity of NYU—to its cafés, bars, jazz clubs, coffeehouses, theaters, and cabarets, not to mention its long row of unpretentious ethnic restaurants.

TIMING
Greenwich Village lends itself to a leisurely pace, so allow yourself most of a day to explore its backstreets and stop at shops and cafés.

Sights to See

★ ❽ **Balducci's.** From the vegetable stand of the late Louis Balducci Sr. sprouted this full-service gourmet food store. Along with more than 80 Italian cheeses and 50 kinds of bread, the family-owned enterprise features imported Italian specialties and first-rate take-out foods. ⊠ *424 6th Ave., at 9th St.,* ☎ *212/673–2600.*

㉒ **Cherry Lane Theatre.** One of the original off-Broadway houses, this 1817 building was converted into a theater in 1923, thanks to Edna St. Vincent Millay and a group of theater artists. Over the years it hosted American premieres of works by O'Neill, Beckett, Ionesco, Albee, Pinter, and Mamet. The playhouse was modernized in 1996, but it still contains the original audience seats. At nearby 48 Commerce Street stands a handsome, renovated Greek Revival building originally constructed in 1844 for merchant prince Alexander T. Stewart. ⊠ *38 Commerce St.,* ☎ *212/989–2020.*

⑭ **Christopher Park.** Sometimes mistaken for ☞ **Sheridan Square,** this pleasant triangular oasis contains a bronze statue of Civil War general Philip Sheridan and striking sculptures designed by George Segal of a lesbian couple sitting on a bench and gay male partners standing near them; both couples appear to be having a conversation. ⊠ *Bordered by Washington Pl. and Grove and Christopher Sts.*

⑲ **Chumley's.** A speakeasy during the Prohibition era, this still-secret tavern behind an unmarked door on Bedford Street retains its original ambience with oak booths, a fireplace once used by a blacksmith, and subdued lighting. For years Chumley's attracted a literary clientele (John Steinbeck, Ernest Hemingway, Edna Ferber, Simone de Beauvoir, and Jack Kerouac), and the book covers of their publications were proudly displayed (and still appear) on the walls. There's another "secret" entrance in Pamela Court, accessed at 58 Barrow Street around the corner. ⊠ *86 Bedford St., near Barrow St.,* ☎ *212/675–4449.*

⑥ **Church of the Ascension.** A mural depicting the Ascension of Jesus and stained-glass windows by John LaFarge, as well as a marble altar sculpture by Augustus Saint-Gaudens, are the highlights of this 1841 Gothic Revival–style brownstone church designed by Richard Upjohn. In 1844 President John Tyler married Julia Gardiner here. ⊠ *36–38 5th Ave., at W. 10th St.,* ☎ *212/254–8620.*

⑬ **51–53 Christopher Street.** On June 27, 1969, a gay bar at this address named the Stonewall Inn was the site of a clash between gay men and women (some in drag) and the New York City police. As the bar's patrons were being forced into police wagons, sympathetic gay onlookers protested and started fighting back, throwing beer bottles and garbage cans. Every June the Stonewall Riots are commemorated around the world with parades and celebrations that honor the gay rights movement. A clothing store now occupies 51; a bar named Stonewall is next door at No. 53.

★ ☕ ⑦ **Forbes Magazine Galleries.** The late publisher Malcolm Forbes's idiosyncratic personal collection fills the ground floor of the limestone Forbes Magazine Building, once the home of Macmillan Publishing. Exhibits change in the large painting gallery and one of two autograph galleries, while permanent highlights include U.S. presidential papers, more than 500 intricate toy boats, 12,000 toy soldiers, and some of the oldest Monopoly game sets ever made. Perhaps the most memorable permanent display contains exquisite items created by the House of Fabergé, including 12 jeweled eggs designed for the last of the Russian czars. ⊠ *62 5th Ave., at 12th St.,* ☎ *212/206–5548.* ☐ *Free.* ☉ *Tues.–Wed. and Fri.–Sat. 10–4.*

NEED A BREAK?	If you're yearning for a *pain au chocolat* or a madeleine, stop by **Marquet Patisserie** (⊠ 15 E. 12th St., ☎ 212/229–9313), a sleek, friendly café that serves irresistible French pastries, great coffee, and satisfying sandwiches, salads, and quiches.

OFF THE BEATEN PATH	**GANSEVOORT MARKET –** Each morning, otherwise undistinguished warehouse buildings become the meat market for the city's retailers and restaurants. Racks of carcasses make a fascinating, if not very pretty, sight. Action peaks on weekdays between 5 AM and 9 AM. ⊠ *Between 9th Ave. and the Hudson River, from Gansevoort St. north to 14th St.*

⑪ **Gay Street.** A curved lane lined with small row houses from circa 1810, one-block-long Gay Street was originally a black neighborhood and later a strip of speakeasies. In the 1930s the short thoroughfare and nearby Christopher Street became famous nationwide when Ruth McKinney published her somewhat zany autobiographical stories in the *New Yorker,* based on what happened when she and her sister moved to Greenwich Village from Ohio (they appeared in book form as *My Sister Eileen* in 1938). McKinney wrote in the basement of No. 14. Also on Gay Street, Howdy Doody was designed in the basement of No. 12. ⊠ *Between Christopher St. and Waverly Pl.*

❸ Grey Art Gallery. On the east side of Washington Square, New York University's main building contains a welcoming street-level space with changing exhibitions usually devoted to contemporary art. ⊠ *100 Washington Sq. E,* ☎ *212/998–6780.* ▱ *$2.50 (suggested donation).* ☼ *Tues. and Thurs.–Fri. 11–6, Wed. 11–8, Sat. 11–5.*

⓲ Grove Court. Built between 1853 and 1854, this enclave of brick-front town houses was intended originally as apartments for employees at neighborhood hotels. Grove Court used to be called Mixed Ale Alley because of the residents' propensity to pool beverages brought from work. It now houses a more affluent crowd. ⊠ *10–12 Grove St.*

⓴ Isaacs-Hendricks House. Originally built as a Federal-style wood-frame residence in 1799, this immaculate structure is the oldest remaining house in Greenwich Village. Its first owner, Joshua Issacs, a wholesale merchant, lost the farmhouse to creditors; the building then belonged to copper supplier Harmon Hendricks. The village landmark was re-modeled twice; it received its brick face in 1836, and the third floor was added in 1928. ⊠ *77 Bedford St., at Commerce St.*

❾ Jefferson Market Library. Critics variously termed this magnificent towered courthouse's hodgepodge of styles Venetian, Victorian, or Italian; Villagers, noting the alternating wide bands of red brick and narrow strips of granite, dubbed it the "lean bacon style." Over the years the structure has housed a number of government agencies (public works, civil defense, census bureau, police academy); it was on the verge of demolition when local activists saved it and turned it into a public library in 1967. Note the fountain at the corner of West 10th Street and 6th Avenue, and the seal of the City of New York on the east front; inside are handsome interior doorways and a graceful circular stairway. If the gate is open, visit the flower garden behind the library, a project run by local green thumbs. ⊠ *425 6th Ave., at 10th St.,* ☎ *212/243–4334.*

❹ Judson Memorial Church. Designed by celebrated architect Stanford White, this Italian Roman-Renaissance church has long attracted a congregation interested in the arts and community activism. Funded by the Astor family and John D. Rockefeller and constructed in 1892, the yellow-brick and limestone building was the brainchild of Edward Judson, who hoped to reach out to the poor immigrants in adjacent Little Italy. The church has stained-glass windows designed by John LaFarge and a 10-story campanile. ⊠ *55 Washington Sq. S, at Thompson St.,* ☎ *212/477–0351.* ☼ *To gain access to sanctuary weekdays 10–6, inquire at parish office, 243 Thompson St.; also open for Sun. service at 11.*

⓬ Northern Dispensary. Constructed in 1831, this triangular Georgian brick building originally served as a clinic for indigent Villagers. Edgar Allan Poe was a frequent patient. In more recent times the structure has housed a dental clinic and a nursing home for AIDS patients. Note that the Dispensary has *one* side on *two* streets (Grove and Christopher streets where they meet) and *two* sides facing *one* street—Waverly Place, which splits in two directions. ⊠ *165 Waverly Pl.*

⑩ Patchin Place. This little cul-de-sac off 10th Street between Greenwich and 6th avenues has 10 diminutive 1848 row houses. Around the corner on 6th Avenue is a similar dead-end street, **Milligan Place,** consisting of four small homes completed in 1852. The houses in both quiet enclaves were originally built for the waiters (mostly Basques) who worked at 5th Avenue's high-society Brevoort Hotel, long since demolished. Patchin Place later attracted numerous writers, including Theodore Dreiser, e.e. cummings, Jane Bowles, and Djuna Barnes. John Reed and Louise Bryant also lived there. Milligan Place eventually became the address for several playwrights, including Eugene O'Neill.

★ **❷ The Row.** Built from 1829 through 1839, this series of beautifully preserved Greek Revival town houses along Washington Square North, on the two blocks between University Place and MacDougal Street, once belonged to merchants and bankers; now the buildings serve as NYU offices and faculty housing. Developers were not so tactful when they demolished 18 Washington Square North, once the home of Henry James's grandmother, which he later used as the setting for his novel *Washington Square* (Henry himself was born just off the square, in a long-gone house on Washington Place). The oldest building on the block, 20 Washington Square North, was constructed in 1829 in the Federal style, and with Flemish bond brickwork—alternate bricks inserted with the smaller surface (headers) facing out—which before 1830 was considered the best way to build stable walls. ✉ *1–13 Washington Sq. N, between University Pl. and 5th Ave.; 19–26 Washington Sq. N, between 5th Ave. and MacDougal St.*

★ **㉔ St. Luke's-in-the-Fields.** The first warden of St. Luke's, which was constructed in 1822 as a country chapel for downtown's Trinity Church, was Clement (" 'Twas the Night Before Christmas") Clarke Moore, who figured so largely in Chelsea's history (☞ Chelsea, *above*). An unadorned structure of soft-colored brick, the chapel was nearly destroyed by fire in 1981, but a flood of donations, many quite small, from residents of the West Village financed restoration of the square central tower. Bret Harte once lived at 487 Hudson Street (today the St. Luke's parish house), at the end of the row. The Barrow Street Garden on the chapel grounds is worth visiting. ✉ *485 Hudson St., between Barrow and Christopher Sts.,* ☎ *212/924–0562.* ☉ *Grounds open daily 9–dusk.*

★ **㉖ St. Luke's Place.** This often peaceful street has 15 classic Italianate brownstone and brick town houses (1852–53), shaded by graceful gingko trees. Novelist Theodore Dreiser wrote *An American Tragedy* at No. 16, and poet Marianne Moore resided at No. 14. Mayor Jimmy Walker (first elected in 1926) lived at No. 6; the lampposts in front are "mayor's lamps," which were sometimes placed in front of the residences of New York mayors. This block is often used as a film location, too: No. 12 was shown as the Huxtables' home on *The Cosby Show* (although the family lived in Brooklyn), and No. 4 was the setting of the Audrey Hepburn movie *Wait Until Dark.* Before 1890 the playground on the south side of the street was a graveyard where, according to legend, the dauphin of France—the lost son of Louis XVI and Marie Antoinette—is buried. ✉ *Between Hudson St. and 7th Ave. S.*

NEED A BREAK?

The **Anglers and Writers Café** (✉ 420 Hudson St., at St. Luke's Pl., ☎ 212/675–0810) lives up to its name with bookshelves, fishing tackle, and pictures of Door County, Wisconsin, hung on the walls. It's an ideal spot to linger over a pot of tea and a slice of cake.

⑯ 17 Grove Street. William Hyde, a prosperous window-sash maker, built this clapboard residence in 1822; a third floor was added in 1870. Hyde added a workshop behind the house in 1833. The building has since served many functions; it housed a brothel during the Civil War. The structure is the Village's largest remaining wood-frame house. ⊠ *17 Grove St., at Bedford St.*

㉑ 75½ Bedford Street. Rising real estate rates inspired the construction of New York City's narrowest house—just 9½ ft wide—in 1873. Built on a lot that was originally a carriage entrance of the ☞ **Isaacs-Hendricks House** next door, this sliver of a building has been home to actor John Barrymore and poet Edna St. Vincent Millay, who wrote the Pulitzer Prize–winning *Ballad of the Harp-Weaver* during her tenure here from 1923 to 1924. ⊠ *75½ Bedford St., between Commerce and Morton Sts.*

⑮ Sheridan Square. At one time an unused asphalt space, this green triangle was landscaped following an extensive dig by urban archaeologists, who unearthed artifacts dating to the Dutch and Native American eras. ⊠ *Bordered by Washington Pl. and W. 4th, Barrow, and Grove Sts.*

⑰ Twin Peaks. In 1925 financier Otto Kahn gave money to a Village eccentric named Clifford Daily to remodel an 1835 house for artists' use. The building was whimsically altered with stucco, half-timbers, and the addition of a pair of steep roof peaks. The result was something that might be described as an ersatz Swiss chalet. ⊠ *102 Bedford St., between Grove and Christopher Sts.*

㉓ Twin Sisters. These attractive Federal-style brick homes connected by a walled garden were said to have been erected by a sea captain for two daughters who loathed each other. Historical record insists that they were built in 1831 and 1832 by a milkman who needed the two houses and an open courtyard for his work. The striking mansard roofs were added in 1873. ⊠ *39 and 41 Commerce St.*

❺ Washington Mews. This cobblestone private street is lined on one side with the former stables of the houses on The Row on Washington Square North. Writer Walter Lippmann and artist-patron Gertrude Vanderbilt Whitney (founder of the Whitney Museum) once had homes in the mews; today it's mostly owned by NYU. ⊠ *Between 5th Ave. and University Pl.*

★ ☕ ❶ **Washington Square.** The physical and spiritual heart of the Village, 9½-acre Washington Square started out as a cemetery, principally for yellow fever victims—an estimated 10,000–22,000 bodies lie below. In the early 1800s it was a parade ground and the site of public executions; bodies dangled from a conspicuous Hanging Elm that still stands at the northwest corner of the square. Made a public park in 1827, the square became the focus of a fashionable residential neighborhood and a center of outdoor activity. Today it's a maelstrom of playful activity, shared by earnest-looking NYU students, Frisbee players, street musicians, skateboarders, jugglers, stand-up comics, joggers, chess players, and bench warmers, watching the grand opera of it all. A huge outdoor art fair is held here each spring and fall.

Dominating the square's north end, the triumphal **Washington Arch** stands at the foot of glorious 5th Avenue. Designed by Stanford White, a wooden version of Washington Arch was built in 1889 to commemorate the 100th anniversary of George Washington's presidential inauguration and was originally placed about half a block north of its present location. The arch was reproduced in Tuckahoe marble in

1892, and the statues—*Washington at War* on the left, *Washington at Peace* on the right—were added in 1916 and 1918, respectively. The civilian version of Washington was the work of Alexander Stirling Calder, father of the renowned artist Alexander Calder. Bodybuilder Charles Atlas modeled for *Peace*. ⊠ *5th Ave. between Waverly Pl. and W. 4th St.*

㉕ **White Horse Tavern.** Built in 1880, this amiable bar occupies one of the city's few remaining wood-frame structures. Formerly a speakeasy and a seamen's tavern, the White Horse has been popular with artists and writers for decades; its best-known customer was Welsh poet Dylan Thomas, who had a room named for him here after his death in 1953. ⊠ *567 Hudson St., at 11th St.,* ☎ *212/243–9260.*

THE EAST VILLAGE AND THE LOWER EAST SIDE

Numbers in the text correspond to numbers in the margin and on the Greenwich Village, the East Village, and the Lower East side map.

A Good Walk

Begin at the intersection of East 8th Street, 4th Avenue, and Astor Place, where you'll see two traffic islands. One of these contains an ornate cast-iron kiosk, a replica of a Beaux Arts subway entrance, which provides access to the **Astor Place Subway Station** ㉗. Go down into the station to see the authentically reproduced wall tiles with a beaver motif. On the other traffic island stands the **Alamo** ㉘, a huge black cube sculpted by Bernard Rosenthal.

Go straight east from the Alamo to **St. Marks Place** ㉙, the name given to 8th Street in the East Village. This often crowded thoroughfare has long attracted an assortment of street kids, gawkers, and washed-out counterculture types.

Second Avenue, which St. Marks crosses after one block, was called the Yiddish Rialto in the early part of this century. At this time eight theaters between Houston and 14th streets presented Yiddish-language productions of musicals, revues, and heart-wrenching melodramas. Two survivors from that period are the **Orpheum** (⊠ 126 2nd Ave., at 8th St.) and the neo-Moorish Yiddish Arts Theatre, now the multiscreen **Village East Cinemas** (⊠ 189 2nd Ave., at 12th St.), which has preserved the original ornate ceiling. In front of the **Second Avenue Deli** (⊠ 2nd Ave. and 10th St.), Hollywood-style squares have been embedded in the sidewalk to commemorate Yiddish stage luminaries.

Second Avenue is also home to a neighborhood landmark, **St. Mark's-in-the-Bowery Church** ㉚, a stately Episcopal church on the corner of 10th Street that serves as a community cultural center and public meeting hall. From in front of the church, you can take a quiet detour to investigate the facades of handsome redbrick row houses on **Stuyvesant Street,** ㉛ which stretches southwest to 9th Street. If you continue north up 2nd Avenue from St. Mark's-in-the-Bowery, you'll reach the **Ukrainian Museum** ㉜, a modest upstairs gallery celebrating the cultural heritage of Ukraine.

Next, walk south on 2nd Avenue to 9th Street. At 135 2nd Avenue, between 9th Street and St. Marks Place, is the **Ottendorfer Branch of the New York Public Library** ㉝. A leisurely stroll east on 9th Street from 2nd Avenue to Avenue A will take you past a number of cafés and small, friendly shops selling designer and vintage clothing, housewares, toys, herbs, leather goods, recordings, and much more.

At the northeast corner of 1st Avenue and 9th Street stands **P.S. 122** (✉ 150 1st Ave.), a former public school building transformed into a complex of spaces for avant-garde entertainment (☞ Chapter 4). If you continue east on 9th Street or St. Marks Place, you're heading toward **Alphabet City,** the area's nickname; here the avenues are named A, B, C, and D. St. Marks Place between 1st Avenue and Avenue A is lined with inexpensive cafés catering to a late-night younger crowd. Across from St. Marks Place on Avenue A is **Tompkins Square Park** ㉞, a fairly peaceful haven.

If you walk south on Avenue A past Houston Street, you'll run into Manhattan's most recently gentrified neighborhood, the **Lower East Side.** While young hipsters move into apartments on streets like Rivington and Clinton, cutting-edge boutiques such as **Nova** (✉ 100 Stanton St., at Ludlow St.) and **TG 170** (✉ 170 Ludlow St., at Stanton St.) compete with the new generation of shops on Orchard Street, a longtime shopping strip (☞ Chapter 9). There's no shortage of places for trendy locals to eat and be entertained, as restaurants like **Baby Jupiter** (✉ 170 Orchard St., at Stanton St.) and clubs like **Mercury Lounge** (✉ 217 E. Houston St., at Essex St.) prove. But if you look up at the old brick walls of the tenement buildings, here and there you'll see reminders of the old days—the fading signs for defunct Jewish businesses, as well as for a few holdouts that still operate. Historic establishments such as **Katz's Delicatessen** (✉ 205 E. Houston, at Ludlow St.) and **Ratner's Restaurant** (✉ 138 Delancey St., between Norfolk and Suffolk Sts.) anchor the area firmly in its immigrant past; on Orchard Street, the **Lower East Side Tenement Museum** ㉟ brings that era to life.

Head back up into the East Village, to the corner of 1st Avenue and 6th Street. The entire south side of 6th Street between 1st and 2nd Avenues belongs to a dozen or more Indian restaurants serving inexpensive subcontinental fare (New Yorkers joke that they all share a single kitchen). On the other side of 2nd Avenue is the future home of the Ukrainian Museum. Turn right on Taras Shevchenko Place (named for the Ukrainain Shakespeare) to 7th Street and **McSorley's Old Ale House** ㊱, one of New York's oldest bars. Just past McSorley's is **Surma, the Ukrainian Shop** ㊲, selling all sorts of Ukrainian-made goods. Across the street is the copper-domed **St. George's Ukrainian Catholic Church** ㊳, whose interior is lit by impressive stained-glass windows.

Across 3rd Avenue, the massive brownstone **Cooper Union Foundation Building** ㊴ houses a tuition-free school for artists, architects, and engineers and overlooks Cooper Square, a large open space. To the south are the offices of the *Village Voice* newspaper (✉ 36 Cooper Sq.). If you're here from Sunday through Thursday, walk south on Cooper Square and turn right on 4th Street to visit the **Merchant's House Museum** ㊵, where 19th-century family life can be viewed thanks to the preservation of the original furnishings and architecture.

One block west of Cooper Square is Lafayette Street. The long block between East 4th Street and Astor Place contains on its east side a grand Italian Renaissance–style structure housing the New York Shakespeare Festival's **Joseph Papp Public Theater** ㊶; in the 19th century the city's first free library opened here. Across the street note the imposing marble Corinthian columns fronting **Colonnade Row** ㊷, a stretch of four crumbling 19th-century Greek Revival houses. Walking north on Lafayette Street brings you back to Astor Place; heading west brings you to Broadway. To the left (south) is a busy downtown shopping strip, with several clothing shops and chain stores. Above street level the old warehouses here have mostly been converted into residential lofts. North on Broadway from Astor Place lies **Grace Church** ㊸, on the corner of Broadway and 10th Street, which has a striking marble spire. If you continue north on the same side of the street as the church, you'll pass a few of the many antiques stores in the area. You can end your walk at the popular **Strand Book Store** ㊹, the largest secondhand bookstore in the city and an absolutely necessary stop for anyone who loves to read.

TIMING

Allow about three hours for the walk. If you plan to stop at museums, add one hour, and at least another hour to browse in shops along the way. If you end your walk at the Strand Book Store, you may want to stop somewhere for coffee before perusing the bookshelves, which can easily eat up another hour or more of your time.

Sights to See

🐾 ㉘ **Alamo.** Created by Bernard Rosenthal in 1967, this massive black cube made of steel was originally part of a temporary citywide exhibit, but it became a permanent installation thanks to a private donor. Balanced on a post, the "Cube," as it is locally known, was one of the first abstract sculptures in New York City to be placed in a public space. ✉ *On traffic island at Astor Pl. and Lafayette St.*

OFF THE
BEATEN PATH
Alphabet City. Beyond 1st Avenue, the north–south avenues all labeled with letters, not numbers, give this area its commonly used nickname. Until fairly recently, Alphabet City was a burned-out territory of slums and drug haunts, but some blocks and buildings were gentrified during the height of the East Village art scene in the mid-80s. The reasonably priced restaurants with their bohemian atmosphere on avenues A and B, and the cross streets between them, attract a mix of locals, adventurous visitors from other parts of the city, and tourists. A close-knit Puerto Rican community lies east of Avenue A, but amid the Latin shops and groceries Avenue B has become a sort of far-out restaurant row. In Alphabet City you'll find everything from grungy bars, such as **Lakeside Lounge** (✉ 162–4 Ave. B, between 10th and 11th Sts.), to trendy, cheap cafés, such as **Radio Perfecto** (✉ 190 Ave. B, near 12th St.), to excellent bistros like **Le Tableau** (✉ 511 E. 5th St., between Aves. A and B). ✉ *Alphabet City extends approximately from Ave. A to the East River, between 14th and Houston Sts.*

NEED A
BREAK?
Old Devil Moon (✉ 511 E. 12th St., between Aves. A and B, ☎ 212/ 475–4357) is a delightfully snug, dimly lighted hangout with whimsical decor where you can stop for a drink, snack, or something more substantial.

㉗ **Astor Place Subway Station.** At the beginning of this century, almost every Independent Rapid Transit (IRT) subway entrance resembled the ornate cast-iron replica of a Beaux Arts kiosk that covers the stairway leading to the uptown No. 6 train. In the station itself, authentically reproduced ceramic tiles of beavers, a reference to the fur trade that contributed to John Jacob Astor's fortune, line the walls. Milton Glaser, a Cooper Union graduate, designed the station's attractive abstract murals. ✉ *On traffic island at 8th St. and 4th Ave.*

㊷ **Colonnade Row.** Marble Corinthian columns front this grand sweep of four Greek Revival mansions (originally nine) constructed in 1833, with stonework by Sing Sing penitentiary prisoners. In their time these once-elegant homes served as residences to millionaires John Jacob Astor and Cornelius Vanderbilt until they moved uptown. Writers Washington Irving, William Makepeace Thackeray, and Charles Dickens all stayed here at one time or another; more recently, writer Edmund White lived here. Today three houses are occupied on street level by restaurants, while the northernmost building houses the Astor Place Theatre. ⊠ *428–434 Lafayette St., between Astor Pl. and E. 4th St.*

39 **Cooper Union Foundation Building.** This impressive eight-story brown-stone structure dominates Cooper Square, a large open space situated where 3rd and 4th avenues merge into the Bowery. A statue of industrialist Peter Cooper, by Augustus Saint-Gaudens, presides over the square. Cooper founded this college in 1859 to provide a forum for public opinion and free technical education for the working class; it still offers tuition-free education in architecture, art, and engineering. Cooper Union was the first structure to be supported by steel railroad rails—rolled in Cooper's own plant. Two galleries in the building are open to the public, presenting changing exhibitions during the academic year. ⊠ *E. 7th St. to Astor Pl., 4th Ave. to the Bowery at Cooper Sq.,* ☎ *212/353–4200.* 🎫 *Free.* ⊙ *Weekdays noon–7, Sat. noon–5.*

★ **43** **Grace Church.** Topped by a finely ornamented octagonal marble spire, this Episcopal church, designed by James Renwick Jr., has excellent Pre-Raphaelite stained-glass windows. The building—a fine mid-19th-century example of an English Gothic Revival church—fronts a small green yard facing Broadway. The church has been the site of many society weddings (including that of P. T. Barnum show member Tom Thumb). ⊠ *802 Broadway, at E. 10th St.,* ☎ *212/254–2000.* ⊙ *Weekdays 10–6, Sat. noon–4, Sun. 8:30–1.*

41 **Joseph Papp Public Theater.** In 1854 John Jacob Astor opened the city's first free library in this expansive redbrick and brownstone Italian Renaissance–style building, which was renovated in 1967 as the Public Theater to serve as the permanent home of the New York Shakespeare Festival. The theater opened its doors with the popular rock musical *Hair.* Under the leadership of the late Joseph Papp, the Public's five playhouses built a fine reputation for bold and innovative performances; the long-running hit *A Chorus Line* had its first performances here, as have many less commercial plays. Today, director and producer George C. Wolfe heads the Public, which continues to present controversial modern works and imaginative Shakespeare productions. The Public produces the three annual summer productions in Central Park's Delacorte Theater (☞ Central Park, *above,* and Chapter 4). ⊠ *425 Lafayette St., between E. 4th St. and Astor Pl.,* ☎ *212/260–2400.*

🕑 **35** **Lower East Side Tenement Museum.** America's first urban living-history museum preserves and interprets the life of immigrants and migrants in New York's Lower East Side. A guided tour (reservations suggested) takes you to a partially restored 1863 tenement building at 97 Orchard Street, where you can view the apartments of Natalie Gumpertz, a German-Jewish dressmaker (dating from 1878); Adolph and Rosaria Baldizzi, Catholic immigrants from Sicily (1935); the Rogarshevsky family from Eastern Europe (1918); and the Confino family, Sephardic Jews from Kastoria, Turkey, which is now part of Greece (1916). The Confino family apartment has been reconstructed from a child's point of view, and children and adults can actually touch items in the exhibit. The museum also leads historic walking tours around Orchard Street. If you wish to forego the tours, you can watch a free slide show tracing the history of the tenement building and the neighborhood as well as a video with interviews of Lower East Side residents past and present. The gallery (free) has changing exhibits relating to Lower East Side history, in addition to a list of the former residents. ⊠ *90 Orchard St.,* ☎ *212/431–0233.* 🎫 *Tenement tour $8, tenement and Orchard St. walking tours $12.* ⊙ *Museum: Tues.–Fri. noon–5, weekends 11–5; tenement tours: Tues.–Fri. 1, 2, 3, and 4, weekends* *every 30 mins 11–4:30; walking tours: weekends 1:30 and 2:30. Tours are limited to 15 people.*

㊱ McSorley's Old Ale House. One of several pubs that claim to be New York's oldest, this often-crowded saloon attracts many collegiate types enticed by McSorley's own brands of ale. The mahogany bar, gas lamps, and potbelly stove all hark back to decades past. McSorley's asserts that it opened in 1854; it didn't admit women until 1970. Joseph Mitchell immortalized the spot in *The New Yorker.* ✉ 15 E. 7th St., between 2nd and 3rd Aves., ☎ 212/473–9148.

㊵ Merchant's House Museum. Built in 1831–32, this redbrick house, combining Federal and Greek Revival styles, offers a rare glimpse of family life in the mid-19th century. Retired merchant Seabury Tredwell and his descendants lived here from 1835 right up until it became a museum in 1933. The original furnishings and architectural features remain intact; family memorabilia are also on display. The Greek Revival–style parlors have 13-ft ceilings with intricate plasterwork, free-standing Ionic columns, a mahogany pocket-door screen, and black-marble fireplaces. Self-guided tour brochures are always available, and guided tours are given on Sunday. ✉ 29 E. 4th St., between Bowery and 2nd Ave., ☎ 212/777–1089. ☞ $5. ☾ Sun.–Thurs. 1–4.

㉝ Ottendorfer Branch of the New York Public Library. The first Manhattan building to be constructed as a free public library, this 1884 structure designed by William Schickel incorporates elements from several late Victorian styles; the early interior use of molded terra-cotta remains untouched. The rust-color building dates from a time when the East Village was heavily populated by German immigrants and was a gift from Oswald Ottendorfer, a rich German philanthropist and newspaper editor. It began as the German-language branch of the Free Circulating Library (hence the words FREIE BIBLIOTHEK UND LESEHALLE on its facade) and eventually became part of the city's public library system. ✉ 135 2nd Ave., near St. Marks Pl., ☎ 212/674–0947.

㊳ St. George's Ukrainian Catholic Church. Notable for its copper dome and the three brightly colored religious murals on its facade, this ostentatious modern church serves as a central meeting place for the old local Ukrainian population. Built in 1977, it took the place of the more modest Greek Revival–style St. George's Ruthenian Church. An annual Ukrainian folk festival is held here in the spring. ✉ 30 E. 7th St., between 2nd and 3rd Aves., ☎ 212/674–1615.

㉚ St. Mark's-in-the-Bowery Church. A Greek Revival steeple and a cast-iron front porch were added to this 1799 fieldstone country church, which occupies the former site of the family chapel of the old Dutch governor Peter Stuyvesant. St. Mark's is the city's oldest continually used Christian church site (Stuyvesant and Commodore Perry are buried here). Its interior had to be completely restored after a disastrous fire in 1978, and stained-glass windows were added to the balcony in 1982. Over the years St. Mark's has hosted much countercultural activity. In the 1920s a forward-thinking pastor injected the Episcopal ritual with Native American chants, Greek folk dancing, and Eastern mantras. William Carlos Williams, Amy Lowell, and Carl Sandburg once read here, and Isadora Duncan, Harry Houdini, and Merce Cunningham also performed here. During the hippie era St. Mark's welcomed avant-garde poets and playwrights, including Sam Shepard. Today dancers, poets, and performance artists cavort in the main sanctuary, where pews have been removed to accommodate them. ✉ 131 E. 10th St., at 2nd Ave., ☎ 212/674–6377.

NEED A
BREAK?

Bright and bustling **Veselka** (⊠ 144 2nd Ave., at 9th St., ☎ 212/228–9682), a longtime East Village favorite, serves bagels, muffins, Italian coffee, egg creams, and Ben & Jerry's ice cream alongside good, traditional Ukrainian fare such as borscht, kielbasa, and veal goulash.

㉙ St. Marks Place. St. Marks Place, as 8th Street is called between 3rd Avenue and Avenue A, is the longtime hub of the hip East Village. During the 1950s beatniks such as Allen Ginsberg and Jack Kerouac lived and wrote in the area; the 1960s brought Bill Graham's Fillmore East concerts, the Electric Circus, and hallucinogenic drugs. The black-clad, pink-haired, or shaved-head punks followed, and some remain today. St. Marks Place between 2nd and 3rd avenues is lined with ethnic restaurants, jewelry stalls, leather shops, and stores selling books, posters, and eccentric clothing. The street vendors who line the sidewalk daily add to the bazaarlike atmosphere, although a Gap store dilutes the effect.

At 80 St. Marks Place, near 1st Avenue, is the Pearl Theatre Company (☞ see Beyond Broadway *in* Chapter 4), which performs classic plays from around the world. The handprints, footprints, and autographs of such past screen luminaries as Joan Crawford, Ruby Keeler, Joan Blondell, and Myrna Loy are embedded in the sidewalk. At 96–98 St. Marks Place (between 1st Avenue and Avenue A) stands the building that was photographed for the cover of Led Zeppelin's *Physical Graffiti* album. The cafés between 1st Avenue and Avenue A attract customers late into the night.

★ ㊹ **Strand Book Store.** Serious book lovers from around the world make pilgrimages to this secondhand book emporium with a stock of some 2 million volumes, including thousands of collector's items (the store's slogan is "Eight Miles of Books"). Opened in 1929 by Ben Bass, the Strand was originally on 4th Avenue's Book Row until it moved to its present location on Broadway in 1956. Review copies of new books sell for 50% off, and used books are often priced at much less. A separate rare-book room is on the third floor at 826 Broadway, to the immediate north of the main store. ⊠ *828 Broadway, at 12th St., ☎ 212/473–1452. ☉ Main store: Mon.–Sat. 9:30–10:30, Sun. 11–10:30; rare books: Mon.–Sat 9:30–6:30, Sun. 11–6:30.*

★ ㉛ **Stuyvesant Street.** This block-long thoroughfare, the hypotenuse of two triangles bounded by 2nd and 3rd avenues and East 9th and 10th streets, is unique in Manhattan: it is the oldest street laid out precisely along an east–west axis. (This grid never caught on, and instead a street grid following the island's geographic orientation was adopted.) The area was once Governor Peter Stuyvesant's *bouwerie,* or farm; among the handsome redbrick row houses are the Federal-style **Stuyvesant-Fish House** (⊠ 21 Stuyvesant St.), which was built in 1804 as a wedding gift for a great-great-granddaughter of the governor, and **Renwick Triangle**, an attractive group of carefully restored one- and two-story brick and brownstone residences originally constructed in 1861. In 1998, The George Hecht Viewing Gardens were built at 3rd Avenue and 9th Street, with one side of the gardens bordering Stuyvesant Street.

㊲ **Surma, the Ukrainian Shop.** The exotic stock at this charming little store includes Ukrainian books, magazines, cassettes, and greeting cards, as well as musical instruments, painted eggs, and an exhaustive collection of peasant blouses. ⊠ *11 E. 7th St., between 2nd and 3rd Aves., ☎ 212/477–0729.*

㊱ ㉞ **Tompkins Square Park.** This leafy oasis amid the East Village's crowded tenements is the physical, spiritual, and political heart of the radical

East Village. The square takes its name from four-time governor Daniel Tompkins, an avid abolitionist and vice president under James Monroe, who once owned this land from 2nd Avenue to the East River. Its history is long and violent: the 1874 Tompkins Square Riot involved some 7,000 unhappy laborers and 1,600 police. In 1988 riots again broke out, as police followed then-mayor David Dinkins's orders to clear the park of the many homeless who had set up makeshift homes here, and homeless rights and antigentrification activists armed with sticks and bottles fought back. After a yearlong renovation, the park reopened in 1992 with a midnight curfew, still in effect today. The park fills up with locals on clement days year-round, partaking in minipicnics, drum circles, rollerblade basketball, and, for dog owners, a large dog run. East of the park at 151 Avenue B, near 9th Street, stands an 1849 four-story white-painted brownstone, where renowned jazz musician Charlie Parker lived from 1950 to 1954. ⊠ *Bordered by Aves. A and B and 7th and 10th Sts.*

NEED A BREAK? At the northwest corner of the park is **Life Cafe** (⊠ 343 E. 10th St., at Ave. B, ☎ 212/477–8791), a frequently busy local hangout featured in the hit Broadway musical *Rent*. Two of the city's best Italian pastry shops are nearby. **De Robertis Pasticceria** (⊠ 176 1st Ave., between 10th and 11th Sts., ☎ 212/674–7137) offers exceptional cheesecake and cappuccinos in its original 1904 setting, complete with glistening mosaic tiles. Opened in 1894, the popular **Veniero Pasticceria** (⊠ 342 E. 11th St., between 1st and 2nd Aves., ☎ 212/674–7264) has rows and rows of fresh cannoli, fruit tarts, cheesecakes, cookies, and other elaborate desserts on display in glass cases; there's a separate café section.

32 **Ukrainian Museum.** Ceramics, jewelry, hundreds of brilliantly colored Easter eggs, and an extensive collection of Ukrainian costumes and textiles are the highlights of this small collection, nurtured by Ukrainian Americans in exile throughout the years of Soviet domination. At press time, the museum was raising money for the construction of new quarters, at 222 East 6th Street. ⊠ *203 2nd Ave., between 12th and 13th Sts.,* ☎ *212/228–0110.* ⊠ *$3.* ☉ *Wed.–Sun. 1–5.*

SOHO AND TRIBECA

Today the names of these two downtown neighborhoods are virtually synonymous with a certain eclectic elegance—an amalgam of black-clad artists, young Wall Streeters, expansive loft apartments, hip art galleries, and packed-to-the-gills restaurants. It's all very urban, very cool, very now. Twenty-five years ago, though, these two areas were virtual wastelands. SoHo (so named because it is the district *So*uth of *Ho*uston Street, bounded by Broadway, Canal Street, and 6th Avenue) was regularly referred to as "Hell's Hundred Acres" because of the many fires that raged through the untended warehouses crowding the area. It was saved by two factors: first, preservationists here discovered the world's greatest concentration of cast-iron architecture and fought to prevent demolition; and second, artists discovered the large, cheap, well-lighted spaces that cast-iron buildings provide.

All the rage between 1860 and 1890, cast-iron buildings were popular because they did not require massive walls to bear the weight of the upper stories. Since there was no need for load-bearing walls, these buildings had more interior space and larger windows. They were also versatile, with various architectural elements produced from standardized molds to mimic any style—Italianate, Victorian Gothic, neo-

SoHo, TriBeCa, Little Italy, Chinatown

Leroy St.

Downing St.

Clarkson St.

1,9 M

**GREENWICH
VILLAGE**

W. Houston St.

Hudson St.

Varick St.

Ave. of the Americas (Sixth Ave.)

MacDougal St.

Sullivan St.

King St.

Charlton St.

C,E M

Washington St.

Vandam St.

Spring St.

Dominick St.

Broome St.

Holland Tunnel
Entrance

Canal St.

1,9 M

A,C,E M

Watts St.

Holland Tunnel
Exit

Varick St.

Desbrosses St.

Greenwich St.

Vestry St.

Laight St.

Ericsson Pl.

Hubert St.

TRIBECA

N. Moore St.

14 Franklin St.

Old New York
Mercantile Exchange 12

West St.

13 Jay St.

Staple St.

11

Harrison St.

15

1,2,3,9 M

Stuyvesant
High School ■

Chambers St.

West Side Hwy.

Warren St.

16

Murray St.

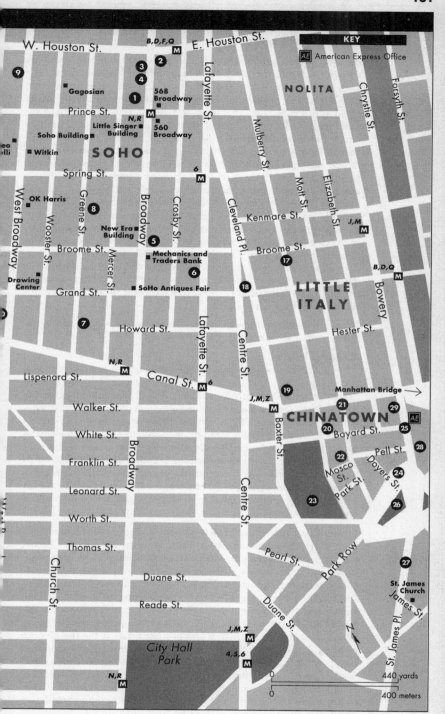

AE American Express Office

W. Houston St.

B,D,F,Q M E. Houston St.

9

3
2 M

4

Gagosian

1 568 Broadway

Prince St.

NOLITA

Chrystie St.

Forsyth St.

N,R M
Little Singer Building
560 Broadway

Soho Building

eo lli
Witkin

SOHO

Mulberry St.

Mott St.

Elizabeth St.

Spring St.

6 M

OK Harris

Greene St.

8

West Broadway

Wooster St.

New Era Building

5

Broadway

Crosby St.

Cleveland Pl.

Kenmare St.

J,M M

Mechanics and Traders Bank

Broome St.

Broome St.

Mercer St.

6

SoHo Antiques Fair

17

LITTLE ITALY

B,D,Q M

Bowery

Drawing Center

Grand St.

18

Hester St.

7

Howard St.

Lafayette St.

Centre St.

N,R M

Canal St. M 6

Lispenard St.

Walker St.

J,M,Z M

19

Manhattan Bridge →

21

29

AE

White St.

Broadway

Franklin St.

Baxter St.

CHINATOWN

20 Bayard St.

25

28

Leonard St.

22

Pell St.

Mosco St.

Doyers St.

24

Worth St.

Park St.

23

26

Thomas St.

Centre St.

Church St.

Duane St.

Reade St.

Pearl St.

Park Row

27

St. James Church

James St.

St. James Pl.

Duane St.

J,M,Z M

City Hall Park

4,5,6 M

N

0 ————— 440 yards

0 ————— 400 meters

N,R M

Grecian, to name but a few visible in SoHo. At first it was technically illegal for artists to live in their loft studios, but so many did that eventually the zoning laws were changed to permit residence.

By 1980 SoHo's galleries, trendy shops, and cafés, together with its marvelous cast-iron buildings and vintage Belgian-block pavements (the 19th-century successor to traditional cobblestones), had made SoHo such a desirable residential area that only the most successful artists could afford it. Seeking similar space, artists moved downtown to another half-abandoned industrial district, for which a new, SoHo-like name was invented: TriBeCa (the *Tri*angle *Be*low *Ca*nal Street, although in effect it goes no farther south than Murray Street and no farther east than West Broadway). The same scenario played itself out again, and TriBeCa's rising rents are already beyond the means of most artists, who have moved instead to west Chelsea, Long Island City, areas of Brooklyn, or New Jersey. But despite their gentrification, SoHo and TriBeCa retain some of their gritty bohemianism—one local store terms it "shabby chic"—that has come to dominate the downtown scene. In the case of SoHo, however, the arrival of large chain stores such as Pottery Barn and J. Crew has given some blocks the feeling of an outdoor suburban shopping mall. As if in response to the influx, independent designers and restaurateurs have pressed east from SoHo to open intriguing spots in the neighborhood that has come to be known as NoLita (for *No*rth of *Li*ttle *Ita*ly.)

Numbers in the text correspond to numbers in the margin and on the SoHo, TriBeCa, Little Italy, Chinatown map.

A Good Walk

Starting at Houston (pronounced *how*-ston) Street, walk south down Broadway, stopping at the many museums that crowd both sides of the street between Houston and Prince streets. The most noteworthy of these is the **Guggenheim Museum SoHo** ①, which opened in 1992—but also worthwhile are the **Alternative Museum** ②, whose political and sociopolitical themes make for lively discussion; the **Museum for African Art** ③, whose handsome two-story building complements its high-quality exhibits; and the **New Museum of Contemporary Art** ④, which is devoted exclusively to living artists. Several art galleries share these blocks as well, most notably at **568 Broadway,** which has 13 galleries and the trendy Armani Exchange store on the ground level. For more on SoHo's galleries, see Chapter 4.

Just south of Prince Street, **560 Broadway** on the east side of the block is another popular exhibit space, home to some 20 galleries. Across the street, Ernest Flagg's 1904 **Little Singer Building** (⊠ 561 Broadway) shows the final flower of the cast-iron style, with wrought-iron balconies, terra-cotta panels, and broad expanses of windows. One block south of the Little Singer Building, between Spring and Broome streets, a cluster of lofts that were originally part of the 1897 **New Era Building** (⊠ 495 Broadway) boast an Art Nouveau copper mansard. At the northeast corner of Broadway and Broome Street is the **Haughwout Building** ⑤, a restored classic of the cast-iron genre. At the southeast corner of Broadway and Broome Street, the former **Mechanics and Traders Bank** (⊠ 486 Broadway) is a Romanesque and Moorish Revival building with half-round brick arches. At the northwest corner of Broadway and Grand Street, the popular **SoHo Antiques Fair** draws about 100 dealers selling everything from used bicycles to vintage posters and prints on weekends from 9 to 5.

For a glimpse of the old SoHo, detour west from Broadway to Mercer Street or east to Crosby Street, where Belgian paving stones, multiple loading docks, and a patchwork of fire escapes recall the days when these streets were used as service thoroughfares. If you head east and you have youngsters in tow, continue one more block to the **Children's Museum of the Arts** ⑥, where the interactive exhibits provide a welcome respite from SoHo's mostly grown-up pursuits. Farther east, along Mulberry, Mott, and Elizabeth streets, is the district known as **NoLita,** the most recent manifestation of downtown's continued gentrification.

As an alternative, you can head west from Broadway on Grand Street, which leads to **Greene Street,** where cast-iron architecture is at its finest. The block between Canal and Grand streets (⊠ 8–34 Greene St.) represents the longest row of cast-iron buildings anywhere. Handsome as they are, these buildings were always commercial, containing stores and light manufacturing firms, principally in the textile trade. Along this street notice the iron loading docks and the sidewalk vault covers that lead into basement storage areas. Two standout buildings on Greene Street are the so-called **Queen of Greene Street** ⑦ and the **King of Greene Street** ⑧. Even the lampposts on Greene Street are architectural gems: note their turn-of-the-century bishop's-crook style, adorned with various cast-iron curlicues from their bases to their curved tops. Several of SoHo's better exhibition spaces run by younger and more innovative dealers and artists are clustered on the south end of Greene and Wooster streets near Grand Street.

Greene Street between Prince and Spring streets is notable for the **SoHo Building** (⊠ 104–110 Greene St.); towering 13 stories, it was the neighborhood's tallest building until the SoHo Grand Hotel went up in 1996. At Prince Street, walk one block west to Wooster Street, which, like a few other SoHo streets, still has its original Belgian paving stones. Going south on Wooster, shoppers will find a retail paradise in the blocks between Prince and Spring streets (☞ Chapter 9). Also in this vicinity is one of Manhattan's finest photography galleries, **Howard Greenberg** (⊠ 120 Wooster St.). Proceeding even farther south on Wooster, between Broome and Grand streets and Grand and Canal streets, you'll find more art worth checking out at the **Drawing Center** (⊠ 35 Wooster St.), **Spencer Brownstone** (⊠ 39 Wooster St.), and **Basilico Fine Arts and Friedrich Petzel** (⊠ 26 Wooster St.). Right nearby, between Wooster and Greene streets, also stop at **Deitch Projects** (⊠ 76 Grand St.).

Now head back north on Wooster Street to the blocks between West Houston and Prince streets. Here you may investigate the **New York Earth Room** ⑨ and the **Gagosian Gallery** (⊠ 136 Wooster St.), operated by prominent uptown dealer Larry Gagosian.

From Wooster Street walk one block west on Prince Street to SoHo's main drag, West Broadway, with galleries and stores galore. In the block between Prince and Spring streets alone, you'll find **Nancy Hoffman** (⊠ 429 W. Broadway); the gallery complex at 415 West Broadway, which includes the **Witkin Gallery** for photography; and 420 West Broadway, with six separate galleries, including two of the biggest SoHo names, **Leo Castelli** and the **Sonnabend Gallery.**

Continue south on West Broadway to the blocks between Spring and Broome streets, where there's more beauty to be had; the immense **OK Harris** is one of the area's major art galleries (⊠ 383 W. Broadway). Stay on West Broadway on the west side of the street and proceed south; between Grand and Canal streets stands the **SoHo Grand Hotel** ⑩, the first major hotel to be built in the neighborhood since the 1880s.

From here TriBeCa is less than one block away; just follow West Broadway south to Canal Street, the neighborhood's official boundary. Stop to marvel at the life-size iron Statue of Liberty crown rising above the kitschy white-tile entrance to **El Teddy's** (✉ 219 W. Broadway), a popular Mexican restaurant. Continuing south on West Broadway to Duane Street, you'll pass Worth Street, once the center of the garment trade and the 19th-century equivalent of today's 7th Avenue. Turn right on Duane Street to Hudson Street and you'll find the calm, shady **Duane Park** ⑪. When you walk one block north on Hudson Street, on the right-hand side you'll see the Art Deco **Western Union Building** (✉ 60 Hudson St.), where 19 subtly shaded colors of brick are laid in undulating patterns.

The area to the west (left), near the Hudson River docks, was once the heart of the wholesale food business. Turn off Hudson Street onto quiet Jay Street and pause at narrow **Staple Street** ⑫, whose green pedestrian walkway overhead links two warehouses. Gaze up Harrison Street toward the ornate old **New York Mercantile Exchange.** If you continue west on Jay Street, you'll pass the loading docks of a 100-year-old food wholesaler, **Bazzini's Nuts and Confections,** where an upscale retail shop peddles nuts, coffee beans, and candies; there are also a few tables where you can enjoy a light snack.

Jay Street comes to an end at Greenwich Street; at the intersection is a surprising row of early 19th-century town houses nestled in the side of **Independence Plaza** ⑬, a huge high-rise apartment complex. Two blocks north on Greenwich Street, at Franklin Street, is the **TriBeCa Film Center** ⑭, owned by Robert De Niro. Two blocks south of Jay Street on Greenwich Street lies 2½-acre **Washington Market Park** ⑮, a pleasant, landscaped oasis.

At the corner of the park, turn west on Chambers Street, heading west toward the Hudson River. A five-minute walk will bring you to the overpass across the West Side Highway. Here, behind the huge Stuyvesant High School building, you'll reach the north end of the **Hudson River Park** ⑯, a great place for a stroll.

TIMING

To see SoHo and TriBeCa at their liveliest, visit on a Saturday, when the fashionable art crowd is joined by smartly dressed uptowners and suburbanites who come down for a little shopping and gallery hopping. If you want to avoid crowds, take this walk during the week. Keep in mind that most galleries are closed on Sunday and Monday. If you allow time for leisurely browsing in several galleries and museums, as well as a stop for lunch, this tour can easily take up to an entire day.

Sights to See

❷ **Alternative Museum.** As the sign outside says, this two-room gallery SEEKS TO EXHIBIT THE WORK OF THOSE ARTISTS WHO HAVE BEEN DISENFRANCHISED BECAUSE OF IDEOLOGY, RACE, GENDER, OR ECONOMIC INEQUALITY. It presents some of the most interesting and engaging (and occasionally offensive or confrontational) art in SoHo. ✉ *594 Broadway, near E. Houston St.,* ☎ *212/966–4444.* ✑ *$3 (suggested donation).* ☉ *Tues.–Sat. 11–6.*

- -

OFF THE BEATEN PATH   **CHARLTON STREET –** The city's longest stretch of redbrick town houses preserved from the 1820s and 1830s runs along the north side of this street, which is west of 6th Avenue and south of West Houston Street and has high stoops, paneled front doors, leaded-glass windows, and narrow dormer windows all intact. While you're here, stroll along the parallel King and Vandam streets for more fine Federal houses. This quiet enclave was once an estate called Richmond Hill, whose various residents included George Washington, John and Abigail Adams, and Aaron Burr.

🖐 **❻ Children's Museum of the Arts.** In a bi-level space in SoHo, children 1–10 have the chance to become actively involved in visual and performing arts (☞ Chapter 3). ⊠ *182 Lafayette St., between Grand and Broome Sts.,* ☎ *212/274–0986.* 🎫 *$4 weekdays, $5 weekends.* ⊙ *Wed.– Sun. noon–5.*

⓫ Duane Park. The city bought this calm, shady triangle from Trinity Church (☞ Wall Street and the Battery, *below*) in 1797 for $5. Cheese, butter, and egg warehouses have surrounded this oasis for more than 100 years. ⊠ *Bordered by Hudson, Duane, and Staple Sts.*

NEED A BREAK? For a real New York story, duck into the **Odeon** (⊠ 145 W. Broadway, ☎ 212/233–0507), an Art Deco restaurant-bar. With black-and-red banquettes, chrome mirrors, neon-lighted clocks, and ceiling fans, this place has a distinctively slick atmosphere. Come for a drink at the bar or a snack anytime from noon to 2 AM.

★ **❶ Guggenheim Museum SoHo.** Since it opened in 1992, this downtown branch of the uptown museum has displayed a revolving series of exhibitions, both contemporary work and pieces from the Guggenheim's permanent collection. The museum occupies space in a landmark 19th-century redbrick structure with its original cast-iron storefronts and detailed cornice. Arata Isozaki designed the two floors of stark, loft-like galleries as well as the museum store facing Broadway. ⊠ *575 Broadway, at Prince St.,* ☎ *212/423–3500.* 🎫 *$8.* ⊙ *Wed.–Fri. and Sun. 11– 6, Sat. 11–8.*

NEED A BREAK? Diagonally across from the Guggenheim Museum SoHo, **Dean & DeLuca** (⊠ 560 Broadway, at Prince St., ☎ 212/431–1691), the gourmet emporium, brews superb coffee and tea, but it gets crowded early.

❺ Haughwout Building. Nicknamed the Parthenon of Cast Iron, this Venetian palazzo–style structure was built in 1857 to house Eder Haughwout's china and glassware business. Inside, the building once contained the world's first commercial passenger elevator, a steam-powered device invented by Elisha Graves Otis. ⊠ *488 Broadway, at Broome St.*

★ 🖐 **⓰ Hudson River Park.** A landscaped oasis with playgrounds, promenades and walkways, handball and basketball courts, and grassy areas, this park on the river at the corner of Chambers and West streets and north of the World Financial Center fills with downtown residents soaking up rays on sunny days. Be sure not to overlook *The Real World* sculpture garden at its north end, by Tom Otterness, which playfully pokes fun at the area's capitalist ethos. The Stuyvesant High School building (1992) is also at this end of the park; on its north side begins the paved river esplanade that extends to Gansevoort Street in the West Village. The esplanade is full of skaters, joggers, and strollers at all hours, and the benches along the path are terrific spots from which to watch the sunset over New Jersey. The park is part of plans for an even larger park to extend north to midtown, managed by the Hudson River Park Trust (☞ A New Breeze Is Blowing Down by the Riverside, *in* The Seaport and the Courts, *below*).

⓭ Independence Plaza. These high-rise towers at the intersection of Greenwich and Harrison streets are the fruit of a pleasant, if somewhat utilitarian, project of the mid-1970s that was supposed to be part of a wave of demolition and construction—until the preservationists stepped in. For several years Independence Plaza remained a middle-class island stranded downtown, far from stores, schools, and neighbors. With TriBeCa's increasingly chic reputation, however, plus the development of Battery Park City to the south, it has become a much more desirable address. The three-story redbrick houses that share Harrison Street with Independence Plaza were moved here from various sites in the neighborhood when, in the early 1970s, the food wholesalers' central market nearby was razed and moved to the Bronx. ⊠ *Greenwich St. between Duane and N. Moore Sts.*

❽ King of Greene Street. This five-story Renaissance-style 1873 building has a magnificent projecting porch of Corinthian columns and pilasters. Today the King (now painted ivory) houses the M-13 art gallery, Alice's Antiques, and Bennison Fabrics. ⊠ *72–76 Greene St., between Spring and Broome Sts.*

❸ Museum for African Art. Dedicated to contemporary and traditional African art, this small but expertly conceived museum is housed in a handsome two-story space designed by Maya Lin, who also designed Washington, D.C.'s Vietnam Veterans Memorial. Exhibits may include contemporary sculpture, ceremonial masks, architectural details, costumes, and textiles. The entertaining museum store features African crafts, clothing, and jewelry. ⊠ *593 Broadway, near Houston St.,* ☎ *212/966–1313.* ▣ *$5.* ☉ *Tues.–Fri. 10:30–5:30, Sat. noon–8, Sun. noon–6.*

❹ New Museum of Contemporary Art. The avant-garde exhibitions here, all by living artists (many from outside the United States), are often radically innovative and socially conscious. A 1997 renovation added a second-floor gallery, a bookstore, and no-admission-charge exhibition space in the basement devoted to participatory art (all of which can be touched). ⊠ *583 Broadway, between Houston and Prince Sts.,* ☎ *212/219–1222.* ▣ *$5; free Thurs. 6 PM–8 PM.* ☉ *Wed. and Sun. noon–6, Thurs., Fri., and Sat. noon–8.*

NEED A BREAK? **Space Untitled Espresso Bar** (⊠ 133 Greene St., near W. Houston St., ☎ 212/260–8962) serves coffee, tea, sweets, and lunch sandwiches, as well as wine and beer, in a minimalist gallery setting.

❾ New York Earth Room. Walter de Maria's 1977 avant-garde work consists of 140 tons of gently sculpted soil (22 inches deep) filling 3,600 square ft of space of a second-floor gallery. ⊠ *141 Wooster St., between Houston and Prince Sts.,* ☎ *212/473–8072.* ▣ *Free.* ☉ *Jan.–mid-June and mid-Sept.–Dec., Wed.–Sat. noon–3 and 3:30–6.*

OFF THE BEATEN PATH **NoLita** Mulberry, Mott, and Elizabeth streets between Houston and Spring streets are the core of this up-and-coming neighborhood whose name comes from "North of Little Italy." Trendy clothing, design, and secondhand boutiques as well as restaurants and cafés have opened up and down these few blocks, and many new ventures continue to debut, making this area a sort of new SoHo. Though the neighborhood lacks big-draw exploring sights, its unique stores are worth exploring (☞ Chapter 9).

❼ Queen of Greene Street. The regal grace of this 1873 cast-iron beauty is exemplified by its dormers, columns, window arches, projecting central bays, and Second Empire–style roof. ⊠ *28–30 Greene St., between Grand and Canal Sts.*

10 **SoHo Grand Hotel.** The first major hotel to appear in the area since the 1800s, the 15-story SoHo Grand, which opened in 1996, was designed to pay tribute to the neighborhood's architectural history, particularly the cast-iron historic district. Serving as a "dog bar," a 17-century French stone basin stands at the hotel's entrance, signalling that pets are welcome. A staircase—made of translucent bottle glass and iron and suspended from the ceiling by two cables—links the entryway with the second-floor 7,000-square-ft lobby, which has 16-ft-high windows and massive stone columns supporting the paneled mercury mirror ceiling (☞ Chapter 6). ⊠ *310 W. Broadway, at Grand St.,* ☎ *212/965–3000.*

NEED A BREAK?   For a taste of SoHo shabby chic, head for **Scharmann's** (⊠ 386 W. Broadway, between Spring and Broome Sts., ☎ 212/219–2561), where the hip drink tea from gleaming brass pots on oversize couches, mismatched chairs, and a bean bag or two.

12 **Staple Street.** Little more than an alley, Staple Street was named for the eggs, butter, cheese, and other staple products unloaded here by ships in transit that didn't want to pay duty on any extra cargo. Framed at the end of the alley is the redbrick New York Mercantile Exchange (⊠ 6 Harrison St.), its square corner tower topped by a bulbous roof. On the ground floor is the acclaimed French restaurant Chanterelle (☞ Chapter 5).

14 **TriBeCa Film Center.** Robert De Niro created this complex of editing, screening, and production rooms, where Miramax Films, Stephen Spielberg, Quincy Jones, and De Niro keep offices. Like many of the other chic buildings in this area, it's inside a former factory, the old Coffee Building. On the ground floor is the TriBeCa Grill restaurant (☞ Chapter 5), also owned by Robert De Niro. ⊠ *375 Greenwich St., between Franklin and N. Moore Sts.*

15 **Washington Market Park.** This much-needed recreation space for TriBeCa was named after the great food market that once sprawled over the area. It is now a green, landscaped oasis with a playground and a gazebo. Just across Chambers Street from the park, P.S. 234, a public elementary school, has opened to serve TriBeCa's younger generation. At the corner, a stout little red tower resembles a lighthouse, and iron ship figures are worked into the playground fence—reminders of the neighborhood's long-gone dockside past. ⊠ *Greenwich St. between Chambers and Duane Sts.*

LITTLE ITALY AND CHINATOWN

Mulberry Street is the heart of Little Italy; in fact, at this point it's virtually the entire body. In 1932 an estimated 98% of the inhabitants of this area were of Italian birth or heritage, but since then the growth and expansion of neighboring Chinatown have encroached on the Italian neighborhood to such an extent that merchants and community leaders of the Little Italy Restoration Association (LIRA) negotiated a truce in which the Chinese agreed to let at least Mulberry remain an all-Italian street.

In the second half of the 19th century, when Italian immigration peaked, the neighborhood stretched from Houston Street to Canal Street and the Bowery to Broadway. During this time Italians founded at least three Italian parishes, including the Church of the Transfiguration (now almost wholly Chinese); they also operated an Italian-language newspaper, *Il Progresso.*

In 1926 immigrants from southern Italy celebrated the first Feast of San Gennaro along Mulberry Street—a 10-day street fair that still takes place every September. Dedicated to the patron saint of Naples, the festival transforms Mulberry Street into a virtual alfresco restaurant, as wall-to-wall vendors sell traditional fried sausages and pastries. Today the festival is one of the few reminders of Little Italy's vibrant history as the neighborhood continues to change. If you want the flavor of a truly Italian neighborhood, you'd do better to visit Carroll Gardens in Brooklyn or Arthur Avenue in the Bronx (☞ Chapter 2)—or rent a video of the Martin Scorsese movie *Mean Streets,* which was filmed in Little Italy in the early 1970s.

Throughout Little Italy, fire escapes project over the sidewalks from the facades of many tenements. In these late-19th-century, six-story buildings on 25- by 90-ft lots, most of the apartments are railroad flats: their rooms are laid out along a straight line, so the dwellings resemble railroad cars. This style was common in the densely populated immigrant neighborhoods of lower Manhattan until 1901, when the city passed an ordinance requiring air shafts in the interior of buildings.

Visually exotic, Chinatown is a popular tourist attraction, but it is also a real, vital community where about half the city's population of 300,000 Chinese still live. Its main businesses are restaurants and garment factories; some 55% of its residents speak little or no English. Historically, Chinatown was divided from Little Italy by Canal Street, the bustling artery that links the Holland Tunnel (to New Jersey) and the Manhattan Bridge (to Brooklyn). However, in recent years an influx of immigrants from the People's Republic of China, Taiwan, and especially Hong Kong has swelled Manhattan's Chinese population, and Hong Kong residents have poured capital into Chinatown real estate. Chinatown now spills over its traditional borders into Little Italy to the north and the formerly Jewish Lower East Side to the east.

The first Chinese immigrants were primarily railroad workers who came from the West in the 1870s to settle in a limited section of the Lower East Side. For nearly a century anti-immigration laws prohibited most men from having their wives and families join them; the neighborhood became known as a "bachelor society," and for years its population remained static. It was not until the end of World War II, when Chinese immigration quotas were increased, that the neighborhood began the outward expansion that is still taking place today.

Chinatown is now livelier than ever—a thriving marketplace crammed with souvenir shops and restaurants in funky pagoda-style buildings and crowded with pedestrians day and night. From fast-food noodles or dumplings to sumptuous Hunan, Szechuan, Cantonese, Mandarin, and Shanghai feasts, every imaginable type of Chinese cuisine is served here. Sidewalk markets burst with stacks of fresh seafood and strange-shaped vegetables in extraterrestrial shades of green. Food shops proudly display their wares: if America's motto is "A chicken in every pot," then Chinatown's must be "A roast duck in every window."

Numbers in the text correspond to numbers in the margin and on the SoHo, TriBeCa, Little Italy, Chinatown map.

A Good Walk

Start your tour at the intersection of Spring and Mulberry streets, which still has a residential feel. Take a moment to poke your nose into the **DiPalma Bread Outlet** (⌂ 45 Spring St.), one of the last coal-oven bakeries in the United States. Walk down **Mulberry Street** ⑰ to Broome Street, a gastronomic thoroughfare. East of Mulberry Street, the building at 375 Broome Street is known for its sheet-metal cornice that bears the face of a distinguished, albeit anonymous, bearded man.

To see the ornate Renaissance Revival former **New York City Police Head-quarters** ⑱, walk west on Broome Street to Centre Street, between Broome and Grand streets. Then work your way back to the corner of Grand and Mulberry streets and stop to get the lay of the land. Facing north (uptown), on your right you'll see a series of multistory houses from the early 19th century, built long before the great flood of immigration hit this neighborhood between 1890 and 1924. Turn and look south along the east side of Mulberry Street to see Little Italy's trademark railroad-flat-style tenement buildings.

On the southeast corner of Grand Street, **E. Rossi & Co.** (✉ 191 Grand St.), established in 1902, is an antiquated little shop that sells house-wares, espresso makers, embroidered religious postcards, and jocular Italian T-shirts. Two doors east on Grand Street is **Ferrara's** (✉ 195 Grand St.), a pastry shop opened in 1892 that ships its creations—can-noli, peasant pie, Italian rum cake—all over the world. Another sur-vivor of the pre-tenement era is the two-story, dormered brick Van Rensselaer House, now **Paolucci's Restaurant** (✉ 149 Mulberry St.); built in 1816, it is a prime example of the Italian Federal style.

One block south of Grand Street, on the corner of Hester and Mul-berry streets, you'll reach the site of what was once **Umberto's Clam House** (✉ 129 Mulberry St.), best known as the place where mobster Joey Gallo was munching scungilli in 1973 when he was fatally sur-prised by a task force of mob hit men. Turn left onto Hester Street to visit yet another Little Italy institution, **Puglia** (✉ 189 Hester St.), a restaurant where guests sit at long communal tables, sing along with house entertainers, and enjoy southern Italian specialties with quanti-ties of homemade wine. (For other Little Italy restaurants, *see* Chap-ter 5.) One street west, on Baxter Street about three-quarters of a block toward Canal Street, stands the **San Gennaro Church** ⑲, which each autumn sponsors Little Italy's keynote event, the annual Feast of San Gennaro.

To reach Chinatown from Little Italy, cross Canal Street at Mulberry Street. A good place to get oriented is the **Museum of Chinese in the Americas** ⑳, in a century-old schoolhouse at the corner of Bayard and Mulberry streets. For a taste of Chinatown-style commercialism, walk one block north to Canal Street, where restaurants and markets abound. If Chinese food products intrigue you, stop to browse in **Kam Man** (✉ 200 Canal St.) and then head east to **Mott Street** ㉑, the principal busi-ness street of the neighborhood.

Turn right from Canal Street onto Mott Street and walk three blocks. On the corner of Mott and Mosco streets, you'll find the **Church of the Transfiguration** ㉒, where the faithful have worshiped since 1801. From here turn right from Mott Street onto Mosco Street, proceeding down-hill to Mulberry Street, where you'll see **Columbus Park** ㉓. This peace-ful spot occupies the area once known as the **Five Points,** a tough 19th-century slum ruled by Irish gangs.

Across Mott Street from the church is a sign for Pell Street, a narrow lane of wall-to-wall restaurants whose neon signs stretch halfway across the thoroughfare. Halfway up Pell is **Doyers Street** ㉔ the site of turn-of-the-century gang wars. At the end of Doyers you'll find the **Bowery** ㉕ Cross the street to **Chatham Square** ㉖, where the Kimlau Arch honors Chinese casualties in American wars, and a statue pays homage to Lin Zexu, a 19th-century Chinese official who banned opium from the mainland. From Chatham Square cross over the east side, past Park Row. Take a sharp right turn onto St. James Place to find two remnants of this neighborhood's pre-Chinatown past. On St. James Place is the **First Shearith Israel graveyard** ㉗, the first Jewish cemetery in the United States. Walk a half block farther, turn left on James Street, and you'll see **St. James Church** (✉ 32 James St.), a stately 1837 Greek Revival edifice where Al Smith, who rose from this poor Irish neighborhood to become New York's governor and a 1928 Democratic presidential candidate, once served as altar boy.

Return to Chatham Square once again and walk north up the Bowery to **Confucius Plaza** ㉘, where a statue of the Chinese sage stands guard. Then cross the Bowery back to the west side of the street; at the corner of Pell Street stands 18 Bowery, which is one of Manhattan's oldest homes—a Federal and Georgian structure built in 1785 by meat wholesaler Edward Mooney. Farther north up the Bowery, a younger side of Chinatown is shown at the **Asian American Arts Centre** ㉙, which displays current work by Asian-American artists.

Continue north. At the intersection of the Bowery and Canal Street, a grand arch and colonnade mark the entrance to the **Manhattan Bridge,** which leads to Brooklyn. This corner was once the center of New York's diamond district. Today most jewelry dealers have moved uptown, but you can still find some pretty good deals at jewelers on the Bowery and the north side of Canal Street.

TIMING
Since Little Italy consists of little more than one street, a tour of the area shouldn't take more than one hour. Most attractions are food-related, so plan on visiting around lunchtime. Another fun time to visit is during the San Gennaro Festival, which runs for two weeks each September, starting the first Thursday after Labor Day. For more information, call ☎ 212/768–9320. Come on a weekend to see Chinatown at its liveliest; locals crowd the streets from dawn until dusk, along with a slew of tourists. For a more relaxed experience, opt for a weekday instead. Allowing for stops at the two local museums and a lunch break, a Chinatown tour will take about three additional hours.

Sights to See

㉙ **Asian American Arts Centre.** This space offers impressive contemporary works by Asian-American artists, annual Chinese folk-art exhibitions during the Chinese New Year, Asian-American dance performances, and videotapes of Asian-American art and events. The center also sells unique art objects from Asia. There's no sign out front, and the door reads KTV-CITY; ring buzzer No. 1. ✉ 26 Bowery, between Bayard and Canal Sts., ☎ 212/233–2154. 🖭 Free. ♡ Tues.– Fri. 1–6, Sat. 4–6.

㉕ **Bowery.** Now a commercial thoroughfare lined with stores selling light fixtures and secondhand restaurant equipment, in the 17th century this broad boulevard was a farming area north of the city; its name derives from *bowerij,* the Dutch word for farm. As the city's growing population moved northward, Bowery became a broad, elegant avenue lined with taverns and theaters. In the late 1800s the placement of an elevated subway line over Bowery and the proliferation of saloons and brothels led to its demise as an elegant commercial thoroughfare; by the early 20th century it had become infamous as a skid row full of indigents and crime. After 1970 efforts at gentrification had some effect, and some of the neighborhood's indigent population dispersed. Today Bowery is poised for futher gentrification.

㉖ **Chatham Square.** Ten streets converge at this labyrinthine intersection, creating pandemonium for cars and a nightmare for pedestrians. A memorial, the **Kimlau Arch,** honoring Chinese casualties in American wars, stands on an island in the eye of the storm. A statue on the square's eastern edge pays tribute to a Quin Dynasty official named Lin Zexu. Erected in late 1997, the 18-ft, 5-inch tall granite statue reflects Chinatown's growing population of mainland immigrants and their particular national pride: the Fujianese minister is noted for his role in sparking the Opium War by banning the drug. The base of his statue reads, SAY NO TO DRUGS. On the far end of the square, at the corner of Catherine Street and East Broadway, there's a Republic National Bank—originally a branch of the Manhattan Savings Bank. It was built to resemble a pagoda.

㉒ **Church of the Transfiguration.** Built in 1801 as the Zion Episcopal Church, this is an imposing Georgian structure with Gothic windows. It is now a Chinese Catholic church distinguished by its trilingualism: here Mass is said in Cantonese, Mandarin, and English. ⊠ *29 Mott St.,* ☎ *212/962–5157.*

| NEED A BREAK? | Right across from the Church of the Transfiguration, at the corner of Mott and Mosco Streets, you'll see a red shack, **Cecilia Tam's Hong Kong Egg Cake Company,** where Ms. Tam makes mouthwatering small, round egg cakes for $1 a portion, between Tuesday and Sunday from early morning until 5. At 35 Pell Street, off Mott Street, is **May May Chinese Gourmet Bakery** (☎ 212/267–0733), a local favorite, with Chinese pastries, rice dumplings wrapped in banana leaves, yam cakes, and other sweet treats. A colorful flag hangs outside the entrance of the **Chinatown Ice Cream Factory** (⊠ 65 Bayard St., between Mott and Elizabeth Sts., ☎ 212/608–4170), where the flavors range from red bean to litchi to green tea. Prepare to eat your scoop on the run, since there's no seating. |

㉓ **Columbus Park.** Mornings bring groups of elderly Chinese practicing the graceful movements of tai chi to this shady, paved space; during afternoons the park's tables fill for heated games of mah-jongg. One hundred years ago the then-swampy area was known as the **Five Points**—after the intersection of Mulberry Street, Anthony (now Worth) Street, Cross (now Park) Street, Orange (now Baxter) Street, and Little Water Street (no longer in existence)—and was notoriously ruled by dangerous Irish gangs. In the 1880s a neighborhood-improvement campaign brought about the park's creation.

㉘ **Confucius Plaza.** At this open area just north of ☞ Chatham Square, a bronze statue of Confucius presides before the redbrick high-rise apartment complex named for him. The statue was originally opposed by leftist Chinese immigrants, who considered the sage a reactionary symbol of Old China. ⊠ *Intersection of Bowery and Division St.*

㉔ **Doyers Street.** The "bloody angle"—a sharp turn halfway down this little alleyway—was the site of turn-of-the-century battles between Chinatown's Hip Sing and On Leon tongs, gangs who fought for control over the local gambling and opium trades. Today the street is among Chinatown's most colorful, lined with tea parlors and barbershops.

㉗ **First Shearith Israel graveyard.** Consecrated in 1656 by the country's oldest Jewish congregation, this small burial ground bears the remains of Sephardic Jews (of Spanish-Portuguese extraction) who emigrated from Brazil in the mid-17th century. The second and third Shearith Israel graveyards are in Greenwich Village and Chelsea, respectively. ⊠ *55 St. James Pl.*

㉑   **Mott Street.** The main commercial artery of Chinatown, Mott Street has appeared in innumerable movies and television as the street that exemplifies the neighborhood. Chinatown began in the late 1880s when Chinese immigrants (mostly men) settled in tenements in a small area that included the lower portion of Mott Street as well as nearby Pell and Doyer streets. Today the street is often crowded during the day and especially on weekends; it overflows with fish and vegetable markets, restaurants, bakeries, and souvenir shops.

Opened in 1891, **Quong Yuen Shing & Co.** (✉ 32 Mott St.), also known as the Mott Street General Store, is one of Chinatown's oldest curio shops, with porcelain bowls, teapots, and cups for sale. Next door is one of Chinatown's best and oldest bakeries, **Fung Wong** (✉ 30 Mott St.), where you can stock up on almond cookies, sticky rice cakes, sweet egg tarts, roast pork buns, and other goodies. If you've never tried dim sum (Chinese dumplings and other small dishes), now's your chance; *see* Chapter 5 for recommended restaurants.

⑰   **Mulberry Street.** Crowded with restaurants, cafés, bakeries, imported-food shops, and souvenir stores, Mulberry Street is where Little Italy lives and breathes. The blocks between Houston and Spring streets fall within the neighborhood of NoLita and are home to an increasing number of up-to-the-moment stores and restaurants, which are side by side with others that seem dedicated to staying exactly as their old customers remember them.

NEED A BREAK?	You can savor cannoli and other sweet treats at **Caffè Roma** (✉ 385 Broome St., at Mulberry St., ☎ 212/226–8413), a traditional neighborhood favorite with wrought-iron chairs and a pressed-tin ceiling.

★ ☕ ⑳   **Museum of Chinese in the Americas (MCA).** In a century-old schoolhouse that once served Italian-American and Chinese-American children, MCA is the only U.S. museum devoted to preserving the history of the Chinese people throughout the western hemisphere. The permanent exhibit—*Where's Home? Chinese in the Americas*—explores the Chinese-American experience by weaving together displays of artists' creations and personal and domestic artifacts with historical documentation. Slippers for binding feet, Chinese musical instruments, a reversible silk gown (circa 1900) worn at a Cantonese opera performance, items from a Chinese laundry, and antique business signs are some of the unique objects on display; changing exhibits fill a second room. MCA sponsors workshops, walking tours, lectures, and family events. Its archives (open by appointment only) dedicated to Chinese-American history and culture include 2,000 volumes. ✉ 70 *Mulberry St., at Bayard St., 2nd floor,* ☎ 212/619–4785. 🎫 *$3.* ☺ *Tues.–Sat. noon–5.*

⑱   **New York City Police Headquarters.** This magnificent Renaissance Revival structure with baroque embellishments and a striking dome served as the New York City police headquarters from its construction in 1909 until 1973; in 1988 it was converted into a high-priced condominium complex. Known to New Yorkers today as "240 Centre Street," its big-name residents have included Cindy Crawford, Winona Ryder, and Steffi Graf, among others. ✉ *240 Centre St., between Broome and Grand Sts.*

⑲   **San Gennaro Church.** Every autumn San Gennaro Church—officially called the Most Precious Blood Church, National Shrine of San Gennaro—sponsors the Feast of San Gennaro, the biggest event in Little Italy (☞ Festivals and Seasonal Events *in* Smart Travel Tips). (The community's other big festival celebrates St. Anthony of Padua in June; the church connected to the festival is at Houston and Sullivan streets, in what is now SoHo.) ⊠ *113 Baxter St., near Canal St.*

WALL STREET AND THE BATTERY

Island city that it is, much of Manhattan strangely turns its back on the rushing waters that surround it—not so the Battery. From waterside walks in Battery Park, you can look out on the confluence of the Hudson and East River estuaries where bustling seaborne commerce once glutted the harbor that built the "good city of old Manhatto," Herman Melville's moniker from the second chapter of *Moby-Dick.* It was here that the Dutch established the colony of Nieuw Amsterdam in 1625; in 1789 the first capitol building of the United States found itself here. The city did not really expand beyond these precincts until the middle of the 19th century. Today this historic heart of New York continues to be dominated by Wall Street, which is both an actual street and a shorthand name for the vast, powerful financial community that clusters around the New York and American stock exchanges. A different but equally awe-inspiring type of sight can be found at the tip of the island as you gaze across the great silvery harbor to the enduring symbols of America: the Statue of Liberty and Ellis Island, port of entry for countless immigrants to a new land.

Numbers in the text correspond to numbers in the margin and on the Lower Manhattan map.

A Good Walk

The immediate vicinity of the Staten Island Ferry Terminal (just outside the South Ferry subway station on the 1 and 9 lines) is a little unsightly, but that doesn't detract from the pleasure of a ride on the **Staten Island Ferry** ①. The 20- to 30-minute ride across New York Harbor provides great views of the Manhattan skyline, Ellis Island, the Statue of Liberty, the Verrazano-Narrows Bridge, and the New Jersey coast—and the blue-and-orange boats are a delight (plus, rides are free).

Just north of the Staten Island Ferry Terminal, the tall white columns and curved brick front of the 1793 **Shrine of St. Elizabeth Ann Seton at Our Lady of the Rosary** ② are a dignified sight. The house was one of many mansions lining State Street. To the left of the shrine, the verdant **Battery Park** ③, Manhattan's green toe, curves up the west side of the island. It is filled with sculpture and monuments, including the circular **Castle Clinton** ④. The venerable fort is where you buy tickets for the ferries to the **Statue of Liberty** ⑤ and **Ellis Island** ⑥. From Castle Clinton follow the rose-color walk toward **Bowling Green,** ⑦ an oval greensward at the foot of Broadway that became New York's first public park in 1733. Across State Street, facing the south flank of Bowling Green, is the Beaux Arts Alexander Hamilton U.S. Custom House, home of the **National Museum of the American Indian** ⑧.

Next follow Whitehall Street down the east side of the American Indian museum. A left turn onto Bridge Street will bring into focus a block of early New York buildings. As you approach Broad Street, the two-tone Georgian **Fraunces Tavern** ⑨ will appear. The complex of five largely 19th-century buildings houses a museum, restaurant, and bar. Across Pearl Street, **85 Broad Street** pays homage to urban archaeology with a transparent panel in the sidewalk showing the excavated foundations of the 17th-century Stadt Huys, the Old Dutch City Hall. The course of old Dutch Stone Street is marked in the lobby with a line of brown paving stones.

Lower Manhattan

CHINATOWN

South Street Seaport

Pier 17

Pier 16

Catherine Slip

Henry St.

Mott St.

Mulberry St.

Baxter St.

Worth St.

Hogan Pl.

Lafayette Pl.

Madison St.

St. James Pl.

Hayes Pl.

Pearl St.

Pearl St.

Worth St.

Elk St.

Centre St.

Foley Square

Fulton Fish Market

Dover St.

Peck Slip

Beekman St.

Pearl St.

Fulton St.

Burling Slip

Titanic Memorial

Gold St.

Pace University

Spruce St.

Beekman St.

John St.

Platt St.

Fletcher St.

Louise Nevelson Plaza

William St.

Maiden Lane

Old New York Life Insurance Company Headquarters

Federal Plaza

Duane St.

Reade St.

Chambers St.

Brooklyn Bridge Walkway

Park Row

City Hall Park

Ann St.

Fulton St.

John St.

J,M,Z

4,5,6

A,C

J,M,Z

2,3

Broadway

Murray St.

N,R

2,3

Leonard St.

Worth St.

Thomas St.

Church St.

West Broadway

Dey St.

Cortlandt St.

Liberty St.

N,R

C,E

4,5

Hudson St.

Chambers St.

1,2,3,9

Warren St.

Park Pl.

Barclay St.

Vesey St.

World Trade Center

1,9

Staple St.

Harrison St.

Jay St.

Greenwich St.

Franklin St.

Independence Plaza

West St.

Vesey St.

West Side Highway

A,E

Stuyvesant High School

Warren St.

Park Pl. W.

Murray St.

North End Ave.

Vesey St.

World Financial Center

Promenade

Hudson River Park

North Cove Yacht Harbor

Hoboken Ferry Terminal

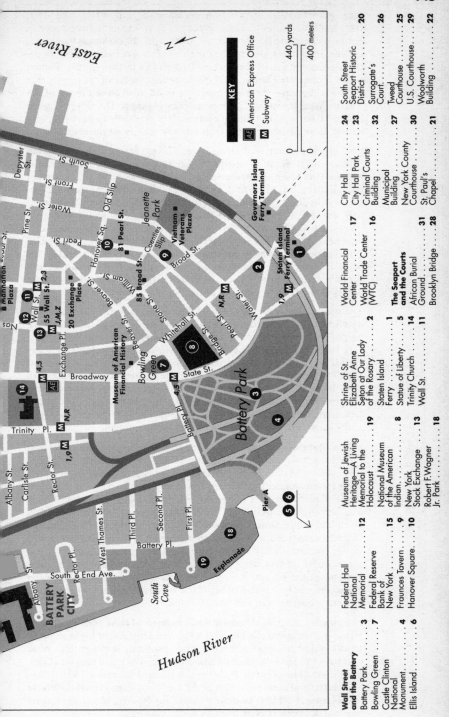

East River

Hudson River

KEY

AE American Express Office

M Subway

0 _____ 440 yards

0 _____ 400 meters

Wall Street and the Battery

Battery Park	3
Bowling Green	7
Castle Clinton National Monument	4
Ellis Island	6
Federal Hall National Memorial	12
Federal Reserve Bank of New York	15
Fraunces Tavern	9
Hanover Square	10
Museum of Jewish Heritage—A Living Memorial to the Holocaust	19
National Museum of the American Indian	8
New York Stock Exchange	13
Robert F. Wagner Jr. Park	18
Shrine of St. Elizabeth Anne Seton at Our Lady of the Rosary	2
Staten Island Ferry	1
Statue of Liberty	5
Trinity Church	14
Wall St.	11
World Financial Center	17
World Trade Center (WTC)	16

The Seaport and the Courts

African Burial Ground	31
Brooklyn Bridge	28
City Hall	24
City Hall Park	23
Criminal Courts Building	32
Municipal Building	27
New York County Courthouse	30
St. Paul's Chapel	21
South Street Seaport Historic District	20
Surrogate's Court	26
Tweed Courthouse	25
U.S. Courthouse	29
Woolworth Building	22

Head north on Pearl Street to **Hanover Square** ⑩, a quiet tree-lined plaza, then head inland on William Street to the triangular convergence of South William and Beaver streets. On the right, **20 Exchange Place** towers and adds street-level interest with weighty Art Deco doorways depicting the engines of commerce. Two blocks farther north, William Street crosses **Wall Street** ⑪, a jaw-dropping display of the money that built Manhattan—the massive arcade of **55 Wall Street,** home of the Regent Wall Street hotel, alone speaks volumes. Developers' greed backfired here—they built on every inch of land only to have property values decrease once people realized how stultifying the results were.

One block west on Wall Street, where Broad Street becomes Nassau Street, a regal statue of George Washington stands on the steps of the **Federal Hall National Memorial** ⑫. Across the street is an investment bank built by J. P. Morgan in 1913. By building only four stories, Morgan was in effect declaring himself above the pressures of Wall Street real estate values. Now **Morgan Guaranty Trust,** the building bears pockmarks near the fourth window on the Wall Street side; these were created when a bomb that had been placed in a pushcart exploded in 1920. The temple-fronted **New York Stock Exchange** ⑬ is the central shrine of Wall Street (even though its address is officially on Broad Street). From its visitor center you can watch stressed-out traders gesture wildly in the name of making deals.

The focal point at the west end of Wall Street is the brownstone **Trinity Church** ⑭. Just north of the church is tiny Thames Street, where a pair of skyscrapers playfully called the **Thames Twins**—the Trinity and U.S. Realty buildings—display early 20th-century attempts to apply Gothic decoration to skyscrapers. Across the street at 120 Broadway, the 1915 **Equitable Building** rises 30 stories straight from its base with no setback; its overpowering shadow on the street helped persuade the city government to pass the nation's first zoning law. Large public plazas around the bases of skyscrapers have helped to alleviate this problem, at the same time creating space for public sculpture.

Four **sculpture installations** make for an interesting side tour. The first is on Broadway between Cedar and Liberty streets, where the black-glass Marine Midland Bank (1971) heightens the drama of the red-and-silver Isamu Noguchi sculpture *Cube* in its plaza. Two blocks east, near the William Street edge of the plaza surrounding the 65-story Chase Manhattan Bank Building (1960), stands Jean Dubuffet's striking black-and-white *Group of Four Trees.* Inset in the plaza is another Noguchi installation, a **circular sculpture garden** with his signature carved stones, located slightly south of the Dubuffet. Just north of the Chase plaza, where Liberty Street converges with William Street and Maiden Lane under the Federal Reserve Bank, the triangular **Louise Nevelson Plaza** contains four pieces of her black-welded-steel abstract sculpture: three of moderate size and one 70-footer.

The massive, rusticated **Federal Reserve Bank of New York** ⑮, directly across the street, recalls Florence's Palazzo Strozzi and looks the way a bank ought to: solid, imposing, and absolutely impregnable. Walk west back toward Broadway on Maiden Lane, which will turn into Cortland Street. The contrast between the Federal Reserve's 1924 vision of architectural power and that of the 1,350-ft-tall towers of the **World Trade Center** ⑯ couldn't be more striking. The 16-acre, 12-million-square-ft complex contains New York's tallest buildings.

During the towers' construction more than a million cubic yards of rock and soil were excavated—then moved across West Street to help beget **Battery Park City.** An impressive feat of urban planning, this complete

92-acre neighborhood houses more than 5,000 residents and 20,000 workers. It is almost like a separate city within the city, with high-rises, town houses, shops, and green squares—though it's not a very exciting place to visit. The pedestrian overpass north of 1 World Trade Center leads to Battery Park City's centerpiece, the **World Financial Center** ⑰, a four-tower complex designed by Cesar Pelli. Just north of the basin is the terminal for ferry service to Hoboken, New Jersey. Beyond the ferry terminal is the south end of **Hudson River Park** (☞ SoHo and TriBeCa, *above*). To the south, a longer riverside esplanade begins in the residential part of Battery Park City and connects with **Robert F. Wagner Jr. Park** ⑱, home to the **Museum of Jewish Heritage—A Living Memorial to the Holocaust** ⑲. Especially noteworthy among the artwork populating the Esplanade are Ned Smyth's columned plaza with chessboards and the **South Cove** (a collaborative effort), a romantic curved stage set of wooden piers and a steel-frame lookout.

TIMING

The Manhattan side of this tour takes most of a day—allow more time to ferry out to the Statue of Liberty and Ellis Island. Visit on a weekday to capture the district's true vitality—but expect to be jostled on the crowded sidewalks if you stand too long, peering at the great buildings that surge skyward on every corner. If you visit on a weekend, on the other hand, you'll feel like a lone explorer in a canyon of buildings. Either way, winds from the harbor whipping around the buildings can make this area feel markedly colder than other parts of the city—a great thing in summer—so dress accordingly. Start early, preferably making the first ferry, to try to beat the crowds to Liberty and Ellis islands. Get tickets by lunchtime if you plan to visit the Stock Exchange, which is open only on weekdays until 4. The best place to end the day is looking west over the Hudson for the sunset.

Sights to See

❸ **Battery Park.** Jutting out as if it were Manhattan's green toe, Battery Park (so named because a battery of 28 cannons was placed along its shore in Colonial days to fend off the British) is built on landfill and has gradually grown over the centuries. The park's main structure is ☞ **Castle Clinton National Monument**, the takeoff point for ferries to the ☞ **Statue of Liberty** and ☞ **Ellis Island**. The park is loaded with various other monuments and statues, some impressive, some downright obscure. Starting near the Staten Island Ferry Terminal, head north along the water's edge to the East Coast Memorial, a statue of a fierce eagle that presides over eight granite slabs inscribed with the names of U.S. servicemen who died in the western Atlantic during World War II. Climb the steps of the East Coast Memorial for a fine view of the main features of **New York Harbor**; from left to right: **Governors Island,** a former Coast Guard installation whose future, as of press time, was undecided; hilly **Staten Island** (☞ Chapter 2) in the distance; the ☞ **Statue of Liberty**, on Liberty Island; ☞ **Ellis Island**, gateway to the New World for generations of immigrants; and the old railway terminal in **Liberty State Park,** on the mainland in Jersey City, New Jersey. On crystal-clear days you can see all the way to Port Elizabeth's cranes, which seem to mimic Lady Liberty's stance. Continue north past a romantic **statue of Giovanni da Verrazano,** the Florentine merchant who piloted the ship that first sighted New York and its harbor in 1524. The **Verrazano-Narrows Bridge,** between Brooklyn and Staten Island—so long that the curvature of the earth had to be figured into its dimensions—is visible from here, just beyond Governors Island. At the park's northernmost edge, Pier A, the last Victorian fireboat pier in the city, was undergoing restoration at press time; it is slated to offer a visitor center and restaurant. Its clock tower, erected in 1919, was the nation's first World War I memorial. ⊠ *Broadway at Battery Pl.*

❼ Bowling Green. This oval greensward at the foot of Broadway became New York's first public park in 1733. On July 9, 1776, a few hours after citizens learned about the signing of the Declaration of Independence, rioters toppled a statue of British king George III that had occupied the spot for 11 years; much of the statue's lead was melted down into bullets. In 1783, when the occupying British forces fled the city, they defiantly hoisted a Union Jack on a greased, uncleated flagpole so it couldn't be lowered; patriot John Van Arsdale drove his own cleats into the pole to replace the flag with the Stars and Stripes. The entrance to the subway station here is the original one, built in 1904–05.

☝ ❹ Castle Clinton National Monument. This circular red-stone fortress first stood on an island 200 ft from shore as a defense for New York Harbor. In 1824 it became Castle Garden, an entertainment and concert facility that reached its zenith in 1850 when more than 6,000 people (the capacity of Radio City Music Hall) attended the U.S. debut of the Swedish Nightingale, Jenny Lind. After landfill connected it to the city, Castle Clinton became, in succession, an immigrant processing center, an aquarium, and now a restored fort, museum, and ticket office for ferries to the ☞ **Statue of Liberty** and ☞ **Ellis Island.** (The ferry ride is one loop; you can get off at Liberty Island, visit the statue, then reboard any ferry and continue on to Ellis Island, boarding another boat once you have finished exploring the historic immigration facility there.) Inside the old fort are dioramas of lower Manhattan in 1812, 1886, and 1941. Outside the landward entrance is a statue titled *The Immigrants,* at the beginning of a broad mall that leads back across the park to the **Netherlands Memorial Flagpole,** which depicts the bead exchange that bought from the Native Americans the land to establish Fort Amsterdam in 1626. Inscriptions describe the event in English and Dutch. ☎ *212/344–7220 Castle Clinton; 212/269–5755 ferry information.* ⊡ *Castle Clinton: free; ferry: $7 round-trip.* ☉ *Daily 8:30–5; ferry departures daily every 30 mins 9:15–3:15 (more departures and extended hrs in summer).*

★ ☝ ❻ Ellis Island. Approximately 16 million men, women, and children first set foot on U.S. soil at this 27½-acre island's federal immigration facility between 1892 and 1924. In all, by the time Ellis Island closed for good in 1954, it had processed the ancestors of more than 40% of Americans living today. The island's main building, now a national monument, reopened in 1990 as the **Ellis Island Immigration Museum.** At its heart is the **Registry Room,** where inspectors once attempted to screen out "undesirables"—polygamists, criminals, the utterly destitute, and people suffering from contagious diseases. The cavernous **Great Hall,** where immigrants were registered, has gorgeous tiled arches by Rafael Guastavino; white-tile dormitory rooms overlook this grand space. The **Railroad Ticket Office** at the back of the main building houses exhibits on the *Peopling of America,* recounting 400 years of immigration history, and *Forced Migration,* focusing on the slave trade. The old kitchen and laundry building has been stabilized rather than restored so you can see what the island's buildings looked like prior to the restoration. Perhaps the most moving exhibit is the **American Immigrant Wall of Honor,** where the names of 420,000 immigrant Americans are inscribed along an outdoor promenade overlooking the Statue of Liberty and the Manhattan skyline. The names include Miles Standish, Priscilla Alden, George Washington's grandfather, Irving Berlin—and possibly an ancestor of yours. In 1998 the Supreme Court ruled that about 90% of Ellis Island is in New Jersey. For ferry information *see*

Castle Clinton National Monument, *above.* ☎ *212/363–3200 for Ellis Island; 212/883–1986 for Wall of Honor information.* 📷 *Free.*

⓬ **Federal Hall National Memorial.** On the steps of this Greek Revival building stands a regal statue, created in 1883, of George Washington, who on that site—then also Federal Hall—was sworn in as the nation's first president in 1789. The likeness was made by noted sculptor and relative of the president, John Quincy Adams Ward. After the capital moved to Philadelphia in 1790, the original Federal Hall became New York's City Hall, then was demolished in 1812 when the present City Hall (☞ The Seaport and the Courts, *below*) was completed. The current structure, built as a U.S. Customs House in 1842, was modeled on the Parthenon, a potent symbol for a young nation striving to emulate classic Greek democracy. It's now a museum featuring exhibits on New York and Wall Street. Guided site tours are sometimes available on request, and you can also pick up brochures that lead you on differently themed self-guided walking tours of downtown. ✉ *26 Wall St., at Nassau St.,* ☎ *212/825–6888.* 📷 *Free.* ☉ *Weekdays 9–5.*

⓯ **Federal Reserve Bank of New York.** Built in 1924, and enlarged in 1935, this neo-Renaissance structure made of sandstone, limestone, and ironwork goes five levels underground. The gold ingots in the vaults here are worth roughly $140 billion—reputedly a third of the world's gold reserves. Tours of the bank end at the $750,000 visitor center, which opened in 1997. Its dozen or so interactive computer terminals and displays provide almost as much information as an Economics 101 course—explaining such points as what the Federal Reserve Bank does (besides store gold), what the money supply is, and what causes inflation. ✉ *33 Liberty St., between Willaim and Nassau Sts.,* ☎ *212/ 720–6130.* 📷 *Free.* ☉ *1-hr tour by advance (at least 5 days) reservation, weekdays at 10:30, 11:30, 1:30, and 2:30.*

🖐 ⑨ **Fraunces Tavern.** Redbrick along one side, cream-color brick along another, the tavern's main building is a stately Colonial house with a white-marble portico and coffered frieze, built in 1719 and converted to a tavern in 1762. It was the meeting place for the Sons of Liberty until the Revolutionary War, and in 1783 George Washington here delivered a farewell address to his officers celebrating the British evacuation of New York. Later the building housed some offices of the fledgling U.S. government. Today a museum, restaurant, and bar compose this historic five-building complex. Fraunces Tavern contains two fully furnished period rooms and other displays of 18th- and 19th-century American history. The museum also offers family programs (such as crafts workshops and a scavenger hunt), lectures, workshops, and concerts. ✉ *54 Pearl St., at Broad St.,* ☎ *212/425–1778.* 📷 *Museum $2.50.* ☉ *Museum weekdays 10–4:45, weekends noon–4.*

NEED A BREAK? | The **brick plaza behind 85 Broad Street** is flanked by a variety of small restaurants. Order a take-out meal or snack and eat it out here on the benches, where you can watch busy office workers milling past and enjoy not being one of them.

⓾ **Hanover Square.** When the East River ran past present-day Pearl Street, this quiet tree-lined plaza stood on the waterfront and was the city's original printing-house square—on the site of 81 Pearl Street, William Bradford established the first printing press in the colonies. The pirate Captain Kidd lived in the neighborhood, and the graceful brownstone **India House** (1851–54), a private club at No. 1, used to house the New York Cotton Exchange.

OFF THE
BEATEN PATH

MUSEUM OF AMERICAN FINANCIAL HISTORY – On the site of Alexander Hamilton's law office (today the Standard Oil Building), this four-room museum displays artifacts of the financial market's history, including vintage ticker-tape machines and ticker tape from "Black Tuesday," October 29, 1929—the worst crash in the stock market's history. ⊠ *28 Broadway, just north of Bowling Green,* ☎ *212/908–4110.* ⊡ *$2.* ⊙ *Weekdays 11:30–3:30, or by appointment.*

★ ⑲ **Museum of Jewish Heritage–A Living Memorial to the Holocaust.** Housed in a granite hexagon rising 85 ft above ☞ **Robert F. Wagner Jr. Park,** just below ☞ **Battery Park City,** downtown's newest museum, opened in late 1997 after more than 15 years of planning, pays tribute to the 6 million Jews who perished in the Holocaust. Architect Kevin Roche's Star of David–shape building has three floors of exhibits demonstrating the dynamism of 20th-century Jewish culture. Artifacts of early 20th-century Jewish life are on the first floor: elaborate screens painted by a Budapest butcher for the fall harvest festival of Sukkoth, wedding invitations, and tools used by Jewish tradesmen. *The War Against the Jews,* on the second floor, details the rise of Nazism, the period's anti-Semitism, and the ravages of the Holocaust. A gallery covers the doomed voyage of the *St. Louis,* a ship of German Jewish refugees that crossed the Atlantic twice in 1939 in search of a safe haven. Signs of hope are on display, as well, including a trumpet that Louse Bannet (the "Dutch Louis Armstrong") played for three years in the Auschwitz-Birkenau inmate orchestra, and a pretty blue-and-white checked dress sewn in 1945 by Fania Bratt at the newly liberated Dachau concentration camp. The third floor covers postwar Jewish life and is devoted to the theme of Jewish renewal. The exhibition space's final gallery leads to a usually light-filled room lined with southwest-facing windows with a view of the harbor and the Statue of Liberty. ⊠ *18 1st Pl., Battery Park City,* ☎ *212/968–1800.* ⊡ *$7.* ⊙ *Sun.–Wed. 9–5, Thurs. 9–8, Fri. and eve of Jewish holidays 9–2.*

★ ☝ ⑧ **National Museum of the American Indian.** This museum, a branch of the Washington, D.C.–based Smithsonian Institution, is the first of its kind to be dedicated to Native American culture. Well-mounted exhibits examine the history and the current cultures of native peoples from all over the Americas through literature, dance, lectures, readings, film, and crafts. Contemporary Native Americans participate in visiting programs and work at all levels of the staff. George Gustav Heye, a wealthy New Yorker, amassed most of the museum's collection—more than a million artifacts including pottery, weaving, and basketry from the southwestern United States, painted hides from the Plains Indians of North America, carved jade from the Mexican Olmec and Maya cultures, and contemporary Native American paintings. The museum is in one of lower Manhattan's finest buildings: the ornate Beaux Arts **Alexander Hamilton U.S. Custom House** (1907). Above its base, massive granite columns rise to a pediment topped by a double row of statuary. Daniel Chester French, better known for the sculpture of Lincoln in the Lincoln Memorial in Washington, D.C., carved the lower statues, which symbolize various continents (left to right: Asia, the Americas, Europe, Africa). The upper row represents the major trading cities of the world. Inside, the display of white and colored marble couldn't be more remarkable. The semicircular side staircases are equally breathtaking. ⊠ *1 Bowling Green,* ☎ *212/668–6624.* ⊡ *Free.* ⊙ *Mon.–Wed. and Fri.–Sun. 10–5, Thurs. 10–8.*

⑬ **New York Stock Exchange (NYSE).** The largest securities exchange in the world, the NYSE nearly bursts from this relatively diminutive neoclassical 1903 building with an august Corinthian entrance—a fitting temple to the almighty dollar. Today's "Big Board" can handle a trillion shares of stock per day; in today's market-obsessed media, how those stocks do each day is news broadcast around the world. The third-floor interactive education center, which was completely renovated in 1997, has a self-guided tour, touch-screen computer terminals, video displays, a 15-minute-long film detailing the history of the exchange, and live guides to help you interpret the seeming chaos you'll see from the visitors' gallery overlooking the immense (50-ft-high) trading floor. ⊠ *Tickets available at 20 Broad St., between Wall St. and Exchange Pl.,* ☎ *212/656–5165.* ☜ *Free tickets distributed beginning at 8:45; come before 1 PM to assure entrance.* ☉ *Weekdays 9–4.*

★ ⑱ **Robert F. Wagner Jr. Park.** The link in the chain of parks that stretch from ☞ **Battery Park** to above the ☞ **World Financial Center,** this newest addition to the downtown waterfront may be the best of the bunch. Lawns, walks, gardens, and benches spill right down to the river. Behind these, a brown-brick structure rises two stories to provide river and harbor panoramas. A stream of runners and bladers flows by, making it a toss-up which is better: the people-watching or the views of the Statue of Liberty and Ellis Island. ⊠ *Between Battery Pl. and the Hudson River.*

❷ **Shrine of St. Elizabeth Ann Seton at Our Lady of the Rosary.** The rectory of the shrine is a redbrick Federal-style town house, an example of the mansions that used to line the street, with a distinctive portico shaped to fit the curving street. This house was built in 1793 as the home of the wealthy Watson family; Mother Seton and her family lived here from 1801 to 1803. She joined the Catholic Church in 1805, after the death of her husband, and went on to found the Sisters of Charity, the first American order of nuns. In 1975 she became the first American-born saint. Masses are held here daily. ⊠ *7–8 State St., near Whitehall St.,* ☎ *212/269–6865.* ☉ *Weekdays 6:30–5, weekends by appointment.*

★ ☟ ❶ **Staten Island Ferry.** The best transit deal in town is the Staten Island Ferry, a free 20- to 30-minute ride across New York Harbor, which provides great views of the Manhattan skyline, the Statue of Liberty, the Verrazano-Narrows Bridge, and the New Jersey coast. The classic blue-and-orange ferries embark on various schedules: every 15 minutes during rush hours, every 20–30 minutes most other times, and every hour after 11 PM and on weekend mornings. A word of advice, however: the ferry service runs swift, new low-slung craft that ride low in the water and have no outside deck space, so wait for one of the higher, more open old-timers. ☎ *718/390–5253.*

★ ☟ ❺ **Statue of Liberty.** Millions of immigrants to America first glimpsed their new land when they laid eyes on the Statue of Liberty, a monument that still ennobles all those who encounter it. *Liberty Enlightening the World,* as the statue is officially named, was sculpted by Frederic-Auguste Bartholdi and presented to the United States as a gift from France in 1886. Since then she has become a near-universal symbol of freedom and democracy, standing a proud 152 ft high on top of an 89-ft pedestal (executed by Richard Morris Hunt), on Liberty Island in New York Harbor. Emma Lazarus's sonnet *The New Colossus* ("Give me your tired, your poor, your huddled masses . . .") is inscribed on a bronze plaque attached to the statue's base. Gustav Eiffel designed the statue's iron skeleton. In anticipation of her centennial, Liberty underwent a long-overdue restoration in the mid-'80s and reemerged with great fanfare on July 4, 1986.

The top of the statue is accessible in two ways: an elevator ascends 10 stories to the top of the pedestal, or if you're in good shape, you can climb 354 steps (the equivalent of a 22-story building) to the crown. (Visitors cannot go up into the torch.) Be forewarned that in summer, two- to four-hour waits to walk up to the crown have become commonplace; come prepared to contend with the heat, both outside waiting in line (where there is no overhead protection) and inside the statue. Because the park service occasionally closes off the line to the crown as early as 2, it is vital to catch an early ferry out of ☞ **Castle Clinton National Monument**; the earliest leaves at 9:30 (9:15 in summer). Exhibits inside illustrate the statue's history, including videos of the view from the crown for those who don't make the climb. There are also life-size models of the Liberty's face and foot for the blind to feel and a pleasant outdoor café. ⊠ *Liberty Island,* ☎ *212/363–3200; 212/269–5755 for ferry information.* ⊠ *Free; ferry: $7 round-trip.*

🔟 **Trinity Church.** The present Trinity Church, the third on this site since an Anglican parish was established here in 1697, was designed in 1846 by Richard Upjohn. It ranked as the city's tallest building for most of the second half of the 19th century. The three huge bronze doors were designed by Richard Morris Hunt to recall Lorenzo Ghiberti's doors for the Baptistery in Florence, Italy. The church's Gothic Revival interior is surprisingly light and elegant. On the church's north side is a 2½-acre graveyard: Alexander Hamilton is buried beneath a whitestone pyramid, and a monument commemorates Robert Fulton, the inventor of the steamboat (he's actually buried in the Livingstone family vault, with his wife). ⊠ *74 Trinity Pl. (Broadway at the head of Wall St.),* ☎ *212/602–0872.* ⊙ *Weekdays 7–6, Sat. and Sun. 7–4.*

<table>
<tr><td>OFF THE
BEATEN PATH</td><td>**VIETNAM VETERANS MEMORIAL** – At this 14-ft-high, 70-ft-long rectangular memorial (1985), moving passages from news dispatches and the letters of servicemen and servicewomen have been etched into a wall of greenish glass. The brick plaza around it is often desolate on weekends. ⊠ *At end of Coenties Slip, between Water and South Sts.*</td></tr>
</table>

🔟 **Wall Street.** Named after a wooden wall built across the island in 1653 to defend the Dutch colony against the native Indians, ⅓-mi-long Wall Street is arguably the most famous thoroughfare in the world—shorthand for the vast, powerful financial community that clusters around the New York and American stock exchanges. "The Street," as it's also widely known, began its financial career with stock traders conducting business along the sidewalks or at tables beneath a sheltering buttonwood tree. Today it's a dizzyingly narrow canyon—look to the east, and you'll glimpse a sliver of East River waterfront; look to the west, and you'll see the spire of Trinity Church, tightly framed by skyscrapers, at the head of the street. For a startlingly clear lesson in the difference between Ionic and Corinthian columns, look at 55 **Wall Street**, now the location of the Regent Wall Street hotel. The lower stories were part of an earlier U.S. Customs House, built in 1836–42; it was literally a bullish day on Wall Street when oxen hauled its 16 granite Ionic columns up to the site. When the National City Bank took over the building in 1899, it hired architects McKim, Mead & White to redesign the building and in 1909 added the second tier of columns but made them Corinthian.

🔟 **World Financial Center.** The four towers of this complex, 34–51 stories high and topped with different geometric shapes, were designed by Cesar Pelli and serve as headquarters for companies including Merrill Lynch, American Express, and Dow Jones. The highlight for visitors is the soaring **Winter Garden** atrium, where pink-marble steps cascade into a vaulted plaza with 16 giant palm trees. A vast arched window overlooking the Hudson fills the Winter Garden's west facade, and 45 shops and restaurants surround the atrium, which is a great place to beat the summer heat. The center hosts traveling exhibits and performances in the atrium and in a nearby gallery. The outdoor plaza right behind the Winter Garden curls around a tidy little yacht basin; take in the view of the Statue of Liberty and read the stirring quotations worked into the iron railings. Or hop aboard one of the **Water Taxi**'s bright yellow boats for a sightseeing tour of the harbor or a quick trip across the Hudson to New Jersey's Liberty State Park (a great place for a picnic). The boats are tied up on the north side of the yacht basin, or you can call (☎ 201/985–1164) for more information.

At the northwest corner of the World Financial Center, the **New York Mercantile Exchange,** opened in 1997, houses the world's largest energy and precious metals market. A ground-floor museum details the history of the exchange; a second-floor gallery with a 150-ft-long window overlooks the trading floors. ⊠ *1 North End Ave.,* ☎ *212/299– 2000.* 🎟 *Free.* ☉ *Weekdays 9–5.*

At the end of North End Avenue, on the water's edge, is the terminal for **ferry service** to Hoboken, New Jersey (☎ 212/564–8846), across the Hudson River. It's a $2, eight-minute ride to Frank Sinatra's hometown, with a spectacular view of lower Manhattan. ⊠ *World Financial Center: West St. between Vesey and Liberty Sts.,* ☎ *212/945–0505.*

★ ☕ ⑯ **World Trade Center (WTC).** The mammoth WTC boasts New York's two tallest buildings, the third tallest in the world. Unlike some of the city's most beloved skyscrapers—the Empire State, the Chrysler, or the Flatiron buildings—the WTC's two 1,350-ft towers, designed by Minoru Yamasaki and built in 1972–73, are more engineering marvel than architectural masterpiece. To some they are an unmitigated design disaster—"totalitarian-modernist monstrosity," complains the *Wall Street Journal*'s Raymond Sokolov; to others their brutalist design and sheer magnitude give them the beauty of modern sculpture, and at night when they're lighted from within, they particularly dominate the Manhattan skyline.

The WTC, though, is much more than its most famous twins: it's a 16-acre, 12-million-square-ft complex resembling a miniature city, with a daytime population of 140,000 (including 40,000 employees and 100,000 business and leisure visitors). The WTC has seven buildings in all, arranged around a plaza modeled after, and larger than, Venice's Piazza San Marco; summer concerts are held on the plaza. Underground is a giant mall with 70 stores and restaurants and a network of subway and other train stations. A TKTS booth sells discount tickets to Broadway and off-Broadway shows (☞ Chapter 4) in the mezzanine of 2 WTC.

The WTC's biggest draw is **Top of the World,** the 107th-floor observation deck at 2 World Trade Center, from which the view potentially extends 55 mi (signs at the ticket window disclose how far you can see that day and whether the outdoor deck is open). The elevator ride alone is worth the price of admission, as you hurl a quarter of a mile into the sky in only 58 seconds. Recent additions to the deck include three helicopter simulation theaters with moving seats and a nightly laser light show. On nice days you can ride up another few floors to the Rooftop Observatory, the world's highest outdoor observation platform. It's offset 25 ft from the edge of the building and surrounded with a barbed-wire electric fence. Notice that planes and helicopters are flying *below* you. ⊠ *Ticket booth: 2 World Trade Center, mezza-*

nine level, ☎ *212/323–2340.* 🖭 *$12.* ☉ *June–Aug., daily 9:30 AM–11:30 PM; Sept.–May, daily 9:30–9:30.*

THE SEAPORT AND THE COURTS

New York's role as a great seaport is easiest to understand downtown, with both the Hudson River and East River waterfronts within walking distance. Although the deeper Hudson River came into its own in the steamship era, the more sheltered waters of the East River saw most of the action in the 19th century, during the age of clipper ships. This era is preserved in the South Street Seaport restoration, centered on Fulton Street between Water Street and the East River. Only a few blocks away you can visit another seat of New York history: the City Hall neighborhood, which includes Manhattan's magisterial court and government buildings.

Numbers in the text correspond to numbers in the margin and on the Lower Manhattan map.

A Good Walk

Begin at the intersection of Water and Fulton streets. Water Street was once the shoreline; the latter thoroughfare was named after the ferry to Brooklyn, which once docked at its foot (the ferry itself was named after its inventor, Robert Fulton [1765–1815]). On the 19th-century landfill across the street is the 11-block **South Street Seaport Historic District** ㉙, where you can catch a harbor cruise, visit a boat-building shop at the **South Street Seaport Museum,** shop along **Pier 17,** or simply take in the sea breezes.

Return to Fulton Street and walk away from the river to Broadway, to **St. Paul's Chapel** ㉑, the oldest (1766) surviving church building in Manhattan. Forking off to the right is **Park Row,** which was known as Newspaper Row from the mid-19th to early 20th centuries, when most of the city's 20 or so daily newspapers had offices there. In tribute to that past, a statue of Benjamin Franklin (who was, after all, a printer) stands in front of **Pace University,** farther up on Park Row. Two blocks north on Broadway is one of the finest skyscrapers in the city, the Gothic **Woolworth Building** ㉒, for which Frank Woolworth paid $13 million—in cash.

Between Broadway and Park Row is triangular **City Hall Park,** ㉓ originally the town common, which gives way to a slew of government offices. **City Hall** ㉔, built between 1803 and 1812, is unexpectedly modest. Lurking directly behind it is the **Tweed Courthouse** ㉕, named for the notorious politician William Marcy "Boss" Tweed. The small plaza east of Tweed Courthouse is used as a farmers' market on Tuesday and Friday, and it contains a Big Apple novelty that just might be worth the 25¢ it costs to get in—a public-toilet kiosk, like those found in Paris.

Directly opposite the Tweed Courthouse on the north side of Chambers Street incongruously sits an eight-story Beaux Arts château, the 1911 **Surrogate's Court** ㉖, also called the Hall of Records (✉ 31 Chambers St.). Across Centre Street from the château is the city government's first skyscraper, the imposing **Municipal Building** ㉗, built in 1914 by McKim, Mead & White. Just steps south of the Municipal Building, a ramp curves up into the pedestrian walkway over the **Brooklyn Bridge** ㉘. How romantic it would be to look out from the bridge on the docks of the "mast-hemmed Manhattan" of Walt Whitman's "Crossing Brooklyn Ferry." By the time the bridge was built, the Fulton Ferry was making more than 1,000 crossings per day. The

A NEW BREEZE IS BLOWING, DOWN BY THE RIVERSIDE

NEW YORK IS A CITY OF IS-LANDS, surrounded by ocean, bay, river, and sound. The entire waterfront of the five boroughs measures 578 mi, making it the longest and most diverse of any municipality in the country. Down by the water, the air is salty and fresh, the views exhilarating, the mood peaceful and quiet. Yet New Yorkers only recently recognized the potential pleasures of their waterfront. Today the waterfront's history is being rediscovered and its leisure opportunities invented anew.

New York grew up on the water, a shipping and shipbuilding town. After the opening of the Erie Canal in 1825, which connected it to the Great Lakes and the West for trade, the city became the preeminent port in the country, the gateway to the continent for exports and imports, the "golden door" for immigrants. At the turn of the last century, New York Harbor, crisscrossed with ferries, barges, tugs, canal boats, freighters, and passenger liners, was the busiest in the world.

The waterfront still resonates with its illustrious past. At the southern tip of Manhattan, near ☞ **Battery Park,** the street names suggest the contours of the island before settlers began to fill in the wetlands: Pearl Street, where mother-of-pearl shells were collected; Water Street, Front Street. The Port of New York was first centered near the ☞ **South Street Seaport** on the East River, where the preserved 18th-century streetscape and historic sailing vessels recall the clipper ship era. The port then moved to the wider, less turbulent Hudson River, named in 1609 by the explorer Henry Hudson; it was

here that Robert Fulton launched the first steamboat, where the ironclad Civil War ship *Monitor* was built, and where generations of Americans boarded ever grander transatlantic ocean liners from vast and ornate piers.

New York's rivers still churn with cruise ships, freighters, barges, and tugs, but work is underway to create a new greenbelt around Manhattan's edges, where industry once ruled. When the project is finished there will be long promenades for cyclists, rollerbladers and joggers, marinas for boating, and an expanded 500-acre ☞ **Hudson River Park.** Today, moving north from ☞ **Battery Park City,** you can stroll along an interim greenway the length of the proposed park—just imagine the tow pounds and parking lots as leafy spaces with playgrounds and beaches. At Christopher Street, walk out on ☞ **Greenwich Village**'s popular pier and take in the view back toward the fading vestiges of a Victorian-era waterfront: a panorama of warehouses (many converted to apartments and clubs) and smaller buildings that house cheap hotels and seedy bars. At 14th Street, remember Herman Melville, who worked as a customs inspector nearby. Just south of the ☞ **Chelsea Piers Sports and Entertainment Complex,** note the remains of the pier house where the *Titanic* was scheduled to conclude its maiden voyage. In summer, some old piers spring to life with public events— movies, dances, food festivals. (Call the **Hudson River Park Conservancy** [☎ 212/353–0366] for information.) For kayaking, boating, and parasailing on the Hudson, *see* Chapter 9.

—Elizabeth Hawes

East River is far quieter now, but the river-and-four-borough views from the bridge are no less wondrous.

Foley Square, a name that has become synonymous with the New York court system, opens out north of the Municipal Building. On the right, the orderly progression of the Corinthian colonnades of the **U.S. Courthouse** ㉙ and the **New York County Courthouse** ㉚ is a fitting reflection of the epigraph carved in the latter's frieze: THE TRUE ADMINISTRATION OF JUSTICE IS THE FIRMEST PILLAR OF GOOD GOVERNMENT. Turn to look across Foley Square at **Federal Plaza,** which sprawls in front of the grid-like skyscraper of the Javits Federal Building. The black-glass box to the left houses the U.S. Court of International Trade. Just south of it, at the corner of Duane and Elk streets, is the site of the **African Burial Ground,** ㉛ where thousands of African-Americans from the Colonial period were laid to rest.

Continue north up Centre Street past neoclassical civic office buildings to 100 Centre Street, the **Criminal Courts Building** ㉜, a rather forbidding construction with Art Moderne details. In contrast, the **Civil and Municipal Courthouse** (1960), across the way at 111 Centre Street, is an uninspired modern cube, although it, too, has held sensational trials. On the west side of this small square is the slick black-granite **Family Court,** built in 1975 (✉ 60 Lafayette St.), with its intriguing angular facade.

Turn left onto Leonard Street, which runs just south of the Family Court, and take a look at the ornate Victorian building that runs the length of the block on your left. This is the old **New York Life Insurance Company** headquarters (✉ 346 Broadway), an 1870 building that was remodeled and enlarged in 1896 by McKim, Mead & White. The ornate clock tower facing Broadway is now occupied by the avant-garde **Clocktower Gallery,** which is currently used as rehearsal space by various artists and is therefore not open to the public. The stretch of Broadway south of here is the subject of what is believed to be the oldest photograph of New York. The picture focuses on a paving project— to eliminate the morass of muddy streets—that took place in 1850.

From here a tasty day's-end meal in Chinatown (☞ Little Italy and Chinatown, *above*) is only a few blocks north and east. Or continue on Leonard Street to reach TriBeCa (☞ SoHo and TriBeCa, *below*).

TIMING
You can easily spend a half day at the Seaport, or longer if you browse in shops. The rest of the tour is just walking and takes about 1½ hours. The real Seaport opens well before the sun rises and clears out not much after, when fishmongers leave to make way for the tourists. Unless you're really interested in wholesale fish, however, you're best off visiting the Seaport when its other attractions are open. Try to do this during the week, so that the government offices will be open, too. Also, consider walking across the Brooklyn Bridge in the late afternoon for dramatic contrasts of light.

Sights to See

㉛ **African Burial Ground.** This grassy corner is part of the original area used to inter the city's earliest African-Americans—an estimated 20,000 were buried here until the cemetery was closed in 1794. The site was discovered during a 1991 construction project, and by an act of Congress it was made into a National Historical Landmark, dedicated to the people who were enslaved in the city between 1626 and Emancipation Day in New York, July 4, 1827. ✉ *Duane and Elk Sts.*

★ 28　**Brooklyn Bridge.** "A drive-through cathedral" is how the critic James Wolcott describes this engineering marvel, one of New York's noblest landmarks. Spanning the East River, the Brooklyn Bridge connected Manhattan island to the then-independent city of Brooklyn; before its opening, Brooklynites had only the Fulton Street Ferry to shuttle them across the river. John Augustus Roebling—a visionary architect, legendary engineer, metaphysical philosopher, and fervid abolitionist—is said to have first conceived of the bridge on an icy winter's day in 1852, when the frozen river prevented him from getting to Brooklyn, although, to be sure, he was by no means the first person so inconvenienced. Roebling spent the next 30 years designing, raising money for, and building the bridge. Alas, its construction was fraught with peril. Work began in 1867; two years later Roebling died of gangrene, after a wayward ferry boat rammed his foot while he was at work on a pier. His son, Washington, took over the project and was himself permanently crippled—like many others who worked on the bridge, he suffered from the bends. With the help of his wife, Emily, Washington nonetheless saw the bridge's construction through to completion.

The long struggle to build the span so captured the imagination of the city that when it opened in 1883 it was promptly crowned the "Eighth Wonder of the World." Its twin Gothic-arched towers, with a span of 1,595½ ft, rise 272 ft from the river below; the bridge's overall length of 6,016 ft made it four times longer than the longest suspension bridge of its day. From roadway to water is about 133 ft, high enough to allow the tallest ships to pass. The roadway is supported by a web of steel cables, hung from the towers and attached to block-long anchorages on either shore.

A walk across the bridge's promenade—a boardwalk elevated above the roadway and shared by pedestrians, in-line skaters, and bicyclists—takes about 40 minutes, from Manhattan's civic center to the heart of Brooklyn Heights (☞ Chapter 2); it is well worth traversing for the astounding views. Midtown's jumble of spires loom to the north, to the left of the Manhattan Bridge, and are especially scenic at night, when bright, variously hued lights show off the buildings to great effect. Mostly newer skyscrapers crowd lower Manhattan, while the tall ships docked at their feet, at South Street Seaport, appear to have sailed in straight from the 19th century. Governors Island sits forlornly in the middle of the harbor, which sweeps open dramatically toward Lady Liberty and off in the distance, the Verrazano-Narrows Bridge (its towers are more than twice as tall as those of the Brooklyn Bridge). A word of caution to pedestrians: do obey the lane markings on the promenade—pedestrians on the north side, bicyclists on the south—as the latter often pedal furiously.

24　**City Hall.** Reflecting not big-city brawn but the classical refinement and civility of Enlightenment Europe, New York's surprisingly decorous City Hall is a diminutive palace with a facade punctuated by arches and columns and a cupola crowned by a statue of Lady Justice. Built between 1803 and 1812, it was originally clad in white marble only on its front and sides, while the back was faced in more modest brownstone because city fathers assumed the city would never grow farther north than this. Limestone now covers all four sides. A sweeping marble double staircase leads from the domed rotunda to the second-floor public rooms. The small, clubby Victorian-style **City Council Chamber** in the east wing, has mahogany detailing and ornate gilding; the **Board of Estimate chamber,** to the west, has Colonial paintings and church-pew-style seating; and the **Governor's Room** at the head of the stairs, used for ceremonial events, is filled with historic portraits and furniture, including a writing table that George Washington used in 1789 when New York was the U.S. capital. The **Blue Room,** which was traditionally the mayor's office, is on the ground floor; it is now used for mayoral press conferences. On either side of the building are free interactive videos that dispense information on area attractions, civic procedures, City Hall history, mass transit, and other topics.

Although the building looks genteel, the City Hall politicking that goes on there can be rough and tumble. News crews can often be seen jockeying on the front steps, as they attempt to interview city officials, and frequent demonstrations and protests are staged immediately outside. One current political fracas involves City Hall itself: in late 1998, Mayor Giuliani closed the building to the public for security reasons. This action drew fire from City Council members who, as of this writing, were lobbying to re-open the building to visitors. ✉ *City Hall Park,* ☎ *212/788–6865 for tour information.* 🎟 *Free.* ☉ *Normally open weekdays 9–5 with public tours given at 10, 11, and 2 (reservations required), City Hall was closed to visitors and tours suspended until further notice in late 1998. Call for the latest information.*

㉓ City Hall Park. Originally used as a sheep meadow, this green spot was known in Colonial times as the Fields or the Common. It went on to become a graveyard for the impoverished, the site of an almshouse, and then the site of the notorious Bridewell jail before it became a park. As a park, the site was far from peaceful: it hosted hangings, riots, and political demonstrations. A bronze statue of patriot Nathan Hale, who was hanged in 1776 as a spy by the British troops occupying New York City, stands on the Broadway side of the park. In conjunction with the 1999 restoration of the park's 19th-century grandeur, archaeologists uncovered human bones, coins, clay pipes, and other remnants of the 17th and 18th centuries. ✉ *Between Broadway, Park Row, and Chambers St.*

㉜ Criminal Courts Building. Fans of crime fiction, whether on television, in the movies, or in novels, may recognize this rather grim Art Deco tower, which is connected by a skywalk (New York's Bridge of Sighs) to the detention center known as the Tombs. In *The Bonfire of the Vanities,* Tom Wolfe wrote a chilling description of this court's menacing atmosphere. ✉ *100 Centre St.*

㉗ Municipal Building. Who else but the venerable architecture firm McKim, Mead & White would the city government trust to build its first skyscraper in 1914? The roof section alone is 10 stories high, bristling with towers and peaks and topped by a 25-ft-high gilt statue of Civic Fame. New Yorkers come here to pay parking fines and get marriage licenses (and to get married, in a civil chapel on the second floor). An immense arch straddles Chambers Street (traffic used to flow through here). ✉ *1 Centre St., at Chambers St.*

㉚ New York County Courthouse. With its stately columns, pediments, and 100-ft-wide steps, this 1912 classical temple front is yet another spin-off on Rome's Pantheon. It deviates from its classical parent in its hexagonal rotunda, shaped to fit an irregular plot of land. The courtroom drama *Twelve Angry Men* was filmed here; the courthouse also hosts thousands of marriages a year. ✉ *60 Centre St., Foley Sq.*

㉑ St. Paul's Chapel. The oldest (1766) extant church in Manhattan, this Episcopal house of worship, built of rough Manhattan brownstone, was modeled on London's St. Martin-in-the-Fields (a columned clock tower and steeple were added in 1794). A prayer service here followed George Washington's inauguration as president; Washington's pew is in the north aisle. The gilded crown adorned with plumes above the pulpit is thought to be the only vestige in the city of British rule. In the adjoining cemetery, 18th-century headstones crumble in the shadows of glittering skyscrapers. ⊠ *Broadway and Fulton St.,* ☎ *212/602–0874.* ⊙ *Weekdays 9–3, Sun. 8–3.*

★ ☜ ❷⓿ **South Street Seaport Historic District.** Had it not been declared a historic district in 1967, this charming, cobblestone corner of the city would likely have been gobbled up by skyscrapers. The Rouse Corporation, which had already created Boston's Quincy Market and Baltimore's Harborplace, was hired to restore and adapt the existing historic buildings, preserving the commercial feel of centuries past. The result is a hybrid: part historic museum and part shopping mall. Many of its streets' 18th-, 19th-, and early 20th-century architectural details re-create the city's historic seafaring era.

At the intersection of Fulton and Water streets, the gateway to the Seaport, stands the ***Titanic* Memorial,** a small white lighthouse that commemorates the sinking of the RMS *Titanic* in 1912. Beyond it, Fulton Street, cobbled in blocks of Belgian granite, turns into a busy pedestrian mall. Just to the left of Fulton, at 211 Water Street, is **Bowne & Co.,** a reconstructed working 19th-century print shop. Continue down Fulton around to Front Street, which has wonderfully preserved old brick buildings—some dating from the 1700s. On the south side of Fulton Street is the seaport's architectural centerpiece, **Schermerhorn Row,** a redbrick terrace of Georgian- and Federal-style warehouses and countinghouses built in 1811–12. Today the ground floors are occupied by upscale shops, bars, and restaurants, and the **South Street Seaport Museum** (☎ 212/748–8600, ⊙ Apr.–Sept., daily 10–6, Thurs. 10–8; Oct.–Mar., Wed.–Mon. 10–5), which hosts walking tours and fantastic programs for kids (☞ Chapter 3). ⊠ *12 Fulton St.,* ☎ *212/732–7678 for events and shopping information.* ▨ *$6 (to ships, galleries, walking tours, Maritime Crafts Center, films, and other seaport events).*

Cross South Street under an elevated stretch of the FDR Drive to **Pier 16,** where historic ships are docked, including the *Pioneer,* a 102-ft schooner built in 1885; the *Peking,* the second-largest sailing ship in existence; the full-rigged *Wavertree*; and the lightship *Ambrose.* The Pier 16 ticket booth provides information and sells tickets to the museum, ships, tours, and exhibits. Pier 16 hosts frequent concerts and performances, has an ice rink in winter, and is the departure point for the one-hour Seaport Liberty Cruise (☎ 212/630–8888), which runs from late March through mid-December (▨ $12), as well as "The Beast," a 30-minute speedboat ride out to the Statue of Liberty (▨ $15).

To the north is **Pier 17,** a multilevel dockside shopping mall featuring standard-issue national chain retailers like the Gap, Banana Republic, and Nine West, among many others. Its weathered-wood rear decks make a splendid spot from which to sit and contemplate the river.

As your nose will surmise, the blocks along South Street north of the museum complex still house a working fish market, which has been in operation since the 1770s. More than 200 species of fish—from swordfish to sea urchin roe—are sold by the hundreds of fishmongers of the **Fulton Fish Market.** Get up early (or stay up late) if you want to see it: the action begins around 3 AM and ends by 8 AM. ☎ *212/748–8590.* ▨ *$10.* ⊙ *1st and 3rd Thurs. every month May–Oct. at 6 AM; tours by reservation only.*

NEED A
BREAK?
The cuisine at the fast-food stalls on Pier 17's third-floor **Promenade Food Court** is nonchain eclectic: Pizza on the Pier, Wok & Roll, Simply Seafood, and Salad Mania. What's really spectacular is the view from the tables in a glass-walled atrium.

㉖ **Surrogate's Court.** Also called the **Hall of Records**, this 1911 building is the most ornate of the City Hall court trio. In true Beaux Arts fashion, sculpture and ornament seem to have been added wherever possible to the basic neoclassical structure, yet the overall effect is graceful rather than cluttered. Filmmakers sometimes use its ornate lobby in opera scenes. A courtroom here was the venue for *Johnson v. Johnson,* where the heirs to the Johnson & Johnson fortune waged their bitter battle. ✉ *31 Chambers St., at Centre St.*

㉕ **Tweed Courthouse.** Under the corrupt management of notorious politician William Marcy "Boss" Tweed (1823–78), this Anglo-Italianate gem, one of the finest designs in the City Hall area, took some $12 million and nine years to build (it was finally finished in 1872, but the ensuing public outrage drove Tweed from office). Although it is imposing, with its columned classical pediment outside and seven-story rotunda inside, almost none of the boatloads of marble that Tweed had shipped from Europe made their way into this building. Today it houses municipal offices; it has also served as a location for several films, most notably *The Verdict.* ✉ *52 Chambers St.*

㉙ **U.S. Courthouse.** Cass Gilbert built this in 1936, convinced that it complemented the much finer nearby Woolworth Building, which he had designed earlier. Granite steps climb to a massive columned portico; above this rises a 32-story tower topped by a gilded pyramid, not unlike that with which Gilbert crowned the New York Life building uptown (☞ Murray Hill, Flatiron District, and Gramercy, *above*). This courthouse has been the site of such famous cases as the tax-evasion trial of hotel queen Leona Helmsley. ✉ *40 Centre St., Foley Sq.*

★ ㉒ **Woolworth Building.** Called the Cathedral of Commerce, this ornate white terra-cotta edifice was, at 792 ft, the world's tallest building when it opened in 1913. The Woolworth Company (now Venator Group), whose eponymous stores closed in 1997, sold the building and now leases only a few floors. The spectacular **lobby**'s extravagant Gothic-style details include sculptures set into arches in the ceiling; one of them represents an elderly F. W. Woolworth pinching his pennies, while another depicts the architect, Cass Gilbert, cradling in his arms a model of his creation. ✉ *233 Broadway, at Park Pl.*

2 EXPLORING THE OUTER BOROUGHS

Trips to the city's four outer boroughs offer very different experiences: a free ride on the Staten Island Ferry, a bracing walk across the noble Brooklyn Bridge, a subway ride along elevated tracks to Queens. Once you arrive, the pleasures are many: the Bronx's Wave Hill and world-renowned zoo; Brooklyn's world-class botanical garden and blocks of historic brownstones; Queens' movie museum and lively Greek community; and Staten Island's far-from-the-madding-crowd Tibetan Museum and historic Richmondtown.

By Amy
McConnell
and Matthew
Lore

Updated by
Margaret
Mittelbach and
Melisse Gelula

MANY VISITORS TO MANHATTAN notice the four outer boroughs—Brooklyn, Queens, the Bronx, and Staten Island—only from an airplane window or the deck of a Circle Line cruise. "Don't fall asleep on the subway," the wary tourist tells himself, "or you may end up in the Bronx!"

Driven over the river by astronomical rents, many Manhattanites discovered the outer boroughs in the late 1970s and 1980s. They found sky, trees, and living space among the 19th-century brownstones, converted industrial lofts, Art Deco apartment palaces, and tidy bungalows. They also found fascinating ethnic enclaves and a host of museums and parks. In fact, Manhattan's population of about 1.48 million is smaller than that of either Brooklyn (2 million) or Queens (1.95 million) and only slightly larger than that of the Bronx (1.2 million). Staten Island may be less populous (391,000), but it's 2½ times the size of Manhattan.

There are things to see and do in the outer boroughs that you simply won't find in Manhattan, and most are just a subway ride from midtown. Some Manhattanites may think the world begins and ends in their borough, but after a couple of beers they'll rave about their favorite place for cheesecake (Junior's in Brooklyn) or a great outdoor barbecue they had at their sister's mock-Tudor house (in Forest Hills, Queens); you may even have to listen to a story about a peak experience in the bleachers of Yankee Stadium . . . in the Bronx.

THE BRONX

The only one of New York's boroughs attached to the North American mainland, the Bronx has been an emblem of urban decay for the past 30 years, but it is actually as diverse and rich in personality as the rest of the city. The borough is home to a famous botanical garden and a world-renowned zoo. In addition, there's the friendly Italian neighborhood of Belmont; wealthy Riverdale, with its riverside estates; and of course, Yankee Stadium, the home of the New York Yankees.

The New York Botanical Garden, the Bronx Zoo, and Belmont

Within the 5-mi vicinity covered in this tour, you can stroll among gardens of roses (250 kinds), peonies (58 varieties), and medicinal herbs; watch red pandas swing from tree to tree; and sample biscotti at a third-generation bakery where patrons greet customers by name.

Numbers in the text correspond to numbers in the margin and on the New York Botanical Garden and Bronx Zoo map.

A Good Walk

The most direct route to the **New York Botanical Garden** ① is via Metro North to the Botanical Garden stop, which is right across from the garden's pedestrian entrance (cross Kazimiroff Boulevard to the garden's Mosholu Gate). As an alternative, take the D train or the No. 4 to Bedford Park Boulevard. From the subway station continue east on Bedford Park Boulevard (a 10-minute walk) to the Kazimiroff Boulevard entrance of the garden. You may be tempted to spend the whole day here; when you do decide to leave the garden grounds, exit via the main gate. Turn left and walk along Southern Boulevard (10 minutes); turn left onto Fordham Road and continue (5 minutes) to the Rainey

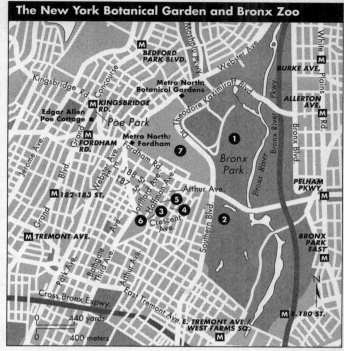

Gate entrance of the **Bronx Zoo** ② —another must-see sight that could easily hold you for most of the day.

Exit the zoo via Southern Boulevard, turn right, and walk two blocks to East 187th Street; this will lead you straight into the heart of **Belmont** ③, an Italian neighborhood. You'll know you're in the right place when you see the imposing brick structure of **Our Lady of Mt. Carmel Roman Catholic Church** ④ (at Belmont Avenue and East 187th Street), the spiritual heart of the neighborhood—but for the true Belmont experience, a walk through the **Arthur Avenue Retail Market** ⑤ and a dish of pasta at **Dominick's** ⑥ are essential.

Fordham University ⑦ occupies a large plot of land north of Belmont. To get here, backtrack on Arthur Avenue to East Fordham Road (head toward the tall Gothic tower in the distance) and turn left. For a peek at the handsome inner campus, turn right on Bathgate Avenue, which leads to a college gate manned by a security guard. Otherwise, continue on East Fordham Road three blocks to chaotic Fordham Plaza, nicknamed the Times Square of the Bronx. To return to Manhattan take the Metro North at East Fordham Road and Webster Avenue, or continue on East Fordham Road about four blocks up to the Fordham Road subway station (at the Grand Concourse) for the D train.

TIMING

The Bronx Zoo and the New York Botanical Garden are each vast and interesting enough to merit half a day or more. If you plan to visit both, start early and plan on a late lunch or early dinner in Belmont. Saturday is the best day to see the Italian neighborhood at its liveliest; on Sunday most stores are closed. The zoo and the garden are less crowded on weekdays—except Wednesday, when admission to both is free.

The Five Boroughs

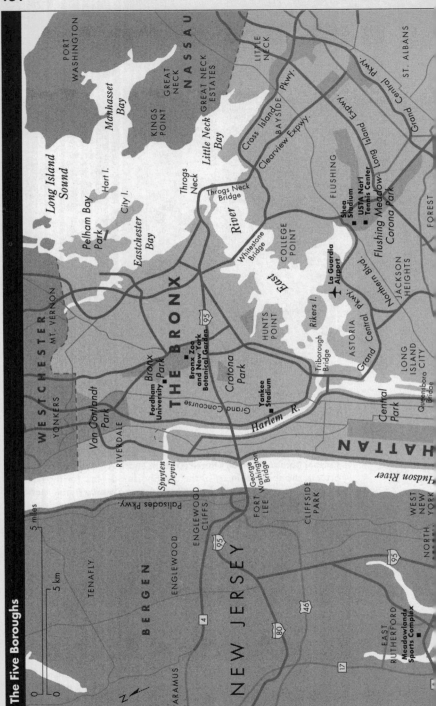

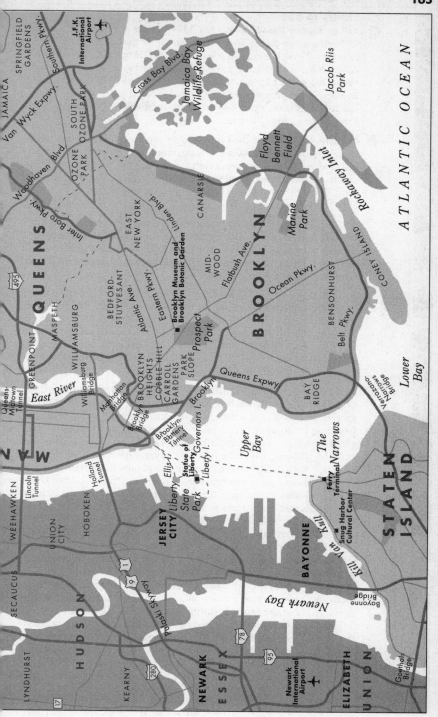

JAMAICA

SPRINGFIELD GARDENS

Southern Pkwy.

J.F.K. International Airport

Cross Bay Blvd

Jamaica Bay Wildlife Refuge

Jacob Riis Park

ATLANTIC OCEAN

Van Wyck Expwy.

Woodhaven Blvd.

SOUTH OZONE PARK

OZONE PARK

Inter Boro Pkwy.

EAST NEW YORK

Linden Blvd.

CANARSIE

Floyd Bennett Field

Rockaway Inlet

495

QUEENS

MASPETH

BEDFORD-STUYVESANT

Atlantic Ave.

Eastern Pkwy.

Brooklyn Museum and Brooklyn Botanic Garden

MID-WOOD

Flatbush Ave.

Marine Park

CONEY ISLAND

GREENPOINT

WILLIAMSBURG

Williamsburg Bridge

BROOKLYN HEIGHTS

COBBLE HILL

CARROLL GARDENS

PARK SLOPE

Prospect Park

Ocean Pkwy.

BENSONHURST

Belt Pkwy.

Queens-Midtown Tunnel

East River

Manhattan Bridge

Brooklyn Bridge

Brooklyn-Battery Tunnel

Brooklyn

Queens Expwy

BAY RIDGE

Lower Bay

N W

WEEHAWKEN

Lincoln Tunnel

UNION CITY

HOBOKEN

Holland Tunnel

Ellis I.

Statue of Liberty

Liberty State Park

Liberty I.

Governors I.

Upper Bay

The Narrows

Verrazano-Narrows Bridge

Ferry Terminal

Snug Harbor Cultural Center

STATEN ISLAND

SECAUCUS

HUDSON

UNION CITY

1

9

Pulaski Skyway

JERSEY CITY

BAYONNE

Kill Van Kull

LYNDHURST

KEARNY

280

Newark Bay

Bayonne Bridge

17

78

95

NEWARK

ESSEX

Newark International Airport

ELIZABETH

UNION

Goethals Bridge

Sights to See

❺ Arthur Avenue Retail Market (⊠ 2344 Arthur Ave.), an indoor shed sheltering more than a dozen stalls, is one of the last bastions of old-time New York. Here, amid piles of fresh produce, market vendors still sell fresh beef hearts and occasionally burst into song. There's also fresh rabbit and tripe, 15 types of olives, gnocchi *freschi, bufula* mozzarella, and low-price ceramic ware imported from Italy. Stop for a quick lunch—or at least a pizza square with toppings fresh from the market—at the Café al Mercato.

❸ Belmont. Often called the Little Italy of the Bronx, Belmont is where some 14,500 families socialize, shop, work, and eat, eat, eat. On Saturday afternoons, as residents rush around buying freshly baked bread and homemade salami, you may as well be in a small market town in Italy. Don't be surprised to hear people speaking Italian in the neighborhood's tidy streets.

On Arthur Avenue, the gastronomic temptations include the brick ovens at **Madonia Bros. Bakery** (⊠ 2348 Arthur Ave.), which have been turning out golden-brown loaves since 1918; the staff will fill cannoli fresh on request. ⊠ *Bordered by E. Fordham Rd., Southern Blvd., and Crescent and 3rd Aves.*

Around the corner at **Mount Carmel Wines & Spirits** (⊠ 612 E. 187th St.), there's a tremendous selection of Italian wines and grappas in beautiful bottles. One block down, **Danny's Pork Store** (⊠ 626 E. 187th St.) has homemade sausages. The **Catholic Goods Center** (⊠ 630 E. 187th St.) sells multilingual Bibles and greeting cards as well as religious art. Next to the Catholic Goods Center, **Borgatti's Ravioli & Egg Noodles** (⊠ 632 E. 187th St.) is known for its homemade pastas.

★ ☺ **❷ Bronx Zoo.** Opened in 1899, this 265-acre spread is the world's largest urban zoo. The zoo's nearly 6,500 animals, representing more than 600 species, mostly live in naturalistic, parklike settings, often separated from you by no more than a moat. Among the best exhibits are "Jungle World," an indoor Asian tropical rain forest filled with white-checked gibbons, tree kangaroos, Malayan tapirs, and other exotic critters; "Wild Asia," where tigers and elephants roam free on nearly 40 acres of open meadows and dark forests; and "the World of Darkness," a windowless building that offers a rare glimpse into the nightlife of such nocturnal creatures as fruit-eating bats and naked mole rats. From late May to early October, a thousand butterflies and moths of 35 species dazzle visitors to the "Butterfly Zone." In 1999 the zoo's most ambitious exhibit to date opened: the "Congo Gorilla Forest," a 6.5-acre re-creation of an African rain forest with treetop lookouts, wooded pathways, lush greenery, and 300 animals—including two lowland gorilla troops, okapi, and red-river hogs. Three different rides, including a shuttle bus, a monorail, and an aerial tram, offer various perspectives of the grounds during summer. The **Children's Zoo** (⊠ $1), open from April to October, has many hands-on learning activities, as well as a large petting zoo. Youngsters can see the world from an animal's perspective by crawling through a prairie dog tunnel and trying on a turtle's shell for size. If you're visiting the city with children during the holidays, don't miss the zoo's spectacular **Holiday Lights** show. Every evening between Thanksgiving and New Year's, the zoo is ablaze with thousands of twinkling lights decorating 50 giant-sized animal sculptures—from frogs to meercats (⊠ $6; ☉ Sun.–Thurs. 5:30–9, Fri.–Sat. 5:30–9:30). To get to the zoo, take the No. 2 subway to Pelham Parkway and walk three blocks west to the zoo's Bronx Parkway entrance. You can also take the **Metro North** train (☎ 212/532–4900) from Grand Central Terminal (☞ 42nd Street *in* Chapter 1) or catch the **Liberty Line** Bronx M11 express bus (☎ 718/652–8400) from mid-Manhattan. ⊠ *Bronx River Pkwy. and Fordham Rd.,* ☎ *718/367– 1010.* ⊠ *Apr.–Oct., Thurs.–Tues. $7.75; Nov.–Dec., Thurs.–Tues. $6; Jan.–Mar., Thurs.–Tues. $4; free Wed.* ☯ *Apr.–Oct., weekdays 10– 5, weekends 10–5:30; Nov.–Mar., daily 10–4:30; last ticket sold 1 hr before closing.*

❻ Dominick's. (☞ Chapter 5) There are no menus and no wine lists at this neighborhood favorite, where the question "What do you have?" is most often answered with "What do you want?" What you'll want is a heaping dish of traditional spaghetti with meatballs—some of the best you'll find in New York City—along with crusty bread and wine poured from a jug. The same family has been cooking at Dominick's since the 1940s, serving loyal fans at congested communal tables with red-and-white checked cloths. Expect to pay about $50 for two people. ⊠ *2335 Arthur Ave., at 187th St.,* ☎ *718/733–2807. Closed Tues.*

OFF THE
BEATEN PATH

EDGAR ALLAN POE COTTAGE – If you finish your tour while it's still light out, venture up Fordham Road to East Kingsbridge Road, turn right, and walk the short block to Poe Park, where the Bronx County Historical Society maintains the Edgar Allan Poe Cottage, open weekends only. It was here that Poe and his sickly wife, Virginia, sought refuge from Manhattan and from the vicissitudes of the writerly life between 1846 and 1849. Poe wandered the countryside on foot and listened to the sound of the church bells at nearby St. John's College Church (now Fordham University); word has it that these bells inspired one of his most famous poems, "The Bells." At night the park attracts loiterers; visit only by day. ⊠ *E. Kingsbridge Rd. and Grand Concourse,* ☎ *718/881–8900.* ⊠ *$2.* ☯ *Mid-Jan.–mid-Dec., Sat. 10–4, Sun. 1–5.*

❼ Fordham University. A small enclave of distinguished Collegiate Gothic architecture in the midst of urban sprawl, this university opened in 1841 as a Jesuit college and was, for a time, one of the country's preeminent schools. Fordham now has an undergraduate enrollment of nearly 6,000 and a second campus near Lincoln Center. Enter the grounds via Bathgate Avenue, a few blocks west of Arthur Avenue (the security guard may require you to show ID), to see **Old Rose Hill Manor Dig**; the **University Church,** whose stained glass was donated by King Louis Philippe of France (1773–1850); the pleasant **Edward's Parade** quadrangle in the center of campus; and **Keating Hall,** sitting like a Gothic fortress in the center of it all. Maps are posted around the campus and are available in the security office on your left inside the gate.

★ ❶ New York Botanical Garden. Considered one of the leading botany centers of the world, this 250-acre garden built around the dramatic gorge of the Bronx River is one of the best reasons to make a trip to the Bronx. The garden was founded by Dr. Nathaniel Lord Britton and his wife, Elizabeth. After visiting England's Kew Gardens in 1889, they returned full of fervor to create a similar haven in New York. The grounds encompass the historic **Lorillard Snuff Mill,** built by two French Huguenot manufacturers in 1840 to power the grinding of tobacco for snuff. Nearby, the Lorillards grew roses to supply fragrance for their blend. A path along the Bronx River from the mill leads to the garden's 40-acre **Forest,** the only surviving remnant of the forest that once covered New York City. Outdoor plant collections include the **Peggy Rockefeller Rose Garden,** with 2,700 bushes of 230 varieties; the spectacular rock garden, which displays alpine flowers; and the **Everett Children's Adventure Garden,** 8 acres of plant and science exhibits for children, including a boulder maze, giant animal topiaries, a wild wetland trail, and a plant discovery center.

In 1997 the historic **Enid A. Haupt Conservatory**—a Victorian-era glass house with 17,000 individual panes—reopened following a four-year renovation. Inside are year-round re-creations of misty tropical rain forests, arid deserts, and the Australian outback. Other indoor attractions can be found at the **Museum Building,** which houses a gardening shop, a library, and a world-renowned herbarium holding 6 million dried plant specimens.

To get to the Botanical Garden, take the **Metro North** train (☎ 212/532–4900) from Grand Central Terminal (☞ 42nd Street *in* Chapter 1) to the Botanical Gardens stop; or take the D or No. 4 trains to the Bedford Park Boulevard stop and walk eight blocks east to the entrance on Kazimiroff Boulevard. ✉ *200th St. and Kazimiroff Blvd.,* ☎ *718/817–8700.* ⊠ *Nov.–Mar. $1.50; Apr.–Oct. $3; free Sat. 10–noon and Wed.; Enid A. Haupt Conservatory $3.50; parking $4.* ☉ *Nov.–Mar., Tues.–Sun. 10–4; Apr.–Oct., Tues.–Sun. 10–6.*

❹ Our Lady of Mt. Carmel Roman Catholic Church. Rising like a beacon of faith above the neighborhood, this is the spiritual center of Belmont. In 1907, an Irish priest successfully petitioned the archdiocese for an Italian church to serve the new Italian immigrant community. Many residents of the neighborhood volunteered to help build the church in order to keep the costs down. ✉ *627 E. 187th St., between Hughes and Belmont Aves.,* ☎ *718/295–3770.* ☉ *Weekdays 9–1 and 2–9, weekends 9–9.*

NEED A
BREAK?

At **Egidio's Pastry Shop** (✉ 622 E. 187th St., ☎ 718/295–6077), a neighborhood favorite, you can sample handmade Italian pastries, washed down with a strong shot of espresso. The homemade gelati next door are top-notch.

OFF THE
BEATEN PATH

CITY ISLAND – At the extreme east end of the Bronx is a bona fide island 230 acres in extent. (To reach City Island, take the No. 6 subway to Pelham Bay Parkway and then catch the No. 29 bus.) Back in 1761, a group of the area's residents planned a port to rival New York's, but when that scheme hit the shoals, they returned to perennial maritime pursuits such as fishing and boatbuilding. City Island–produced yachts have included a number of America's Cup contenders. Connected to Pelham Bay Park by bridge, City Island has a maritime atmosphere, fishing boat rentals, and good seafood restaurants. Worth visiting is the **North Wind Undersea Museum,** with its displays devoted to marine mammal rescue and deep-sea diving. ✉ *610 City Island Ave.,* ☎ *718/885–0701. (Call for hours and fees.)*

WAVE HILL – In the mid- to late-19th century, Manhattan millionaires built summer homes in the Bronx suburb of Riverdale. Perched on a ridge above the Hudson River, the neighborhood commands stirring views of the New Jersey Palisades. Wave Hill, a 28-acre estate built in 1843, is the only one of these old estates open to the public. At various times Theodore Roosevelt, Mark Twain, and Arturo Toscanini all rented the property, which was donated to the city in 1960. Today the greenhouse and conservatory, plus 18 acres of exquisite herb, wildflower, and aquatic gardens, attract green thumbs from all over the world. Grand beech and oak trees adorn wide lawns, and elegant pergolas are hidden along curving pathways. Additional draws are gardening and crafts workshops, a summertime dance series, changing art exhibits, and a popular café overlooking the river and Palisades. From Manhattan you can drive up the Henry Hudson Parkway to Exit 21 and follow the signs to Wave Hill. Or you can take the Metro North Harlem line train to the Riverdale stop and walk up West 254th Street to Indepen-

dence Avenue, turn right and proceed to the main gate. ✉ *W. 249th St. and Independence Ave.,* ☎ *718/549–2055.* 🎫 *Mid-Mar.–mid-Nov. $4; Sat.* AM *and Tues. free; mid-Nov.–mid-Mar. free.* ☉ *Mid-Apr.–mid-Oct., Tues.–Thurs. and weekends 9–5:30, Fri. 9–dusk; mid-Oct.–mid-Apr., Tues.–Sun. 9–4:30; free garden tours Sun. 2:15.*

BROOKLYN

New York City's most populous borough is also its most popular—aside from Manhattan, that is. More people visit Brooklyn than any of the other outer boroughs, and still more come here to live. Several Brooklyn neighborhoods, particularly Brooklyn Heights, Park Slope, Cobble Hill, Carroll Gardens, and Fort Greene, are favored more than ever by young families and professionals, who are drawn by the dignified brownstone- and tree-lined streets, water views, handsome parks, friendly neighborhood businesses, and less than frenetic pace of life.

Brooklyn Heights, Cobble Hill, and Carroll Gardens

"All the advantages of the country, with most of the conveniences of the city," ran the ads for a real-estate development that sprang up in the 1820s just across the East River from downtown Manhattan. Brooklyn Heights—named for its enviable hilltop position—was New York's first suburb, linked to the city originally by ferry and later by the Brooklyn Bridge. Feverish construction led by wealthy industrialists and shipping magnates quickly transformed the airy heights into a fashionable upper-middle-class community. The Heights deteriorated in the 1930s. In the 1940s and 1950s, the area became a bohemian haven, home to writers including Carson McCullers, W. H. Auden, Arthur Miller, Truman Capote, Richard Wright, Alfred Kazin, Norman Mailer, and Hart Crane. Given the neighborhood's European feel and convenient setting, it's not hard to imagine why they came.

Thanks to the vigorous efforts of preservationists in the 1960s, much of the Heights was designated New York's first historic district. Some 600 buildings more than 100 years old, representing a wide range of American building styles, are in excellent condition today. Cranberry and Pineapple are just two of the unusual street names in the Heights. Rumor has it that these names were created by a certain Sarah Middagh, who disliked the practice of naming streets for the town fathers and instead named them after various fruits.

A short hop across Atlantic Avenue from Brooklyn Heights, Cobble Hill is another quiet residential area of leafy streets lined with notable town houses built by 19th-century New York's upper middle class. The neighborhood is rapidly becoming one of Brooklyn's most sought-after; on weekends the sidewalks are busy with residents pushing strollers, walking dogs, or chatting with their neighbors. A bit farther south, around President Street, Cobble Hill turns into the historically Italian, working-class section of Carroll Gardens, a neighborhood distinguished by deep blocks that allow for front yards that are unusually large, at least by New York standards. It might be hard to believe you're in New York City, when, on nice days, residents can be found tending their front-yard gardens or washing their cars.

Numbers in the text correspond to numbers in the margin and on the Brooklyn Heights, Cobble Hill, and Carroll Gardens map.

A Good Walk

Take the No. 2 or 3 subway from Manhattan to Clark Street, or the No. 4 or 5 to Borough Hall and walk up Court Street to Clark Street. From Clark turn left on Henry Street toward Pineapple Street. From here you'll be able to see the blue towers of the **Manhattan Bridge,** linking Brooklyn to Manhattan, and a view of the **Brooklyn Bridge** will soon come into view. (As an alternative, walk across the Brooklyn Bridge (☞ The Seaport and the Courts *in* Chapter 1). At the bridge's Tillary Street terminus, turn right, walk two blocks to Cadman Plaza West, and swing right to Clark Street, where you'll see the No. 2 or 3 subway entrance.)

Turn left onto Orange Street. On the north side of the block (the right-hand side of the street) between Henry and Hicks streets is a formidable institution, the **Plymouth Church of the Pilgrims** ①, the center of abolitionist sentiment in the years before the Civil War. Turn right on Hicks Street and follow it to Middagh Street (pronounced *mid*-awe). At its intersection with Willow Street is **24 Middagh Street** ②, the oldest home in the neighborhood. Venture a few steps west on Middagh to see the Manhattan Bridge reaching over the East River in the shadow of the dominating **Watchtower** building. The area is called DUMBO, a burgeoning artsy and residential neighborhood named for its industrial location—*D*own *U*nder the *M*anhattan *B*ridge *O*verpass.

Backtrack on **Willow Street** ③ and observe the masterful local architecture between Clark and Pierrepont streets (Nos. 149, 155, 157, and 159 are especially notable). As you turn right on Pierrepont Street heading toward the river, glance down **Columbia Heights** ④ to your right, where the brownstones are particularly elegant and well-maintained.

Pierrepont Street ends at the **Brooklyn Heights Promenade** ⑤, one of the most famous vista points in all of New York City. This is a great place for a picnic, with take-out food from one of the many Montague Street restaurants or provisions from the exotic food stores on nearby Atlantic Avenue. After you've soaked in the views from the Promenade, leave it via Montague Street. Look left to see Nos. 2 and 3 Pierrepont Place, two brick-and-brownstone palaces built in the 1850s. On your right lies Montague Terrace, where Thomas Wolfe lived when he was finishing *You Can't Go Home Again.* Auden lived a few doors away. Continue east along this commercial spine of the Heights, past a variety of ethnic restaurants, coffee shops, and retail clothing and gift stores. At the northwest corner of Montague and Clinton streets is **St. Ann's and the Holy Trinity Church** ⑥, known for its early-American stained-glass windows and performing-arts center.

Beyond Clinton on the north side of Montague Street, note an interesting and eclectic row of banks: **Chase** (✉ 177 Montague St.), a copy of the Palazzo della Gran Guardia in Verona, Italy; a **Citibank** (✉ 181 Montague St.) that looks like a latter-day Roman temple; and the Art Deco **Municipal Credit Union** (✉ 185 Montague St.). Farther down the street you'll find the historic **Brooklyn Borough Hall** ⑦, or you can detour a block north up Clinton Street to the elegant Romanesque red-brick **Brooklyn Historical Society** ⑧, slated to be closed for renovation throughout 2000.

Return south along Clinton Street, and then turn right onto Remsen Street. At the corner of Remsen and Henry streets, stop to take in the Romanesque Revival **Our Lady of Lebanon Maronite Church** ⑨. Continue west on Remsen Street and then turn left onto Hicks Street to visit the 1847 Gothic Revival **Grace Church** at No. 254. Across Hicks Street is Grace Court Alley, a traditional mews with a score of beau-

Brooklyn Heights, Cobble Hill, and Carroll Gardens

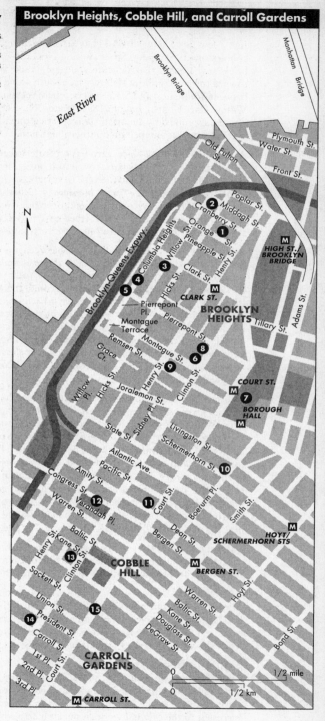

tifully restored redbrick carriage houses, which were once stables for the mansions on Remsen and Joralemon streets.

Just a few more steps down Hicks Street, turn right and stroll down cobblestoned Joralemon Street, noting Nos. 29–75, a row of modest brick row houses that delicately sidestep their way down the hill toward the river. Follow Willow Place south along the peaceful block between Joralemon and State streets, where the quietly elegant former Willow Place Chapel, built in 1876, stands. Nos. 43–49, four redbrick houses, are linked by a majestic two-story colonnade that looks transplanted from an antebellum Southern mansion.

At the end of Willow Place, turn left on State Street and follow it past Hicks and Henry streets back to Clinton Street. If you're so inclined, make a left on Clinton and then the next right on Schermerhorn Street to visit the **New York City Transit Museum** ⑩. Otherwise turn right down Clinton to Atlantic Avenue, a busy thoroughfare crowded with Middle Eastern restaurants and, farther east between Hoyt and Bond streets, more than a dozen antique furniture stores.

Atlantic Avenue is the dividing line between the neighborhoods of Brooklyn Heights and Cobble Hill. For a taste of the latter, go two blocks south down Clinton Street to Amity Street. You may want to turn left to **197 Amity Street,** ⑪ where Jennie Jerome, the mother of Winston Churchill, was born in 1854. Return to Clinton and go one more block south, where on the west side of the street is **Cobble Hill Park** ⑫, bordered by Verandah Place, a graceful row of converted stable buildings. Proceed three blocks south down Clinton Street, which is lined with distinguished Romanesque Revival, neoclassical, and Italianate brownstones. At 320 Clinton Street stands the Episcopal **Christ Church** ⑬, designed by Richard Upjohn.

Another four blocks down Clinton Street, near President Street, Cobble Hill gives way to the largely Italian neighborhood of Carroll Gardens. Wander down President, Carroll, and 1st and 2nd places to see the lovingly tended gardens where the abundance of religious statuary attests to Catholic influence in the neighborhood. Before leaving Clinton Street, stop for a look at the **F. G. Guido Funeral Home** ⑭ (on the northwest corner at Carroll Street), one of the city's finest examples of a Greek Revival town house. Turn left (east) on Carroll Street to **Court Street** ⑮, the main commercial thoroughfare of the neighborhood. Carroll Gardens peters out about five blocks south (to the right); from here it's about 10 blocks back to Atlantic Avenue, to the north.

To continue on to the Park Slope tour, take the F train from the Carroll Street subway station (at the intersection of Carroll and Smith streets) three more stops toward Coney Island, to the 7th Avenue stop.

TIMING
Allow three to four hours for a leisurely tour of these three neighborhoods, more if you plan on stopping for a picnic along the Promenade or a meal along Montague Street. Try to come on a clear, sunny day, when the view from the Promenade is most spectacular.

Sights to See

★ ❼ **Brooklyn Borough Hall.** Built in 1848 and thoroughly restored in the late 1980s, this Greek Revival landmark is arguably Brooklyn's handsomest building. The hammered-brass top of the cast-iron cupola (a successor to the original wooden one, which burned in 1895) was restored by the same French craftsmen who restored the Statue of Liberty. The stately building is adorned with Tuckahoe marble both inside and out; other highlights are the square rotunda and the two-story Beaux

Arts–style courtroom with plaster columns painted to look like wood. Today the hall serves as the office of Brooklyn's borough president. On Tuesday and Saturday a city greenmarket sets up on the flagstone plaza in front. ✉ *209 Joralemon St.,* ☎ *718/875–4047.* ✆ *Free.* ☾ *Tours Tues. 1–2:30; groups should telephone ahead.*

★ ☙ ❺ **Brooklyn Heights Promenade.** Stretching from Orange Street on the north to Remsen Street on the south, this ⅓-mi-long sliver of park hangs above Brooklyn's industrial waterfront like one of Babylon's fabled gardens. Cantilevered over two lanes of the Brooklyn–Queens Expressway, the esplanade offers enthralling views of the Manhattan skyline. Circling gulls squawk, tugboats honk, and the city seems like a magical place. This is a terrific vantage point from which to admire the Brooklyn Bridge, the historic steel suspension bridge designed by John Augustus Roebling and completed in 1883 (☞ The Seaport and the Courts *in* Chapter 1). The small island to your left is Governors Island, a former military installation.

❽ **Brooklyn Historical Society.** Erected in 1878–80, this elegant redbrick museum and library was the first major structure in New York to feature terra-cotta ornamentation, such as capitals, friezes, and lifelike busts. A major renovation that shut the building down is slated for completion by 2000, when its exhibits on Brooklyn history and its impressive library will once again be accessible. Other programs include Saturday neighborhood walking tours, and off-site exhibitions; call for details. ✉ *128 Pierrepont St.,* ☎ *718/624–0890.*

❸ **Christ Church.** This sandstone Episcopal church, with its lean tower-dominated facade, was designed by the prolific architect Richard Upjohn, who lived nearby at 296 Clinton Street. (He also designed Grace Church, at 254 Hicks Street, and ☞ **Our Lady of Lebanon Maronite Church.**) Inside, the pulpit, lectern, and altar are the work of Louis Comfort Tiffany; outside, the tranquil churchyard is enclosed by a wrought-iron fence. ✉ *320 Clinton St., at Kane St.,* ☎ *718/624–0083.* ☾ *Wed. 6:30 PM, Sun. 11 AM.*

☙ ❿ **Cobble Hill Park.** This green oasis, one of the first vest-pocket parks in the city, has marble columns at its entrances, antique benches and tables, and a playground at one end. Bordering the park's south side is **Verandah Place,** a charming row of converted stable buildings; Thomas Wolfe once resided in the basement of No. 40 (one of his many residences in the borough). ✉ *Congress St. between Clinton and Henry Sts.*

NEED A BREAK? Between Court and Clinton streets on Atlantic Avenue are a half dozen Middle Eastern markets and eateries. The best of these is 45-year-old **Sahadi Importing** (✉ 187–189 Atlantic Ave., ☎ 718/624–4550), where serious cooks stock up on cheap and delicious dried fruits, nuts, oils, olives, and spices, among other things. **Damascus Bread & Pastry** (✉ 195 Atlantic Ave., ☎ 718/625–7070) purveys stellar baklava, spinach pie, and still-warm pita bread.

❹ **Columbia Heights.** Among the majestic residences on this street, the brownstone grouping of **Nos. 210–220** is often cited as the most graceful in New York. Norman Mailer lives on this street, and from a rear window in **No. 111,** John Roebling's son Washington, who in 1869 succeeded his father as chief engineer for the Brooklyn Bridge, directed the building of the bridge from his sickbed.

❺ **Court Street.** The main commercial thoroughfare of Cobble Hill and Carroll Gardens, Court Street overflows with activity in its cafés, restaurants, bookstores, old-fashioned bakeries, and a multiplex movie theater. In Cobble Hill, the **Attic** (✉ 220 Court St., ☎ 718/643–9535) is a small antiques store worth seeking out. In Carroll Gardens, fresh pasta, mozzarella, sausages, olives, and prepared dishes are available at a number of shops, including **Pastosa Ravioli** (✉ 347 Court St., ☎ 718/625–9482), where the gnocchi is particularly recommended, and **Caputo's Dairy** (✉ 460 Court St., ☎ 718/855–8852), with a wide selection of homemade pastas and sauces. Italian sausages, *soppressata* (pork sausage), and homemade mozzarella can be had at **G. Esposito's & Sons** (✉ 357 Court St., ☎ 718/875–6863), the neighborhood's best meat store.

NEED A BREAK?   With its whirring ceiling fans, painted tin ceiling, and old wooden tables, the **Roberto Cappuccino Caffè and Tea Room** (✉ 221 Court St., at Wycoff St., ☎ 718/858–7693) is a dimly lit, relaxing spot for soup, sandwiches, coffee, and tea. At **Shakespeare's Sister** (✉ 270 Court St., at Kane St., ☎ 718/694–0084), a café and emporium of scented candles and handmade cards, you can soothe yourself with any one of a great variety of teas and light snacks while viewing art exhibits—usually featuring work by women.

⑭ **F. G. Guido Funeral Home.** Once the John Rankin residence, this freestanding three-story redbrick building, built in 1840, is one of the city's finest examples of a Greek Revival town house. Its recessed portal, bordered by limestone and topped with a fanlight, is particularly distinguished. ✉ *440 Clinton St.*

⑩ **New York City Transit Museum.** Inside a converted 1930s subway station, the Transit Museum displays 18 restored classic subway cars and has an operating signal tower. Its gift shop is a mother lode of subway-inspired memorabilia. ✉ *Boerum Pl. at Schermerhorn St.,* ☎ *718/243–3060.* ⌦ *$3.* ◷ *Tues.–Fri. 10–4, weekends noon–5.*

⑪ **197 Amity St.** Jennie Jerome, the mother of Winston Churchill, was born in this modest house in 1854. A plaque at 426 Henry Street, southwest of here, incorrectly identifies *that* building as the famous woman's birthplace. The Henry Street address is actually where Jennie's parents lived before she was born.

⑨ **Our Lady of Lebanon Maronite Church.** One of the oldest Romanesque Revival buildings in the country, this Congregational church was designed by Richard Upjohn in 1844. Its doors, which depict Norman churches, were salvaged from the 1943 wreck of the ocean liner *Normandie*. ✉ *113 Remsen St., at Henry St.,* ☎ *718/624–7228.* ◷ *Sun. 8:30–noon or by appointment.*

❶ **Plymouth Church of the Pilgrims.** Thanks to the stirring oratory of Brooklyn's most eminent theologian, Henry Ward Beecher (brother of Harriet Beecher Stowe, author of *Uncle Tom's Cabin*), this house of worship was the vortex of anti-slavery sentiment in the years before the Civil War. Because it provided refuge to American slaves, the church, which was built in 1850, is known as the Grand Central Terminal of the Underground Railroad. Its windows, like those of many other neighborhood churches, were designed by Louis Comfort Tiffany. In the gated courtyard beside the church, a statue of Beecher depicts refugee slaves crouched in hiding behind the base. Nearby, at **22 Willow Street,** Beecher's house still stands—a prim Greek Revival brownstone. ✉ *Orange St. between Henry and Hicks Sts.,* ☎ *718/624–4743.* ◷ *Tours Sun. 12:15 or by appointment.*

6 **St. Ann's and the Holy Trinity Church.** The church, a National Historic Landmark, dazzles with 60 of the first stained-glass windows made in the United States. More than two-thirds have been restored to date; through the **St. Ann's Center for Restoration and the Arts,** visitors can see the restoration process up close. In 1980 the church created its own performing arts center, Arts at St. Ann's, where a wide variety of non-classical music—jazz, blues, world and new music, musical theater, and experimental opera—is performed March–May and October–December. The church is open only for performances and Sunday at 11 AM for Episcopal worship services. ⊠ *157 Montague St., at Clinton St.,* ☎ *718/834–8794 for tours; 718/858–2424 for box office.* ☉ *Box office Tues.–Sat. noon–6.*

2 **24 Middagh Street.** This 1824 Federal-style clapboard residence with a mansard roof is the oldest home in the neighborhood. Peer through a door in the wall on the Willow Street side for a glimpse of the cottage garden and carriage house in the rear.

3 **Willow Street.** One of the prettiest and most architecturally varied blocks in Brooklyn Heights is Willow Street between Clark and Pierrepont streets. **Nos. 155–159** are three distinguished brick Federal row houses that were allegedly stops on the Underground Railroad.

OFF THE BEATEN PATH

WILLIAMSBURG – Calling it the new SoHo, New Yorkers are quickly moving into the few remaining converted lofts and affordable apartments in this neighborhood along the East River. Before all the hullabaloo, generations of immigrants—largely Jews, Poles, and Puerto Ricans—settled in this industrial section of Brooklyn, forming autonomous, prosperous communities side by side. Now the area is taking on a distinctly young, white and artsy face, and residents are rallying to beautify a waterfront where they mount frequent outdoor art installations. Today independently owned stores, art galleries, and restaurants line Bedford Avenue, the main drag, revealing Williamsburg's future rather than its past. From Manhattan, take the Carnasie–Rockaway Parkway bound L-train east one stop to **Bedford Avenue,** where everything is close at hand. Shops include the hyper-stylish boutique **Max & Roebling** (189 Bedford Ave., at N. 7th St., ☎ 718/387–0045); vintage housewares purveyor **Ugly Luggage** (214 Bedford Av., between N. 5th and N. 6th Sts., ☎ 718/ 384–0724); and **Beacon's Closet** (110 Bedford Ave., ☎ 718/486– 0816), full of used clothing and accessories. If you're hungry, try the coffee and sandwiches at **L Café** (189 Bedford Ave., between N. 7th and N. 8th Sts., ☎ 718/388–6792); the cheap noodles at **Plan Eat Thailand** (184 Bedford Ave., between N. 7th and N. 8th Sts., ☎ 718/ 599–5758); or the Mexican fare at **Vera Cruz,** (195 Bedford Ave. between N. 6th and N. 7th Sts., ☎ 718/599–7914). For the culturally inclined, there are art galleries such as **Pierogi 2000** (167 N. 9th St., ☎ 718/599–2144) and **Galapagos** (70 N. 6th St., ☎ 718/782–5188), which also shows films.

Park Slope and Prospect Park

Park Slope grew up in the late 1800s and is today one of Brooklyn's most comfortable places to live. The largely residential neighborhood has row after row of immaculate brownstones dating from its turn-of-the-century heyday, when Park Slope had the nation's highest per-capita income. The "Park" in Park Slope refers to Prospect Park, one of New York's most revered green spaces, encompassing 526 acres of meadow and woodland, man-made ponds and lakes, miles of drives and paths, plus a zoo, skating rink, concert bandshell, and much more. Nearby are the Grand Army Plaza, with its Soldiers' and Sailors' Memorial Arch; the stately Brooklyn Museum and Brooklyn Library; and the scenic Brooklyn Botanic Garden, a worthwhile destination virtually any time of year.

Numbers in the text correspond to numbers in the margin and on the Park Slope and Prospect Park map.

A Good Walk

Start your tour at **7th Avenue,** ① the neighborhood's commercial center, accessible by the D or F train (7th Ave. stops) and by the Nos. 2 and 3 (Grand Army Plaza stop). The beginning of this walk is closer to the D, 2, or 3 train. Turn east from 7th Avenue onto Lincoln Place to find the **Montauk Club** ②, whose sumptuous Venetian-palace style proclaims its standing as one of Brooklyn's most prestigious men's clubs. Make your way south along 8th Avenue, sampling the brownstones on various streets along the way (President and Carroll streets are especially handsome), until you reach **Montgomery Place** ③, with its remarkable row of Romanesque Revival brownstones.

From Montgomery Place, walk one block east along Prospect Park West to **Grand Army Plaza** ④, whose center is dominated by the **Soldiers' and Sailors' Memorial Arch,** patterned on the Arc de Triomphe in Paris. Southeast of the plaza is the main entrance to the 526-acre **Prospect Park,** designed by Frederick Law Olmsted and Calvert Vaux. The designers liked it better than their other creation, Manhattan's Central Park (☞ Chapter 1), because no streets divide it and no skyscrapers infringe on its borders. It is regarded by Olmsted aficionados as among his very best work, and a large number of restoration projects are now helping to revitalize the park.

Prospect Park's winding paths and drives, undulating hills, unexpected vistas, and open spaces serve up unanticipated pleasures at every turn. The best way to experience the park is to walk the entirety of its 3.3-mi circular drive and make detours off it as you wish. On summer evenings and weekends year-round, when the drive is closed to vehicular traffic, joggers, skaters, and bicyclists have it to themselves.

Immediately upon entering the park, veer right on the circular drive. Take a moment to admire the 75-acre **Long Meadow,** one of New York's greatest open spaces and a haven for picnickers, kite fliers, and dog owners. Remarkably, more than 130 years after the park's construction, the view down the Long Meadow from here still takes in no buildings—only grass, trees, and sky. A short distance down the drive, just beyond a circular playground on your right, a small access road leads you to **Litchfield Villa** ⑤, an elaborate Italianate mansion and home of the park's administrative offices. Continuing on the circular drive from the villa, you'll next come to two structures on your left—the **Picnic House,** frequently rented for weddings, and, a moment later, the **Tennis House** ⑥, home to the Brooklyn Center for Urban Education.

To the left, beyond the Picnic House and the Tennis House, lies the **Ravine,** the wooded core of the park. The Ravine vividly conveys a sense of wilderness and demonstrates Olmsted's genius at juxtaposing vastly different landscapes. While an ongoing renewal project is underway, it is scheduled to be closed at least through 2000, although one path is open through the area and seasonal guided tours are given (call the Prospect Park hotline for details, ☏ 718/965–8999). Off to the right, just a few steps farther, is the **band shell** ⑦, site of the park's enormously popular free summer performing-arts series.

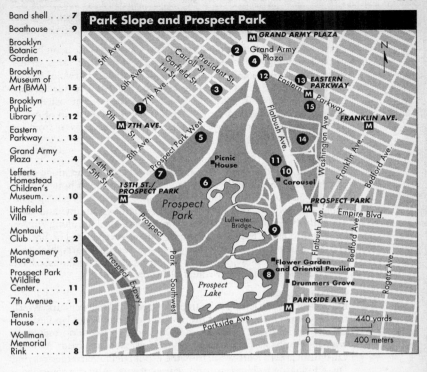

Park Slope and Prospect Park

Continue along the circular drive, which curves to the left around the half dozen baseball diamonds used by local leagues between Memorial Day and Labor Day; the diamonds mark the far southern end of Long Meadow. Down the hill on your left is the glorious 60-acre **Prospect Lake,** a refuge for waterfowl, including a few resident swans. Past the Ocean Parkway/Coney Island Avenue park entrance, as you reach the lake's outer reaches, you'll come upon **Drummers Grove** on the right. Designated an official Prospect Park site in 1996, this area has long been a popular informal weekend gathering spot for Caribbean and African-American musicians, many of whom live in the neighborhood bordering the park's eastern flank. Sunday afternoons from mid-March through mid-September, dozens of drummers, chanters, dancers, and other revelers get down, joined by an audience of bicyclists, joggers, and skaters lulled by the mesmerizing beat.

Just past the grove, on the left, is **Wollman Memorial Rink** ⑧. Moving on, you'll see the **Flower Garden and Oriental Pavilion** and reach the **Boathouse** ⑨. Unfortunately, construction of the Wollman Rink destroyed this area's original close connection with Prospect Lake. In the early days an orchestra would play on an island just offshore while spectators strolled along terraces and radial pathways. Busts of composers including Mozart and Beethoven added to the setting, and visitors sat in the beautiful pavilion, an open shelter supported by eight hand-painted wrought-iron columns and illuminated within by a central stained-glass skylight. Today the area is usually unwelcomingly deserted, and during the winter music blares from the rink.

Not far beyond the Boathouse, off on the eastern edge of the park (to your right) is the **carousel,** and beyond that the **Lefferts Homestead Children's Museum** ⑩ and the **Prospect Park Wildlife Center** ⑪, a small zoo.

From here, you're just a short walk up the circular drive back to Grand Army Plaza, at which point you've come full circle around the park.

East (to your right) of the park's main entrance stands the main branch of the **Brooklyn Public Library** ⑫. A couple of hundred yards farther down the grand **Eastern Parkway** ⑬ lie the entrances to two of Brooklyn's most important cultural offerings: the beautifully tended **Brooklyn Botanic Garden** ⑭, which occupies 52 acres across Flatbush Avenue from Prospect Park, and the world-class **Brooklyn Museum of Art** ⑮. To return to Manhattan, you can take the No. 2 or 3 subway from the station right in front of the museum.

TIMING

You could spend a whole day at the Brooklyn Museum alone—and another day exploring Prospect Park and the Brooklyn Botanic Garden. If you do choose to fit everything into one trip, break up your wanderings with a visit to 7th Avenue, where restaurants and cafés abound. Weekends are the best time to observe local life along 7th Avenue and to enjoy the park, when it's closed to vehicles. The Botanic Garden reaches its prime in the spring, when the cherry blossoms bloom like pink snow, although its gardens and greenhouses have been designed to offer year-round pleasures.

Sights to See

❼ **Band shell.** At the Park's 9th Street entrance (at Prospect Park West), the band shell is the home of the annual **Celebrate Brooklyn Festival,** which from mid-June through Labor Day sponsors free performances—with an emphasis on music—to please every taste, from African-Caribbean jazz to Kurt Weill, from the Brooklyn Philharmonic playing Duke Ellington to bluegrass and zydeco groups. A performance here on a glorious summer evening is *the* best way to enjoy the park and the Slope at their finest. ✉ *Band shell, Prospect Park W and 9th St.,* ☎ *718/965–8999 for park hot line; 718/855–7882 ext. 52 for Celebrate Brooklyn Festival.* ✦ *Free.* ☉ *Concerts late June–Labor Day, Fri.–Sat. 7 PM, some Sun. 2 PM, plus additional times. Call for details.*

NEED A
BREAK?

In the historic Pavilion Theater, the **Living Room Café** (✉ 188 Prospect Park W, at 14th St., ☎ 718/369–0824) is just a short walk from the band shell. Stop for tea and scones, gaze out at the park, and admire the café's mural of Venus, its seashell-encrusted 180-gallon tropical fish tank, and the individually painted chairs. If you prefer coffee and a little quelquechose, stop in at the neighborhood's best bakery, the **Two Little Red Hens** (✉ 1112 8th Ave., at 12th St., ☎ 718/499–8108). The delicately adorned cakes with icing flowers cower before the sinful Brooklyn Blackout, a killer dark-chocolate cake.

❾ **Boathouse.** Styled after Sansovino's 16th-century Library at St. Mark's in Venice, this 1905 lakefront structure in Prospect Park, built about 40 years after the park was first created, sits opposite the **Lullwater Bridge,** setting a lovely scene, particularly on evenings when the light is just right and the lake reflects an exact image of the building. Unfortunately, its white-glazed terra-cotta facade has been heavily water-damaged, and the building has been fenced off and will not reopen until sometime in 2000. Just steps from the Boathouse (on the left as you face the Cleft Ridge Span) and unaffected by its closure is the lovely **Camperdown Elm,** immortalized by the poet Marianne Moore, who in the 1960s was an early park preservationist.

★ ☁ ⑭ **Brooklyn Botanic Garden.** A major attraction at this 52-acre botanic garden, one of the finest in the country, is the beguiling **Japanese Garden**—complete with a blazing red *torii* gate and a pond laid out in the shape of the Chinese character for "heart." The Japanese cherry arbor here turns into a breathtaking cloud of pink every spring. You can also wander through the **Cranford Rose Garden** (5,000 bushes, 1,200 varieties); the **Fragrance Garden,** designed especially for the blind; the **Shakespeare Garden,** featuring more than 80 plants immortalized by the Bard (including many kinds of roses); and **Celebrity Path,** Brooklyn's answer to Hollywood's Walk of Fame, with the names of New York stars—including Mel Brooks, Woody Allen, Mary Tyler Moore, Barbra Streisand, Mae West, and Maurice Sendak—inscribed on stepping-stones. The **Steinhardt Conservatory** (♥ Apr.–Sept., Tues.–Sun. 10–5:30; Oct.–Mar., Tues.–Sun. 10–4), a complex of handsome greenhouses, holds thriving desert, tropical, temperate, and aquatic vegetation, as well as a display charting the evolution of plants over the past 140 million years. The extraordinary C. V. Starr Bonsai Museum in the Conservatory exhibits about 80 miniature Japanese specimens. Free tours are given weekends at 1 PM, except for holiday weekends. ⊠ *1000 Washington Ave., between Empire Blvd. and south side of Brooklyn Museum,* ☎ *718/623–7200.* ☜ *$3; free Tues.* ♥ *Apr.–Sept., Tues.–Fri. 8–6, weekends 10–6; Oct.–Mar., Tues.–Fri. 8–4:30, weekends 10–4:30.*

★ ⑮ **Brooklyn Museum of Art (BMA).** Flanking the entrance to this massive, regal building designed by McKim, Mead & White in 1893 are allegorical figures of Brooklyn and Manhattan, originally carved by Daniel Chester French for the Manhattan Bridge. A world-class museum, BMA was founded in 1823 as the Brooklyn Apprentices' Library Association (Walt Whitman was one of its first directors). Initial plans made this the largest art museum in the world, larger even than the Louvre. With approximately 1.5 million objects, it now ranks as the second-largest art museum in New York—only the Met is larger.

Highlights include **Egyptian Art** (third floor), considered one of the best collections of its kind; and **African and Pre-Columbian Art** (first floor), another collection recognized worldwide. In the gallery of **American painting and sculpture** (fifth floor), *Brooklyn Bridge* by Georgia O'Keeffe hangs alongside nearly 200 first-rate works by Winslow Homer, John Singer Sargent, Thomas Eakins, George Bellows, and Milton Avery. The **Period Rooms** (fourth floor) include the complete interior of the Jan Martense Schenck House, built in the Brooklyn Flatlands section in 1675, as well as a Moorish-style room from the since-demolished 54th Street mansion of John D. Rockefeller (the MoMA sculpture garden now occupies the mansion's former site). **Asian Art** (second floor) includes galleries devoted to Chinese, Korean, Indian, and Islamic works. Outdoors, the **Frieda Schiff Warburg Memorial Sculpture Garden** showcases architectural fragments from demolished New York buildings, including Penn Station. In addition, BMA hosts blockbuster shows, film screenings, readings, and musical performances. ⊠ *200 Eastern Pkwy.,* ☎ *718/638–5000.* ☜ *$4 (suggested donation).* ♥ *Wed.–Fri. 10–5, Sat. 11–9, Sun. 11–6.*

⑫ **Brooklyn Public Library.** Built in 1941, this grand neoclassical edifice was designed to resemble an open book, with a gilt-inscribed spine on Grand Army Plaza that opens out to Eastern Parkway and Flatbush Avenue. Bright limestone walls, perfect proportions, and ornate decorative details make this a rare 20th-century New York building. The 15 bronze figures over the entrance, representing characters in American literature, were sculpted by Thomas Hudson Jones, who also designed the Tomb of the Unknown Soldier in Arlington National Cemetery. ⊠ *Grand Army Plaza at intersection of Flatbush Ave. and*

Eastern Pkwy., ☎ *718/780–7700.* ⊗ *Tues.–Thurs. 9–8; Mon., Fri., and Sat. 10–6; Sun. 1–5.*

⓭ **Eastern Parkway.** The first six-lane parkway in the world originates at Grand Army Plaza. When Frederick Law Olmsted and Calvert Vaux conceived the avenue's design in 1866, in tandem with their plans for Prospect Park, they wanted it to mimic the grand sweep of the boulevards of Paris and Vienna. At that time the parkway ended at Ralph Avenue, then the border of Brooklyn. Today it continues to play an important role in Brooklyn culture: every Labor Day weekend Eastern Parkway hosts the West Indian American Day Parade (☞ Festivals and Seasonal Events *in* Smart Travel Tips), the biggest and liveliest carnival outside the Caribbean.

❹ **Grand Army Plaza.** Prospect Park West, Eastern Parkway, and Flatbush and Vanderbilt avenues radiate out from this geographic star. Crossing the broad streets around here can be hazardous; beware. At the center of the plaza stands the **Soldiers' and Sailors' Memorial Arch,** honoring Civil War veterans and patterned on the Arc de Triomphe in Paris. Three heroic sculptural groupings adorn the arch: atop, a four-horsed chariot by Frederick MacMonnies, so dynamic it seems about to catapult off the arch; to either side, the victorious Union Army and Navy of the Civil War. Inside are bas-reliefs of presidents Abraham Lincoln and Ulysses S. Grant, sculpted by Thomas Eakins and William O'Donovan, respectively. On some spring and fall weekends the top of the arch is accessible; call ☎ 718/965–8999 for information.

To the northwest of the arch, Neptune and a passel of debauched Tritons leer over the edges of the **Bailey Fountain,** a popular spot for tulle-draped brides and grooms in Technicolor tuxes to pose after exchanging vows. On Saturday year-round, a large greenmarket sets up in the plaza; heaps of locally grown produce, flowers and plants, baked goods, and other foodstuffs attract throngs of neighborhood residents.

🐾 ❿ **Lefferts Homestead Children's Museum.** Built in 1783 and moved to Prospect Park in 1918, this gambrel-roof Dutch colonial farmhouse contains a historic house-museum for children. Adults will enjoy the two period rooms furnished with antiques, while children love playing in the four rooms with period reproduction furniture. Nearby is a restored 1912 **carousel** (🎟 50¢ per ride on weekends, closed mid-Oct.–early Apr.). ☎ *718/965–6505 museum.* 🎟 *Free.* ⊗ *Mid-Apr.–mid-Dec., Thurs. and weekends 1–5, Fri. 1–4; mid-Dec.–Mar. by appointment. Hrs vary, so call ahead.*

❺ **Litchfield Villa.** The most important sight on the western border of Prospect Park, this Italianate mansion built in 1857 was designed by Alexander Jackson Davis, considered the foremost architect of his day, for a prominent railroad magnate. It has housed the park's headquarters since 1883, but visitors are welcome to step inside and view the domed octagonal rotunda. Not far from the Litchfield Villa on the park's circular drive is the **Picnic House,** one of the park's less architecturally distinguished buildings, used mostly for private functions. ✉ *Prospect Park W and 3rd St.,* ☎ *718/965–8999 for park hot line.*

❷ **Montauk Club.** The home of a venerable men's club (and newly developed condominium apartments on its upper floors), this 1891 mansion designed by Francis H. Kimball is modeled on Venice's Ca' d'Oro and other Gothic Venetian palaces. It is Park Slope's most impressive building and easily rivals the showcase mansions with more prestigious addresses on Manhattan's Upper East Side. Notice the friezes of Montauk Indians and the 19th-century private side entrance for members' wives. ✉ *25 8th Ave.*

❸ Montgomery Place. This block-long street between 8th Avenue and Prospect Park West is considered to be one of Park Slope's finest thoroughfares; it's lined with picturesque town houses designed by the Romanesque Revival genius C. P. H. Gilbert.

☙ **⓫ Prospect Park Wildlife Center.** Small, friendly, and educational, this children's zoo off the main road of Prospect Park has just the right combination of indoor and outdoor exhibits along with a number of unusual and endangered species among its 390 inhabitants. The central sea-lion pool is a hit with youngsters, as are the indoor exhibits—"Animal Lifestyles," which explains habitats and adaptations, and "Animals in Our Lives," showcasing animals that make good pets and animals used on the farm. There's also an outdoor discovery trail with a simulated prairie-dog burrow and a naturalistic pond. ☎ 718/399–7339. 🎟 $2.50. ☉ Nov.–Mar., daily 10–4:30; Apr.–Oct., weekdays 10–5, weekends 10–5:30.

❶ 7th Avenue. Restaurants, groceries, bookstores, cafés, bakeries, churches, and more line Park Slope's commercial spine from Flatbush Avenue roughly to 15th Street. A few choice spots—beginning at the north (Flatbush) end and moving south—include the **New Prospect** (✉ 52 7th Ave.), a place to pick up some ready-made food or bread; **Prints Charming** (✉ 54 7th Ave.), offering a good selection of both framed and unframed prints; **Leaf & Bean** (✉ 83 7th Ave.), a tea and coffee shop with lots of hard-to-find paraphernalia; **Leon Paley Ltd. Wines & Spirits** (✉ 88 7th Ave.), a fine wine store; and **The Clay Pot** (✉ 162 7th Ave.), known for original wares and ornaments for the home and for one-of-a-kind wedding bands made by local artisans.

On the south end of the Slope, at 15th Street, the **Computer Caffé** is a good place to check your E-mail and have an espresso (✉ 435 7th Ave.); across the street is the **Lucky Bug** (✉ 438 7th Ave.), a riotous mix of toys, kitsch, and folk art that will appeal to kids and adults alike.

NEED A BREAK?
2nd Street Café (✉ 189 7th Ave., at 2nd St., ☎ 718/369–6928) is a homey restaurant with lunch on weekdays, brunch on weekends, and counter service in late afternoons and evenings. Try the raisin-studded bread pudding or heartwarming soups such as curry pumpkin. Two good local coffee joints among the many that line 7th Avenue are **Ozzie's Coffee & Tea** (✉ 57 7th Ave., at Lincoln Pl., ☎ 718/398–6695), a converted drugstore with its apothecary cases still intact, and the **Community Bookstore and Café** (✉ 143 7th Ave., at Garfield, ☎ 718/783–3075) where pastries, quiche, and additional light offerings can be had in the lovely, little garden out back or indoors among the bookcases.

❻ Tennis House. The most prominent of several neoclassical structures in the park, this 1910 limestone and yellow brick building postdates by 40 years the more rustic structures favored by Olmsted and Vaux, few of which survive. The Tennis House's most elegant features are the triple-bay Palladian arches on both its north and south facade, and its airy terra-cotta barrel-vaulted arcade on the south side. The building's large tiled central court has amazing acoustics—shout "hello" and listen to your voice bounce back at you. On the lower level, the **Brooklyn Center for the Urban Environment** houses rotating exhibits about urban issues. ☎ 718/788–8500. 🎟 Free. ☉ Weekdays 8:30–5 (Tennis House only) and weekends noon–4 (Tennis House and BCUE gallery, when an exhibit is up).

☙ **❽ Wollman Memorial Rink.** A cousin to Wollman Rink in Central Park (☞ Chapter 1), this is one of Prospect Park's most popular destinations. Besides skating in the winter, pedal-boat rentals are available here weekends and holidays from April through the middle of October (☎ 718/282–7789 or 718/287–5538); the cost is $10 per hour. The rink is directly across the circular drive from the **Drummers Grove** and adjacent to the **Flower Garden and Oriental Pavilion,** the most formally laid-out part of the park. Once a graceful setting where people strolled to the strains of an orchestra, the area is now rather desolate and ice-skaters are engulfed in loud music. ☎ 718/287–6431. 🎟 $4; $3.50 skate rental. ☾ Mid-Nov.–early Mar., Mon. 8:30–2, Tues. 8:30–5, Wed. 8:30–4, Thurs. 8:30–8, Fri. 8:30–9, Sat. 10–1, 2–6 and 7–10, Sun. 10–1 and 2–6.

Coney Island

Named Konijn Eiland (Rabbit Island) by the Dutch for its wild rabbit population, Coney Island has a boardwalk, a 2½-mi-long beach, a legendary amusement park, the city's only aquarium, and easy proximity to Brighton Beach, a Russian enclave drenched in old-world atmosphere. Coney Island may have declined from its glory days early in this century, when visitors lunched at an ocean-side hotel built in the shape of an elephant, glided across the nation's biggest dance floor at Dreamland, and toured a replica of old Baghdad called Luna Park, But it's still a great place to experience the sounds, smells, and sights of summer: hot dogs, suntan lotion, crowds, fried clams, girls and boys necking under the boardwalk, and old men staring out to sea, not to mention the ponderous turning of the mighty Wonder Wheel and the heart-stopping plunging of the king of roller coasters—the Cyclone.

A Good Walk

Coney Island is the last stop on the B and F trains in Brooklyn. The Coney Island boardwalk remains the hub of the action; amble along it to take in the local color. You'll find standard summer snacks here in the form of ice cream and saltwater taffy, but it is chewy, deep-fried clams, hot dogs with spicy mustard, and ice-cold lemonade—all from **Nathan's Famous**—that are truly synonymous with the Coney Island boardwalk experience. Coney Island is a repository of times gone by, where fire-eaters and sword-swallowers carry on the traditions of what was once billed as the "World's Largest Playground" at **Sideshows by the Seashore and the Coney Island Museum.** The rickety 70-year old Cyclone rollercoaster and, on the north side of the boardwalk, the abandoned space needle–like structure, once the Parachute Jump, are testimony to this waning beachside culture. Today visitors are just as likely to come to Coney Island to see New York City's only aquarium, the **Aquarium for Wildlife Conservation,** where five beluga whales and some 10,000 other creatures of the sea make their home. From here, take a short walk east on Surf Avenue to Brighton Beach Avenue in **"Little Odessa,"** where a community of some 90,000 Russian, Ukrainian, and Georgian emigrés operate fishmarkets, bakeries, and inexpensive restaurants. This is the place to find knishes with every filling imaginable, borscht, blinis, and cups of dark-roast coffee, plus caviar at prices that can put Manhattan purveyors to shame.

TIMING

Coney Island is at its liveliest on weekends, when crowds come out to play, especially in summer. Brighton Beach is a vibrant neighborhood year-round. Allow most of a day for this trip, since the subway ride from Manhattan (one-way) takes at least an hour.

Sights to See

★ ☺ **Aquarium for Wildlife Conservation.** Moved to Coney Island in 1957 from its former digs at Battery Park, New York City's only aquarium is worth a trip in itself. Here otters, walruses, penguins, and seals lounge on a replicated Pacific coast; a 180,000-gallon seawater complex hosts beluga whales; and dolphins and sea lions perform in the Aquatheater. ⊠ *W. 8th St. and Surf Ave.,* ☎ *718/265–3474.* 🎟 *$8.75.* ⊙ *Daily 10–4.*

🍴 **Nathan's Famous** A Coney Island institution since 1916 for hot dogs, fries, and lemonade. Bring your antacid. ⊠ *On the Boardwalk,* ⊙ *May–Sept.; 1310 Surf Ave. at 15th St.,* ⊙ *year-round;* ☎ *both locations 718/ 946–2202.*

🍴 **Sideshows by the Seashore and the Coney Island Museum.** A lively circus sideshow, complete with a fire-eater, sword-swallower, snake charmer, and contortionist, can be seen here. On the first Saturday after summer solstice, the cast of the sideshow and an amazing array of local legends and neighborhood residents take part in the **Mermaid Parade**. In a sometimes beautiful, sometimes absurd spectacle, imaginative floats and participants in wild costumes throng the Boardwalk and Surf Avenue to pay homage to the myth of the mermaid and the legend of the sea. Upstairs from Sideshows, the **Coney Island Museum** (⊠ 1208 Surf Ave., 🎟 99¢) has historic Coney Island memorabilia and a wealth of tourist information. ⊠ *W. 12th St. and Surf Ave.,* ☎ *718/372–5159 for both.* 🎟 *$3.* ⊙ *Memorial Day–Labor Day, Wed.–Sun. noon–midnight; Labor Day–Memorial Day, weekends noon–5.*

QUEENS

Home of the La Guardia and John F. Kennedy International airports and many of Manhattan's bedroom communities, Queens is perhaps New York City's most underappreciated borough. It's certainly the most diverse, for the borough's countless ethnic neighborhoods continue to attract immigrants from all over the world. Its inhabitants represent 117 nationalities and speak scores of languages, from Hindi to Hebrew. Queens communities such as Astoria (Greek and Italian), Jackson Heights (Colombian, Mexican, and Indian), Sunnyside (Turkish and Romanian), and Flushing (Korean and Chinese) are fascinating to explore, particularly if you're interested in experiencing some of the city's tastiest—and least expensive—cuisine. In addition, these areas often feature little-known historic sites, many of them just 10 minutes by subway from Grand Central Terminal.

Note: Queens streets, drives, and avenues—altogether different thoroughfares—sometimes have the same numerical name, e.g., 30th Drive is not the same as 30th Avenue.

Astoria

Home to a vital Greek community, Astoria is a place where people socialize on their front lawns at dusk and where mom-and-pop businesses thrive. Here you can buy Cypriot cured olives and feta cheese from store owners who will tell you where to go for the best spinach pie; or you can sit outside at one of the many *xaxaroplasteion* (pastry shops), eating baklava and watching the subway's elevated trains speed by.

Originally German, then Italian, Astoria earned the nickname Little Athens in the late 1960s; by the early 1990s Greeks accounted for nearly half the population. Today there are also substantial numbers of Asians, Eastern Europeans, Irish, and Hispanic immigrants in Astoria, not to mention an ever-growing contingent of former Manhattan residents in search of cheaper rents and a safer, friendlier atmosphere. But before all this happened, Astoria was the center of America's flashiest indus-

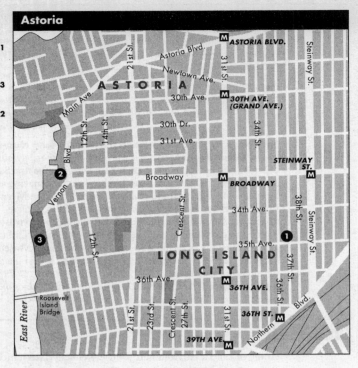

try—namely, show business. In the 1920s, Hollywood was still a dusty small town when such stars as Gloria Swanson, Rudolph Valentino, and the Marx Brothers came to this neighborhood to work at "the Big House," Paramount's moviemaking center in the east. At that time the Kaufman-Astoria Studios were the largest and most important film-making studios in the country; today they remain the largest in the East, and they're still used for major films and television shows.

Numbers in the text correspond to numbers in the margin and on the Astoria map.

A Good Tour

By subway, take the N train from Manhattan to the Broadway stop in Queens. Walk five blocks along Broadway to 36th Street; turn right and walk two blocks to 35th Avenue. Here you'll find the **American Museum of the Moving Image** ①, where you can spend hours studying its exhibits on film production and catching bits of the regularly scheduled film series and directors' talks. Next door, the imposing 13-acre **Kaufman-Astoria Studios** (✉ 34–12 36th St.), has been used for the filming of *The Cotton Club* and *Sabrina* and television series such as *Cosby* and *Sesame Street*.

Head back to the heart of the Greek community by wandering along Broadway between 31st and 36th streets. Here Greek pastry shops and coffeeshops abound, and the elevated subway brings a constant stream of activity. Farther up, 30th Avenue has every kind of food store imaginable; between 35th and 36th streets alone you'll find a *salumeria*, a meat market, a bakery, a wholesale international-food store, and more. The largest Orthodox community outside Greece worships at **St. Demetrios Cathedral** (✉ 30–11 30th Dr.), just off 30th Avenue.

Anyone interested in sculpture won't want to miss the funky **Socrates Sculpture Park** ② and the more refined **Isamu Noguchi Sculpture Museum** ③. From the Broadway subway station, walk eight blocks (about 15 minutes) toward the river. At Vernon and Broadway the Socrates Sculpture Park at first almost appears to be an urban hallucination, with its large, abstract artwork framed by the Manhattan skyline. Three blocks to the left on Vernon Boulevard, with its entrance on 33rd Road, the Isamu Noguchi Sculpture Museum has hundreds of Noguchi's works displayed in an indoor-outdoor setting that evokes the tranquillity of a Zen garden.

TIMING

To see Greek Astoria at its finest, visit on a Saturday, when sidewalk culture comes to life. Weekdays are also pleasant, as the neighborhood's quiet pace offers a welcome alternative to frenetic Manhattan. Allow at least three hours for a leisurely visit to the American Museum of the Moving Image and a tour of Greek Astoria; add another hour or two if you plan to visit the more distant Socrates Sculpture Park and Isamu Noguchi Sculpture Museum (the latter is closed in winter).

Sights to See

★ ❶ **American Museum of the Moving Image.** The nation's only museum devoted to the art, technology, and history of film, TV, and digital media is alone worth a visit to Astoria. Via artifacts, texts, live demonstrations, and video screenings, the core exhibition, "Behind the Screen," takes you step by step through the process of producing, marketing, and exhibiting moving images. Interactive computers allow you to make your own video flip book, edit sound effects, dub dialogue, and create animation. The museum's collection of movie memorabilia includes 70,000 items, including costumes worn by Marlene Dietrich, Marilyn Monroe, and Robin Williams. Movie serials from the '30s and '40s, such as Buck Rogers and Captain America, are shown daily in the 30-seat King Tut's Fever Movie Palace. The museum also presents changing exhibits, lectures, and provocative film programs, including retrospectives, Hollywood classics, experimental videos, and TV documentaries (☞ Film and Video *in* Chapter 4). ✉ *35th Ave. between 36th and 37th Sts.,* ☎ *718/784–0077.* ✑ *$8.50.* ◷ *Tues.–Fri. noon– 5, weekends 11–6.*

NEED A BREAK? | At the **Omonia Café** (✉ 32–20 Broadway, ☎ 718/274–6650) you can watch the constant activity on Broadway while nursing coffee and honey-sweet pastries. At Broadway and 34th Street, **Uncle George's** (✉ 33–19 Broadway, ☎ 718/626–0593) is a 24-hour Greek diner where rotisserie-roasted lamb and other Greek classics can be had for a song.

★ ❸ **Isamu Noguchi Sculpture Museum.** In 1985, this space across the street from the studio of Japanese-American sculptor Isamu Noguchi (1904– 88) became a museum devoted to his sculpture. A large, open-air garden and two floors of gallery space hold more than 250 of Noguchi's pieces in stone, bronze, wood, clay, and steel. Videos document his long career; there are also models, drawings, and even stage sets for dances by Martha Graham. Weekend bus service ($5) from Manhattan to the museum leaves every hour on the half hour, 11:30–3:30, from the northeast corner of Park Ave. and E. 70th St. ✉ *32–37 Vernon Blvd., at 33rd Rd., Long Island City,* ☎ *718/204–7088.* ✑ *$4 (suggested donation).* ◷ *Apr.–Nov., Wed.–Fri. 10–5, weekends 11–6; closed Dec.–Mar.*

OFF THE BEATEN PATH | **FLUSHING MEADOWS–CORONA PARK** – The site of both the 1939 and 1964 World's Fairs, Flushing Meadows–Corona Park is well worth the trek from Manhattan. A ride on the No. 7 subway from Times Square or

Grand Central Station to the Willets Point–Shea Stadium stop puts you within walking distance of some of New York's most exciting cultural and recreational institutions. At the **Queens Museum of Art** check out the knock-your-socks-off New York City panorama, a 9,335-square-ft model of the five boroughs, made for the 1964 World's Fair. It faithfully replicates all five boroughs of the city building by building, on a scale of 1 inch per 100 ft. The model's tiny brownstones and skyscrapers are updated periodically to look exactly like the real things. ⊠ *Flushing Meadows–Corona Park,* ☎ *718/592–9700.* ⊟ *$4 (suggested donation).* ⊘ *Wed.–Fri. 10–5, weekends noon–5.*

In front of the museum is one of the most stunning photo opportunities in the city, the awe-inspiring **Unisphere.** Made entirely of stainless steel for the 1964 World's Fair, this massive sculpture of the Earth is 140 feet high and weighs 380 tons. If you're here with kids, you'll also want to visit the **New York Hall of Science** (☞ Chapter 3) and the very manageable **Queens Zoo.** During baseball season, top the day off with a Mets game at **Shea Stadium,** just north of the park (☎ 718/507–8499 for a game schedule, ☞ Chapter 8). Or if you're into tennis, catch champs like Pete Sampras, Martina Hingis, and Venus Williams at the U.S. Open Tournament on and around Labor Day at the **USTA National Tennis Center** (☞ Chapter 8) opposite the Unisphere. Or play a match yourself at one of the 29 courts open to the public (☎ 718/760–6200, for court reservations and fees).

❷ **Socrates Sculpture Park.** The ancient Greeks excelled in the art of sculpture, which was often displayed in outdoor temples. It is appropriate, then, that Astoria should have an outdoor sculpture park. In 1985 local residents rallied to transform what had been an illegal dump site into this 4.2-acre park, devoted to the display of public art. Today a superb view of the river and the Manhattan skyline beyond frames huge works of art made of scrap metal, old tires, and other recycled products. ⊠ *Vernon Blvd. at Broadway,* ☎ *718/956–1819.* ⊘ *Daily 10–sunset.*

STATEN ISLAND

Even though Staten Island is officially a part of New York City, it is, to many New Yorkers, the forgotten borough. Its claims to fame are as the city's garbage dump, and as the borough that is perpetually agitating to secede from the city. Settled by Dutch farmers in 1661, Staten Island today still feels provincial and even old-fashioned compared with the rest of the city; indeed, time stands still in the two recreated villages of Richmondtown and Snug Harbor. Although it's less convenient to get here than to the other boroughs, the 20-minute ferry ride across New York Harbor affords phenomenal views of lower Manhattan and the Statue of Liberty—and it's free. On weekend mornings (until 11:30 AM), ferries leave the southern tip of Manhattan every hour on the half hour; on weekdays and weekend afternoons you can catch one at least every half hour. Call ☎ 718/815–2628 for schedules and directions.

Snug Harbor and Beyond

Just 2 mi from the ferry terminal, the restored sailor's community of Snug Harbor is by far the most popular of Staten Island's attractions. For a highly enjoyable daytime outing, take the scenic ferry ride from Manhattan and visit Snug Harbor and two small but engaging nearby museums; then stop perhaps for a meal at Adobe Blues.

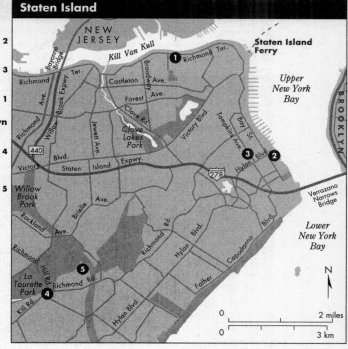

Numbers in the text correspond to numbers in the margin and on the Staten Island map.

A Good Tour

From the Staten Island Ferry terminal, a seven-minute (2-mi) ride on the S40 bus will take you to the **Snug Harbor Cultural Center** ①, an 83-acre complex with an art gallery, a botanical garden, a children's museum, and a colorful history. Signal the driver as soon as you glimpse the black iron fence along the edge of the property.

If the day is still young after you've toured Snug Harbor, return to the ferry terminal and catch the S51–Bay Street bus for the 15-minute ride to Hylan Boulevard to see the turn-of-the-century photographs displayed in the picturesque **Alice Austen House Museum** ②. Italian history buffs should head to the **Garibaldi-Meucci Museum** ③, where war general Giuseppe Garibaldi lived in exile with his friend Antonio Meucci—the true inventor of the telephone.

TIMING

The Snug Harbor Cultural Center alone will take at least half a day, including the ferry commute; add to that the Alice Austen House and the Garibaldi-Meucci Museum, and you're in for a whole-day adventure. If you're interested in visiting all three attractions, plan your visit toward the end of the week, when both the museums are open. The Garibaldi-Meucci Museum is closed in winter.

Sights to See

② **Alice Austen House Museum.** Photographer Alice Austen (1866–1952) defied tradition when, as a girl of 10, she received her first camera as a gift from an uncle and promptly began taking pictures of everything around her. Austen went on to make photography her lifetime avocation, recording on film a vivid social history of Staten Island in the early part of the 20th century; one of the local ferries is actually named for her. The cozy, ivy-covered Dutch-style cottage known as Clear Comfort, where she lived almost all her life, has been restored, and many of her photographs are on display. ⊠ *2 Hylan Blvd.,* ☎ *718/816–4506.* ⊡ *$2.* ⊙ *Mar.–Dec., Thurs.–Sun. noon–5.*

❸ Garibaldi-Meucci Museum. Housed in an altered Federal farmhouse, this small museum is full of the letters and photographs of fiery Italian patriot Giuseppe Garibaldi. It also documents Antonio Meucci's invention of the telephone before Alexander Graham Bell. Appropriately, the museum is in the heart of the Italian neighborhood of Rosebank; the colorful **Our Lady of Mount Saint Carmel Society Shrine** is just around the corner, at 36 Amity Street. Ask the museum curator for directions. ⊠ *420 Tompkins Ave.,* ☎ *718/442–1608.* ⊡ *Free; donations accepted.* ⊙ *Tues.–Fri. 1–5; Sat.–Sun. 12–5 (but it's a good idea to call first).*

★ ⊘ **❶ Snug Harbor Cultural Center.** Once part of a sprawling farm, then a home for "aged, decrepit, and worn-out sailors," this 83-acre property is based around a row of five columned Greek Revival temples, built between 1831 and 1880, and consists of 28 historic buildings, most of which have been restored. The Main Hall—the oldest building on the property, dating from 1833—holds the **Newhouse Center for Contemporary Art,** which features changing exhibitions. Next door is the **John A. Noble Collection,** where an old seaman's dormitory has been transformed into classrooms, a library and archive, a printmaking studio, and galleries displaying maritime paintings, lithographs, photographs, and drawings. ☎ 718/447–6490, call for hours and fees ⊡ $2 (suggested donation), ⊙ Wed.–Sun. 12–5.

Covering the grounds of the cultural center, the **Staten Island Botanical Gardens** include a perennial garden, a greenhouse, a vineyard, 10 acres of natural marsh habitat, a fragrance garden for the physically challenged, and a rose garden. An authentic Chinese Scholars' Garden—hand-created by artisans from China and the only one in the United States—opened in spring 1999, featuring reflecting ponds, waterfalls, pavilions, and a teahouse. The teahouse also offers instruction in the ancient arts of tai chi and calligraphy. ☎ *718/273–8200.* ⊡ *Free.* ⊙ *Dawn–dusk.*

⊘ **Staten Island Children's Museum** is also on the grounds. Five galleries present hands-on exhibitions that introduce topics such as nature's food chains, storytelling, and insects. Portia's Playhouse, an interactive children's theater, invites tykes to step up to the stage and even try on costumes. ☎ *718/273–2060.* ⊡ *$4.* ⊙ *Tues.–Sun. noon–5.*

Snug Harbor's newly renovated **Music Hall,** the second-oldest hall in the city (after Carnegie, built in 1892), offers frequent performances, including an annual music festival, and the former chapel houses the 210-seat **Veterans Memorial Hall,** site of many indoor concerts and gatherings. The complex has a gift shop and a cafeteria. ⊠ *1000 Richmond Terr.,* ☎ *718/448–2500.* ⊡ *Cultural Center grounds free.* ⊙ *Dawn–dusk, guided tours weekends 2 PM Mar.–Nov.*

NEED A
BREAK?

Those with a powerful thirst should head straight to **Adobe Blues** (⊠ 63 Lafayette St., just off Richmond Terr., ☎ 718/720–2583), a Southwestern-style saloon and restaurant with more than 200 beers, 40 types of tequila, and a wicked chili con carne.

Historic Richmondtown

Hilly and full of green space, the scenic southern part of the island is far from the ferry terminal but worth the trip. Sprawling Historic Richmondtown takes you on a vivid journey into Staten Island's past, and the hilltop Jacques Marchais Museum of Tibetan Art transports you to the mountains of Central Asia.

A Good Tour

Take the S74–Richmond Road bus from the ferry terminal to **Historic Richmondtown** ④ (about 25 minutes), whose 27 historic buildings date from the 17th, 18th, and 19th centuries. Afterward, grab lunch at the Parsonage restaurant, or walk about a half mile east on Richmond Road and up steep Lighthouse Avenue to the **Jacques Marchais Museum of Tibetan Art** ⑤, which has the largest collection of its kind outside Tibet.

TIMING

Set aside the better part of a day for a trip to Historic Richmondtown, which is on the opposite end of the island from the ferry terminal; add on a couple of hours for the Tibetan Museum. The latter is closed Monday and Tuesday; in winter its hours are subject to change, so call ahead. Historic Richmondtown hosts a variety of seasonal celebrations, including an autumn crafts fair and a Christmas celebration.

Sights to See

★ ◔ ❹   **Historic Richmondtown.** These 27 buildings, some of them constructed as early as 1685, are situated in a 100-acre complex that was the site of Staten Island's original county seat. The buildings have been restored inside and out; some were built here, while others were relocated from other spots on the island. Many buildings, such as the Greek Revival courthouse, which serves as the **visitor center,** date from the 19th century; other architectural styles on site range from Dutch colonial to Victorian Gothic Revival. During the warmer months costumed staff members demonstrate Early American crafts and trades such as printing, tinsmithing, and fireplace cooking.

The **Voorlezer's House,** built in 1695, is the oldest elementary schoolhouse still standing in the United States; it looks like the mold from which all little red schoolhouses were cast. The **Staten Island Historical Society Museum,** built in 1848 as the second county clerk's and surrogate's office, now houses American china, furniture, toys, and tools, plus a collection of Staten Island photographs.

During a summer visit you might want to make reservations for the 19th-century dinner, cooked outdoors and served with utensils of the period. The Autumn Celebration shows off craftspeople demonstrating their skills; the annual Encampment in July is a reenactment of a Civil War battle; and December brings a monthlong Christmas celebration. Richmondtown regularly hosts other fairs, flea markets, and tours of the historic buildings. A tavern on the grounds of the historic village hosts a Saturday-night concert series showcasing ethnic and folk music; call the visitor center for details. ✉ *441 Clarke Ave.,* ☎ *718/351–1611.* 🎟 *$4.* ☉ *Sept.–June, Wed.–Sun. 1–5; July–Aug., Wed.–Fri. 10–5, weekends 1–5.*

NEED A
BREAK?
    For a taste of Richmondtown cuisine, head to the **Parsonage** (✉ 74 Arthur Kill Rd., ☎ 718/351–7879), which serves rosemary-crusted pork tenderloin strudel and Black Angus steak au poivre in a fully restored 19th-century parish house.

❺   **Jacques Marchais Museum of Tibetan Art.** One of the largest private, nonprofit collections of Tibetan and Himalayan sculpture, scrolls, and paintings outside of Tibet is displayed in a museum resembling a Tibetan monastery. Try to visit on a day when the monks bless the monastery—and you. ⊠ *338 Lighthouse Ave.,* ☎ *718/987–3500.* ⊠ *$3; occasionally an additional $3 charge for special Sun. programs.* ⊗ *Apr.–Nov., Wed.–Sun. 1–5; Dec.–Mar., Wed.–Fri. 1–5 (call for information about special programs and festivals).*

3 EXPLORING NEW YORK CITY WITH CHILDREN

New York is as magical a place for children as it is for adults. Although hotels and restaurants tend to be geared for grown-ups, when provision has been made for children it is usually accomplished in a grand way. The world's best and largest toy store, the biggest park, the nicest city seaport, the most fearsome dinosaur skeletons, the juiciest burgers, the most diverse theme restaurants, kids' stores of every possible description, and, of course, some of the world's tallest buildings are all here.

By Kate
Sekules

Updated by
Mitchell Davis,
Heather Lewis,
Jennifer Paull,
and Tom Steele

CHILD-PLEASING SIGHTS ABOUND in New York City. But on your way to the museums, zoos, and theaters, don't miss out on the everyday pleasures of this vibrant city. You'll find brightly colored pictograms in Chinatown, spectacular four-story-high neon signs in Times Square, Central Park squirrels, and Greenwich Village street musicians good enough to appear on television.

To get children psyched for a New York trip, give them *My New York,* by Kathy Jakobsen; *Next Stop, Grand Central,* by Maira Kalman; *From the Mixed-up Files of Mrs. Basil E. Frankweiler,* by E. L. Konigsburg; *A Cricket in Times Square,* by George Selden; *Eloise,* by Kay Thompson; or *Stuart Little,* by E. B. White.

SIGHTSEEING

In no other city is it easier to entertain offspring simply by wandering: Surprising pockets of street sculpture, graffiti art, quirky or distinguished building facades, and appealing shop windows may be found on almost every block. The sheer size of the buildings is astonishing to children not raised in a large city. Getting around in quintessential New York ways—riding cabs, or even buses and subways (especially in the first or last car, with a view of the track and tunnels)—can also be thrilling. To get a feeling for Old New York, ride in a **horse-drawn carriage** around Central Park. Carriages line up on Grand Army Plaza (at the corner of 5th Avenue and 59th Street) and along 59th Street between 5th and 7th avenues. The city-regulated fare is calculated by time, at a rate of $34 for the first half hour or $54 per hour for up to four people.

Boat rides are great fun. If they have a good attention span, kids will love the narrated three-hour **Circle Line Cruise** (⊠ Pier 83, west end of 42nd St., ☎ 212/563–3200) around Manhattan. Many of the guides who narrate the trip have amazing and humorous tales to tell about the city; they take lengthy breaks, so the kids have plenty of opportunity to let off steam. The fare is $22 for adults and $12 for children. For a special nautical excursion, the restored 19th-century schooner **Pioneer** (⊠ South Street Seaport, ☎ 212/748–8786) sails from May 4 through September 27. The cost for two hours is $20 for adults, $12 for children under 12; reservations are required. For a close-up view of the boats, islands, and other sights of New York Harbor, try the free ride on the **Staten Island Ferry** (⊠ Terminal in Battery Park, ☎ 718/727–2508).

Kids also enjoy New York's opportunities for vertical travel. The favorite midtown high-level view is from the 86th floor of the **Empire State Building** (⊠ 350 5th Ave., at 34th St., ☎ 212/736–3100) (☞ Murray Hill, Flatiron District, and Gramercy *in* Chapter 1). Take the elevator to the 107th floor of the **World Trade Center** (⊠ 1 World Trade Center, ☎ 212/323–2340) for a panoramic view 1,350 ft above the city (☞ Wall Street and the Battery *in* Chapter 1).

Museums

Although almost every major museum in New York City has something to interest children, and many offer special programs, certain ones hold special appeal. At the top of the list is the **American Museum of Natural History** (⊠ Central Park W at 79th St., ☎ 212/769–5100),